BUSINESS DEVELOPMENT FOR LAWYERS:

Strategies for Getting
and
Keeping Clients

Sally J. Schmidt

Cover Design: *Ehren Seeland*

Interior Page Design & Production: *Paige Hinkle*

Library of Congress Cataloging-in-Publication Data

Schmidt, Sally, 1959-
  Business development for lawyers / by Sally Schmidt.
     p. cm.
  ISBN-13: 978-1-58852-136-1 (pbk.)
  1. Lawyers--United States--Marketing. 2. Attorney and client--United States.
3. Practice of law--United States--Economic aspects. 4. Lawyers--Public relations--United States. I. Title.

  KF316.5.S37 2006
  340.068'8--dc22

                                        2006002760

Preface

It seems that marketing has come nearly full circle in the legal industry. When I first started working in the field of law firm marketing, the marketing function was barely recognized within the profession. Lawyers worked individually or teamed with colleagues to generate business and develop a clientele. Then, as law firms adopted, centralized and institutionalized marketing, many lawyers believed—or perhaps hoped—that the marketing function would eliminate the need to do the things that they either didn't like, didn't feel comfortable with or didn't have time for—like networking, speaking, getting involved in organizations and generating business.

Today most people involved in the management or administration of law firms understand that marketing and business development are really two different things, and can finally appreciate why many of their clients have separate "marketing" and "sales" functions. While the two areas need to collaborate and work closely together, they are responsible for different outcomes and their success is measured in very different ways. Marketing is a strategic function involving the design of the law firm's offerings, the way they are priced and packaged, the delivery of legal services to clients, and the communication of the firm's essence and capabilities to its target markets. While in the end, the goal of marketing is to grow and sustain the business, the success of a particular marketing effort might be measured in terms of market share, client satisfaction, awareness level or any number of other metrics. Business development is measured by dollars in the door.

When it comes to developing business, most lawyers—particularly those dealing with institutional, corporate or commercial clients—find that personal efforts to develop both relationships and credibility still rule the day. It is those kinds of efforts that are the subject of this book. It saddens me to see busy lawyers, in their quest to engage in marketing or to develop business, waste their time on ineffective or downright inappropriate activities. I sincerely hope that the information contained in this book will help readers select the right strategies (i.e., those that are the best uses of their time and will produce the best results) and implement them in the most effective fashion.

I also feel that marketing shouldn't be feared or even just tolerated; it should be an integral part of one's practice. This requires that marketing efforts be a good fit with the lawyers' personalities and practices, lifestyles and interests, strengths and contacts.

The information contained in this book has been culled from the hundreds of workshops, speeches and training sessions I have presented to lawyers over the last twenty-plus years. I hope you find the recommendations and ideas practical and relevant—the hallmark of all my consulting activities. The area covered by this book is so vast that I am sure there are things I've overlooked, shortchanged or omitted. But even with that caveat, I believe that every lawyer will be able to find something that he or she can do, or do better, as a result of reading this book.

I would like to thank Bobby Kovich, my husband and number one fan, and Ryan Kovich, for being so supportive; I feel incredibly lucky to have a wonderful family that takes such pride and interest in everything I do. I'd also like to thank Heide Rose and Lisa Kruse, my long-time former associates, whose assistance, support and loyalty contributed enormously to the growth and success of Schmidt Marketing, Inc.; Hallie Mann, Gretchen Semler and Lindsay Hokenson at Schmidt Marketing, Inc. for their diligence, service and personal attention to clients, allowing our company to grow and thrive; Neil Hirsch, Vice President Publications and Editor-in-Chief at the Law Journal Press, a division of

ALM Media, for embracing this book idea; Nancy Stein, my editor there, for her persistence, the value she added and her personal touch; and, of course, my clients. I have had the pleasure and privilege of working with more than 350 law firm clients during my career, and have interacted with hundreds more through networks and conferences; I only hope they have learned as much from me as I have from them. Thank you for the opportunity to contribute to the field of law firm marketing.

CONTENTS

PART I:
INTRODUCTORY COMMENTS

I. INTRODUCTION

If you ask lawyers what they like least about the practice of law, the response frequently will focus on the need to generate business. While undoubtedly there are lawyers who enjoy marketing their practices, many look upon marketing as a necessary evil. Clearly it is necessary.

Why is marketing so important for you? There are many reasons:

• *Control of your own destiny.* The legal world is filled with sad examples of lawyers who relied on their law firms to provide job security only to be left in the cold as the result of a merger, partner defections, firm closure, a major client bankruptcy or other factors. The fact is that only by creating your own sources of work will you truly be secure in the private practice of law.

• *Enjoyment of your practice.* Generally, people who have their own books of business are more satisfied with their practices. This probably can be attributed to several factors. Among them are more control over the type of work they do and closer relationships with their clients.

• *Value to clients.* Lawyers who are actively engaged in marketing activities such as writing for trade associations, getting involved in industry groups, touring client businesses and speaking on legal developments are perceived as more valuable to their clients. As a result of their marketing activities, these lawyers often are more proactive in advising clients about developments, and bring a highly valued external perspective to their engagements (i.e., an understanding of the client's needs, business, industry or situation). These lawyers are in a better position to give advice. In addition, good marketers also tend to be better connected and, consequently, can provide other assistance to clients, like recommending good consultants or helping clients find buyers for their businesses.

•   *Financial benefits.* The bottom line is that, in most law firms, the lawyers who produce the most business and control the relationships with the largest clients make the most money. While money is not the only motivation for engaging in marketing, it certainly is an important consideration.

> *Lawyers who are actively engaged in marketing activities . . . often are more proactive in advising clients about developments, and bring a highly valued external perspective to their engagements.*

The purpose of this book is to help lawyers with their individual marketing efforts. It focuses on "how tos"— offering very practical advice on implementing marketing or business development techniques. It includes many tips to help you determine the activities and approaches that will be right for you.

You can even use this book as a guide for developing an individual marketing plan. At the end of each chapter is a notes page on which you can record your ideas, obstacles, goals or objectives related to the content of that chapter. Part IV of the book provides advice on developing an effective personal marketing plan.

II. MARKETING FUNDAMENTALS

While this book is meant to be a practical guide to marketing and business development, there are some important fundamentals that should be understood up front before you move toward implementation. These are outlined below.

A. Different Aspects of Marketing

If you look at how large companies are organized, most have separate departments to handle "marketing" and "sales." In the legal arena, marketing and sales (or "business development," as it is more commonly described in law firms) are most often performed by the same person (the lawyer—who also handles production, by the way). However, it can be helpful to think about these areas separately when planning your own marketing and business development strategy.

What we call marketing in law firms is often related to "positioning." Most of the "traditional" forms of marketing, such as writing and speaking, serve primarily to position a lawyer as an expert in certain areas. These activities are important when you are trying to get on the "radar screen." Obviously, clients will not consider using you if they are not aware of your expertise. So positioning activities will be effective when you're building the reputation of a practice (e.g., an industry focus in the firm) or when you need to gain awareness for, or create a perception of, expertise. This is especially true for younger or new lawyers.

> *Most of the "traditional" forms of marketing, such as writing and speaking, serve primarily to position a lawyer as an expert in certain areas.*

The second area is "business development." Except in the case of lawyers seeking clients through direct marketing activities like advertising or direct mail, most lawyers get their business (or at least the best business) through relationships. Active and direct activities are needed to build relationships that lead to business, from networking to one-on-one meetings.

While this is a generalization, as a lawyer gets more senior, he or she often should be moving from the more passive and credibility-enhancing activities (such as writing or speaking) toward the more active, relationship-building activities (such as face-to-face contacts).

This book treats positioning and business development in separate sections. Part II is entitled "Positioning Yourself and Your Practice" and covers strategies for developing your reputation and enhancing your visibility. Part III is entitled "Developing Business." It addresses ways to cultivate and develop personal and professional relationships that will help you generate business.

B. Each Practice Is Different

How business is developed can be a complicated issue because every practice gets its business in a different way. For trust and estate planning lawyers, business is often generated through relationships with other professionals, such as accountants and financial advisors. Class action lawyers frequently build substantial practices on referrals from other lawyers. Banking lawyers usually are successful by targeting the prospective clients directly, such as loan officers or the general counsels of financial institutions.

> *How business is developed can be a complicated issue because every practice gets its business in a different way.*

In addition, other factors go into client decision-making. For example, the more specialized the substantive service required by the client, the less important the personal relationship; the more risky the case or transaction, the more important the "brand name" of the firm.

So as you read this book, you will see a theme repeated about the importance of identifying the type of work you are seeking. Only by knowing what kind of work you want and who has it will you be able to develop an effective plan to obtain it.

C. Investment and Return

I've already noted the importance of spending time in positioning and relationship-building activities. The next question is how much time needs to be devoted to these activities. Keep in mind that the "quantity" is not as important as the "quality" of the time invested. However, for those seeking a benchmark, here are some thoughts:

• If you are new to the practice of law and currently spend little or no time on marketing activities, your goal might be 50-100 hours a year. This works out to an hour or two a week—which could be devoted to lunches with colleagues or contacts, seminar preparation, client visits or other very manageable activities like sending notes or making telephone calls.

• If you are a senior associate, you might think about spending somewhere in the 100-200 hour range annually on marketing activities.

- If you are a partner and want to produce good results in business development, most rainmakers will tell you they spend in the range of 250-500 hours on marketing activities per year.

What can you expect from this investment of time? Unfortunately, the answer is not always clear—the results depend on a number of factors. First, the effectiveness of your marketing efforts depends on your situation. If you are developing a new practice, either as a fairly new lawyer or someone trying to create a niche or specialty, it could be years before you see results if measured in terms of new business. Effectiveness also depends on the activity. As you will see throughout in this book, some activities may be very good for one objective (creating awareness) but not another (generating inquiries). You need to understand what a reasonable expectation is for the activities in which you engage.

Finally, all marketing is a long-term endeavor. You rarely will start your marketing efforts by speaking at the plenary session of an industry group's national conference; to receive that invitation, you may first have to speak at local chapter luncheon meetings, then at state meetings, and then at breakout sessions at the national conference. You won't begin your marketing efforts by getting elected to the American Academy of Matrimonial Lawyers.

> *If you are developing a new practice . . . it could be years before you see results if measured in terms of new business.*

You likely will need to spend many years getting active and recognized in your local, state and national bar association family law sections before receiving that honor.

So if you're looking for quick results, you may not find them here. But if you're looking to build a practice and a career, this book will help you. And it certainly should help you improve what you're already doing.

D. Ethical Considerations

Finally, it is important that you consult the Rules of Professional Conduct for the jurisdiction(s) in which you practice before engaging in marketing and business development activities, particularly those addressing direct contact with prospective clients.

III. QUALITIES OF SUCCESSFUL MARKETERS

The Harvard Business School did a study to identify the characteristics of good salespeople. Most of their attributes seem to apply equally well to lawyers who are "rainmakers." The list of traits of good salespeople has been applied to lawyers below:

(1) *Self-confidence.* Good marketers have enough self-confidence that they do not take rejection personally. They will be disappointed if their business development efforts fail, but such failure will not affect their self-esteem or their ability to continue to deal with the individuals who said "no." Rainmakers understand that clients have many relationships and many choices, and that for every ten good contacts, just one or two will likely turn into clients.

(2) *High level of empathy.* Prospective clients feel that these lawyers really care about the prospects' needs. The best rainmakers are good listeners, and are sincere in trying to help their contacts achieve a goal or handle a problem.

(3) *Goal orientation.* Successful business developers have goals, measure their personal progress along the way, and don't allow themselves to get side-tracked by the day-to-day press of the practice.

(4) *Persistence.* Rainmakers follow up with people on an ongoing basis. They make follow-up telephone calls to see if decisions have been made or to reiterate their interest in the prospect. They are very self-disciplined and have systems to remind themselves of what they should be doing.

(5) *Personal accountability for failure.* If they are not successful, rainmakers don't blame other people, the firm's marketing department, the tactics of competitors or the irrational decision of the prospect. They try to learn from the experience and look for ways to overcome the barrier in future business development opportunities.

(6) *Desire to succeed.* The desire to succeed actually makes people successful at business development because it influences their priorities—how they spend their time and with whom, both inside and outside the law firm.

(7) *Ability to approach strangers, even when uncomfortable.* Going to a cocktail party and talking to people you don't know is hard for anyone. But rainmakers generally are able to strike up conversations with strangers. The key? They ask questions and then listen.

> *The best business developers ... aren't trying to "sell" something; they are trying to fill needs.*

(8) *Incredible honesty.* The best business developers admit their weaknesses and praise good competitors. They aren't trying to "sell" something; they are trying to fill needs. This attitude helps them build trust and credibility with prospective clients.

While many people feel great rainmakers are born and not made, it is possible to learn from successful rainmakers and improve your own business development abilities. By using the advice in this book, you can strengthen your skills and create an effective personal marketing plan.

IV. CONCLUSION

Throughout this book, you will see some themes and even some specific points repeated. This is done for two reasons. First, the same principles may apply to multiple areas or activities, so they are discussed where relevant. Second, the chapters are meant to stand alone, so they can be resources for the lawyer seeking advice on a particular activity or technique.

In addition to the advice contained in this book, there are other resources to help you understand how business comes to those in your area(s) of practice and to help you identify the most effective activities for you. You might think about doing the following:

• *Interview a partner with a book of business in your practice area.* You can ask him or her to share with you: How were your biggest clients developed? Who have been your best sources of business or your most important contacts generally? Which organizations did you find most helpful in building a practice in the area? Which publications do you read religiously, or which ones are most important to the practice area?

• *Interview a client.* For example, if you practice in the health care area, ask one or more of your firm's clients the following: What do you look for when selecting a lawyer or law firm? What should I know about a medical practice or the health care industry generally to position myself to serve clients better? Which organizations do you find most helpful in terms of professional development or networking? Might I also get involved in such organizations?

• *Interview a trade or an industry organization contact.* If you handle labor and employment work, for example, ask an officer or the executive director of the local human resource organization for perceptions of trends in the area, what the organization's members are looking for, how human resource departments tend to make decisions, or how you might better understand the needs of the membership.

• *Interview another professional service provider.* If you want to work more in the hospitality industry, for example, invite an accountant with a substantial practice in the area for lunch and ask how he or she successfully built the practice. Ask for thoughts and suggestions as you seek to build a clientele in that industry.

PART II:

POSITIONING YOURSELF AND YOUR PRACTICE

1
Overview: Positioning Yourself and Building Credibility

I. INTRODUCTION

The chapters in Part II of this book focus on a number of marketing activities in which lawyers frequently engage. Lawyers undertake these activities largely to enhance visibility or build awareness—in short, to position themselves, their practice or their firm.

Why is "positioning" important? When seeking counsel, most clients or referral sources will develop a "short list" of lawyers or law firms to consider. The short list is developed in different ways. They may ask colleagues, friends, neighbors or people in their industry for the names of lawyers. They may do some independent research to see which names are associated with a particular type of expertise or a particular industry. They may consider lawyers whom they've read about, heard speak or met through their organizational activities.

"Perception of expertise" is consistently reported by clients to be the most important criterion when selecting a lawyer. Clients are looking for counsel expert in the area in which they need assistance. Your positioning activities play a very big role in creating a perception of expertise. Think about the following examples:

- *"He teaches tax law at the University."*
- *"She is the President of the local trademark association."*
- *"He wrote the book on water law in the region."*

These kinds of statements give comfort both to the person referring a lawyer as well as to the prospective client.

Positioning activities are also important because they can reinforce your existence and expertise. The saying "Timing is everything" is particularly true in lawyer marketing. Most people you target with your marketing activities are either not in need of counsel at that particular moment or have a lawyer with whom they already work. As a result, reinforcement is extremely important to increase the odds that you are "in the right place at the right time" when someone needs counsel or changes lawyers.

> *[R]einforcement is extremely important to increase the odds that you are "in the right place at the right time" when someone needs counsel or changes lawyers.*

So positioning activities are valuable for every lawyer—i.e., creating a perception of expertise among the people you would like to target. But they are especially important for younger lawyers. More senior people have the benefit of perceived expertise; inexperienced lawyers need to put clients and prospects at ease by having credentials to which they can point. Consider, for example, a young lawyer in the real property section of his firm. The following will help create an impression of his expertise:

• Involvement in the local chapter of the National Association of Industrial and Office Parks (NAIOP) or the Building Owners and Managers Association (BOMA).

• Articles and speeches about real-estate related issues, which are noted on his bio, posted on the firm's Web site and distributed with his marketing materials.

• A listing on his résumé and in his bio on the firm's Web site of transactions or representative matters in which he has been involved to show the depth and breadth of his experience.

II. SELECTING THE RIGHT ACTIVITIES

Unfortunately, many lawyers engage in positioning activities with little thought about whether what they are doing is actually effective.

They accept an invitation to speak before evaluating the potential audience or write an article before even determining to which publication it will be submitted.

Most lawyers face a lot of time pressure, both from within and outside the firm. You only have so much time to devote to marketing, so you need to be sure it's used effectively! This Section provides some thoughts on how to select the positioning activities that will be most effective for you.

Lawyers frequently will ask whether a particular activity "works." Let's use speaking at a Continuing Legal Education (CLE) program as an example. Some lawyers will say with conviction that speaking to other lawyers at CLE programs is a "waste of time." But other lawyers who get the bulk of their business through lawyer referrals, such as bankruptcy practitioners, know that presenting at CLE programs can be very effective. So your practice and target market will determine what "works" or what "doesn't work" for you.

> *You only have so much time to devote to marketing, so you need to be sure it's used effectively!*

In addition, some activities, like public speaking or writing, may work well for one lawyer but not another simply because of the individuals' skills. Some lawyers have more contacts than others, some are more social than others, some are better writers or speakers than others, and some have more expertise than others. All of these factors—personality, age, contacts, expertise—will have a bearing on whether a particular marketing activity will work for you.

In other words, every activity has the potential to "work" and has the potential not to "work," depending on you, your targets, your practice and your execution.

So how can you make good decisions about your opportunities? Before engaging in any marketing activity, you should attempt to answer the following questions:

(1) *Who is the audience?* The most important issue is whether you are targeting the right people. For example, some estate planning lawyers will speak to any group—those attending community education programs, Rotary clubs, etc.—believing that everyone is a prospective client. But the estate planners with the highest margin business usually

get their work referred to them by other professionals—accountants, insurance agents, financial planners, etc.

(2) *What is the message?* Once you have determined that you are speaking to or writing for the right people, you need to consider what you are trying to communicate. Is it substance (e.g., a new development in your area of expertise)? Is it practical advice? Is it promotional? Each audience will be interested in different information. For example, a bank general counsel may be more interested in emerging issues related to the financial services industry while a loan officer may be more interested in ideas for improving loan processes.

(3) *What is the most effective medium?* Once you've determined the audience and the information you'd like to convey, you should consider

> *If other lawyers or law firms are already doing one thing, you should think about doing something different.*

what will be the best medium for communicating. For example, a written newsletter or alert may be the best medium if you are targeting highly technical people, like patent coordinators. A full-day seminar may be the best medium if you are targeting people in the public sector. General counsels may attend a roundtable with their peers, but business owners may be too busy to come to seminars. When you are developing your thoughts about the medium, be certain to consider the competition for your audience's time and attention. If other lawyers or law firms are already doing one thing, you should think about doing something different. Competition for your audience's attention also can come from nonlegal venues, such as trade associations and other professional service organizations.

(4) *How will you measure success?* For every activity you undertake, you should try to establish an objective. For example, how will you determine if writing an article was an effective marketing strategy? It is unlikely to generate calls per se unless it is extremely timely. However, it may pique the interest of members of an industry association, who invite you to make a presentation on the topic. Or you may be able to leverage it into a number of other opportunities, from internal seminars to Web site postings.

(5) *How will you follow up?* Finally, and very importantly, for any given activity, before you even start you should be thinking about how you can leverage your effort into additional exposure or activities. If you give a speech, how will you follow up with the attendees and what else can you do with the information you prepared? If you attend an out-of-town conference, how will you follow up with people you meet?

If you answer these questions and follow the steps suggested when evaluating a marketing activity, you will be spending your time and effort much more productively and should see future returns.

III. OTHER CONSIDERATIONS AND TIPS IN POSITIONING YOURSELF AND BUILDING CREDIBILITY

The following are some additional tips and thoughts about selecting positioning activities to help assure that you use your time effectively and maximize your return:

• *Do things you enjoy and are good at.* As marketing opportunities come your way, such as speaking engagements, writing assignments or organizational activities, be honest with yourself in determining your skills and what you really like to do. If you don't like writing or aren't particularly good at it, then focus on opportunities to speak.

• *Pick activities you believe in.* For example, if you want to become active in an association, find one whose purpose you feel strongly about. You will be more likely to attend meetings and make a contribution if you care about the mission.

• *Be selective.* In some cases, opportunities to engage in positioning activities will come to you. For example, a contact may invite you to speak at an industry seminar,[1] or a publication may contact you to submit an article.[2] Be sure to ask the right questions before agreeing to participate. If it's not appropriate for you, you can always help find someone else to take on the job.

---

[1] See Chapter 3 *infra* on Public Speaking.

[2] See Chapter 2 *infra* on Writing for Publication.

• *Be proactive.* Many times, the best positioning opportunities need to be sought out. Contact the executive director of a trade association for your target audience and ask how you can submit a presentation idea for the upcoming annual conference. Call the editor of a bar publication in which you'd like to have an article appear and brainstorm some potential topics.

• *Improve your skills.* If you are weak in a particular area, try to improve. For example, every lawyer will benefit from public speaking, so if that isn't a strength of yours, you can join a Toastmasters chapter or take a class in public speaking. If you're not comfortable working a room, you can attend workshops on networking.

Ideas/Notes: Overview: Positioning Yourself and Building Credibility

My personal challenge(s) or obstacle(s) in this area:

_____

_____

_____

_____

_____

My goal(s) or objective(s) in this area:

_____

_____

_____

_____

_____

What I need to do to get started:

   (1) _____

   _____

   (2) _____

   _____

   (3) _____

   _____

   (4) _____

   _____

   (5) _____

   _____

Writing for Publication

I. INTRODUCTION

Most lawyers like to write. When it comes to marketing activities, many a lawyer's first thought is to write an article. Even practice groups often start their marketing efforts by publishing newsletters.

Writing can be an effective activity if you understand its place in your overall marketing program and what kind of "return on investment" you can expect. Being published builds your credibility and allows you to enhance your résumé. It is one of the building blocks that you use to become better known as an "expert," by contributing to the perception that you are knowledgeable in a particular area. For example, while writing a book may not make you rich, it can provide you with name recognition, a degree of respect and, in some cases, publicity.

However, writing may be the marketing activity least likely to produce business per se. Unless your work is the first to report on a new development, is extremely timely or innovative, or covers a highly specialized niche or substantive area, writing rarely will generate business, or even inquiries, for you.

> [W]riting may be the marketing activity least likely to produce business **per se** [but] can still be a very valuable and worthwhile piece of your overall marketing effort.

That being said, writing can still be a very valuable and worthwhile piece of your overall marketing effort. This is particularly true when you are a younger lawyer trying to establish your credibility and flesh out your résumé, when you can be the "first to market" with a new development or a novel approach, or when you are trying to establish yourself as "the" expert on a particular topic. And writing can often lead to other marketing opportunities, such as speaking.

For any writing project to succeed, you need to reach the right audience. If you are interested in writing as part of your business development or marketing effort, there are different options available to you:

(1) *Books.* You can be an editor or an author of a book. Writing a book, even serving as an editor, requires an enormous commitment of time and effort. If you choose to go down that path, you should look closely at the following issues:

- What are the competing publications? In reviewing them, determine how you might differentiate your book (e.g., substantive detail, intended audience, etc.). Also, look at the strength of the competition (e.g., publishing entity, marketing arm, pricing, audience, etc.).

- Who is the intended audience? Does the publisher have good access to that audience? How will the book be marketed?

- What is the timeframe for publication?

- Will the work be updated on a regular basis? What will your obligations be once the book is published?

After your research, you can conduct a cost-benefit analysis to see whether the royalties or the likelihood of building your reputation as a result of the work will outweigh the cost of your nonbillable time or producing the book.

(2) *Chapters.* Writing a chapter is a less time-intensive endeavor than writing a book, but still involves a substantial commitment. The same considerations of cost, benefit, audience, etc. apply as in the case of writing a book.

(3) *Articles.* Articles can be placed in third-party or firm-produced media. Your writing can include articles submitted to newsletters, Web sites, magazines or other publications, as well as client advisories and

letters to the editor. Again, when considering where to publish, you should focus on whether the publication is highly respected or widely read by the audience you'd like to reach.

II. SELECTING YOUR TOPIC AND PUBLICATION

Perhaps the most common mistake that lawyers make is to start with an outline or even the finished product, for example, writing an article and then trying to find someone to publish it. It is far better to consider topics, do some research to identify the media or publishers that reach the appropriate audience for your message and then approach the publisher. If the publisher is interested in your general topic, you can work through the details together to assure that the end result will be what both you and the publisher want. If you put in all the work ahead of time, you may find your work rejected because you have missed the mark in terms of content; even if the work is accepted, you may be in the position of doing substantial rewriting. The best article, chapter or book will not help promote you if it doesn't reach the people you need to reach or isn't perceived to provide valuable information.

One lawyer decided he was interested in using his marketing efforts to attract and serve family owned businesses. Based on his experience, he wrote an article outlining issues facing family businesses. However, when it came time to publish, he submitted his article to his state bar journal. While there are some practice areas or topics for which other lawyers would be the appropriate target, in this instance, it would have made a lot more sense to publish the article where family business owners would see it, for example in a publication for small business owners or an entrepreneurs' magazine.

With that as a backdrop, here are some thoughts about selecting your topic and the right kind of vehicle.

A. Selecting the Right Vehicle

Even before you pick your topic, you should think about alternative publishing vehicles. Depending on your practice or your firm, there may be a number of media available to you, including firm opportunities, such as newsletters, advisories or client alerts, and outside publications you can investigate.

When selecting the type of publishing vehicle, you should consider these factors:

- *Objective.* What is your objective for writing in the first place? Is it to provide an educational service, increase your visibility or generate inquiries? If, for example, you are interested in generating inquiries, your vehicle will need to be very timely and targeted.

> *What is your objective for writing in the first place? If, for example, you are interested in generating inquiries, your vehicle will need to be very timely and targeted.*

- *Credibility.* Being published in a non-firm medium usually will do more to build your credibility and reputation than being published in a firm-sponsored vehicle.

- *Reach.* Outside publications may have a larger circulation than your in-house publications, providing you with the means to get in front of many more targets (particularly prospective clients or referral sources).

- *Comprehensiveness.* Obviously a book or even a chapter offers the opportunity to cover a subject in more detail than being published in a two-page newsletter article. However, a book, or even a chapter, involves a lot more work.

- *Timeliness.* Publishing schedules vary, but some magazines may have a six-month delay between the submission of your article and the date it hits the newsstands. A book may be two or three years in the making. As a result, if you want to write about breaking news, such as a court ruling, you may want to consider a more timely medium, like an electronic update.

B. Picking a Good Topic

In addition, before beginning to write, you should think generally about your topic. You probably have an idea based on a legal matter or case in which you've been involved, some research you've done, a recent court ruling, or a trend you've noted in an industry you serve.

Whatever the inspiration, here are some ideas to make sure your writing time is spent productively:

(1) *Talk to members of the intended audience.* If you have some topic ideas, run them past a few of your friends, clients or referral sources who represent the kind of people for whom you are writing or who might be interested in the subject. If you are looking for topics or ideas, ask the same kind of people to name the three or four legal issues that are most on their minds or the one thing keeping them up at night.

(2) *Go to the source.* Talk to the editor of a publication serving your target industry or audience, or the executive director of a related professional association, to ask for content ideas.

(3) *Use marketing professionals.* If your firm has a marketing department or access to an outside agency, enlist the help of the marketing staff. They can assist you in determining if you have a good idea, identifying an appropriate publication, and even editing your work for readability.

C. Selecting the Publisher/Medium

Once you have the general idea for your article or publication, you should use the following checklist to hone your product and make it effective for both you and your audience.

(1) *Audience*

The first questions you need to answer are about the audience. For example:

- Who is your audience?
- How sophisticated are the people you are targeting in terms of legal issues?
- What is their level of knowledge?
- What information will be of assistance to them?

Knowing your audience will help you refine your topic, select the appropriate medium, and determine the content of your work. For example, if you want to write about corporate governance issues, you should determine whether you're writing for in-house lawyers, directors and officers, or investors.

Each type of audience will have different information needs, understanding of the law, levels of sophistication, etc. Let's say you are a family law practitioner and you want to write an article on how a particular financial planning tool will help a client retain more income after a divorce. Your article will take a completely different tone depending on whether it is written for financial planners, lawyers in other practice areas or the general public. Similarly, if you are a labor and employment lawyer, an article that you write for in-house lawyers should be very different than an article you write for HR managers.

(2) *Media*

Once you have better defined your audience, you can set about finding an appropriate medium for your writing. This typically involves investigating:

- *Internal or external.* Will you utilize a firm publication or an outside medium?

- *Third-party media.* If you want to place an article in an existing publication and the firm doesn't have one, what outside publications does your audience read? Third-party publications could include subscription newsletters or magazines (electronic or print), as well as publications circulated to members of trade or professional associations, like the ACC Docket for in-house counsel, and even publications developed by other vendors. Web sites are another outside resource.

- *Publishers.* If you are considering new material, such as a book, what publishers can help you reach your target market?

Your firm's library can be an excellent source of information on potential media. Once identified, you should review past issues of the publication or works of the publisher, if possible, to see what topics have been covered recently and to what extent, and to get a sense of the style and format.

(3) *Opportunities to Write*

If you are planning to target outside publishers, before investing your valuable time in writing, you should contact an editor at these publishing houses to determine interest in your submission. Questions you might want to ask include:

• Do they accept and publish articles or other types of treatises written by outside authors? If so, in what areas?

• Are they interested in your proposed topic? If so, what are the editorial guidelines (e.g., length of articles, word count, style, etc.)?

> *If [an editorial calendar] exists, it may guide your decision about the issue in which you want your article to appear.*

• Is there an editorial calendar? If one exists, it may guide your decision about the issue in which you want your article to appear. For example, a business journal may plan a special issue on commercial real estate development in July, which represents a perfect tie-in to your proposed article on property tax appeals.

• What is the deadline?

• Do they publish photos of authors? If so, you should be prepared to submit one.

• Do they provide reprint permission or extra copies to authors? Obviously you would like the ability to leverage your work into future marketing efforts.

After going through this process, you should have a good handle on your audience and subject matter, and will have identified an appropriate and interested medium. Now you're ready to write.

III. WRITING FOR IMPACT

If you are writing for marketing or business development purposes, your overarching objective is to provide useful information so people will consider you knowledgeable in the subject area and, just as important, helpful. The more your work can assist people, by pointing out issues, helping solve a problem or suggesting a course of action, the more likely your writing will have a positive impact on your marketing efforts.

If you are writing for an outside publisher, you will need to follow publication guidelines or style tips that are provided to you. If those guidelines contradict the advice below, they should be followed nonetheless. However, the more you can incorporate the following suggestions, the more you can maximize the impact of your writing by ensuring it is clear and understood by the readers.

> *The more your work can assist people, by pointing out issues, helping solve a problem or suggesting a course of action, the more likely your writing will have a positive impact on your marketing efforts.*

A. Length

If you are using an existing medium, the length of your submission is typically determined by the publication (e.g., 2,500 words for an article). Should you have more latitude (e.g., writing a firm white paper), keep in mind that shorter is often better. If you are targeting business people, in particular, they are very busy and receive more information than they can ever review. For virtually all audiences, however, the author who captures attention quickly, identifies the key issues, and advises what to do about the issues will be seen as a valuable advisor.

B. Interest

Here are some methods you can incorporate into your submission to capture the attention of the readers:

(1) *Use a quote.* Starting an article with a related quote, humorous or otherwise, can be an effective technique.

(2) *Try a "Q&A" format.* This allows you to pose and then answer questions readers might have about your subject matter.

(3) *Lead with a good title.* A strong, clear title will draw readers into the article. For example, an article entitled "How to Keep Employees from Stealing" is more compelling than titles using terms like "malfeasance," "tortuous" or other legal terms.

(4) *Employ case studies.* This can be an effective way to make subjects more interesting and easier for the audience to understand.

C. Organization

The organization of your work is paramount to your ability to convey a message. There are several techniques you can use to make your writing easier for the audience to follow, including:

- *Headings and subheadings.* These should be used to organize your material and help the reader to find content or skim.

- *Bullets.* Instead of sentences or paragraphs, some information lends itself to bullets, for example, names.

- *Sidebars.* These can be used to summarize information or to pull out case studies or examples.

- *Checklists, charts or graphs.* These techniques can be used to present and summarize material visually.

- *Conclusion.* Include a strong ending to your work, either a summary of your key message or a call to action. For example, in an article about the protection of intellectual property, the summary may begin, "To address these concerns, you should consider the following actions: (1) Audit your software; (2) Implement an anti-piracy policy; etc."

D. Relevancy

Obviously, your writing will have more impact if it is germane to the readers. Some ideas for showing the audience the relevance of the material include:

- Profiling a recognized company or providing a case study in the audience's industry

- Discussing how the outcome of a particular case has the potential to affect the audience

- Teaming with a client or referral source (e.g., employee benefits consultant) to provide a more rounded discussion of an issue

- Developing a "point-counterpoint" approach with a colleague or professional acquaintance (e.g., someone in the targeted industry) to offer different perspectives on an issue

- Providing a "checklist" or summary of practical suggestions for implementation

E. Readability

Employing good writing skills is perhaps the most important way to assure that your work is effective. Consider the following tips:

> *Write in language the readers will understand, from your title to your headings to your content. Even lawyers would rather read an article that is easy to understand than one replete with "legalese."*

(1) *Have a clear message.* By the time readers are through with your publication, what do you want them to know?

(2) *Use plain English.* Write in language the readers will understand, from your title to your headings to your content. Even lawyers would rather read an article that is easy to understand than one replete with "legalese." This means using the readers' jargon and lingo, but avoiding legal jargon and buzzwords. This also means eliminating Latin phrases, which are perceived by readers to be pretentious.

(3) *Focus on the readers.* Use the word "you" (not "we" or "the firm"). Identify key issues for the readers and advise them what to do about the issues.

(4) *Write clearly and concisely.* Keep your writing to the point, and write in an active voice with strong verbs. For example:

Instead of: *"The foregoing table is intended to assist readers in understanding the costs and expenses that a shareholder in the fund will bear."*
Say: *"This table describes the fees and expenses you may pay if you buy and hold shares of the fund."*

(5) *Use the passive voice when it strengthens the sentence.* There are times when the passive voice will place the appropriate emphasis, such as "The jury was impressed by her denial of his accusations."

(6) *Avoid nominalizations.* They overcomplicate your message and add unnecessary words. For example:

Instead of: *"The lawyers conducted an investigation into the complaints and made recommendations concerning three changes to the employee handbook."*

Say: *"The lawyers investigated the complaints and recommended three changes to the employee handbook."*

(7) *Use personal pronouns.* If the publication style permits, personal pronouns will improve the readability and make your writing more interesting. For example:

Instead of: *"The document and appendices should be carefully reviewed by the company."*

Say: *"You should read the document and appendices carefully."*

(8) *Write in the positive.*

Instead of: *"Persons other than the primary beneficiary are not required to sign the document."*

Say: *"Only the primary beneficiary must sign the document."*

(9) *Avoid superfluous words.* Replace "in order to" with "to." Replace "in the event that" with "if."

> *[I]t is good practice to have a nonlawyer go over your finished product for readability.*

In fact, it is good practice to have a nonlawyer go over your finished product for readability, whether this is someone from the firm's marketing department, your spouse, a client or a friend. When your selected readers are finished, ask them to tell you what they took away as the key message(s).

F. Writing a Letter to the Editor or Editorial

There are times when a well-written letter to the editor or an editorial can be an excellent way to communicate with your target audience. Your motivation could be one or more of the following:

- To set the record straight
- To present a certain perspective that you feel has been ignored
- To offer solutions to problems
- To generate support for an issue
- To correct erroneous impressions or information

There have been instances when editorials have actually spurred a column or future feature article.

Before submitting anything of an editorial nature, it is important that you consider any potential conflicts of interest, real or perceived. These should be reviewed on behalf of the firm as well as for particular clients who may be affected. It is a good idea to review your idea with firm management before writing.

If you are submitting something of an editorial nature, consider the following tips:

(1) *Open with your subject.* Start your letter or article by communicating your purpose for writing, e.g., "Your editorial, 'Tax cuts threaten quality of life,' requires a response."

(2) *Assert your position.* State your key message clearly, and use facts, statistics or other information to bolster your case. Your message will be received most positively if you do not appear self-serving or defensive.

(3) *Use good writing skills.* As with all writing, your editorial submission will be most effective if it has a clear message, focuses on the readers' needs and is concise.

(4) *Avoid personal attacks.* Your message should be reasoned, and your letter or article should avoid personal criticisms or emotional reactions.

(5) *Sign your letter.* Include your name, firm name and title, and your phone number for the publication.

(6) *Expect a response.* Due to the nature of editorial writing, many authors will receive reactions—both positive and negative.

IV. LEVERAGING YOUR EFFORT

To get the best return from your writing efforts, you need to think about activities you can engage in after publication. Some ideas are outlined below.

A. Communicating with the Publisher

If you had your work published in a third-party medium, you can use your submission as an opportunity to build a relationship with the editor or your contact at the publication or publisher. For example:

• *Thank the person responsible for publishing your work.* Send a thank-you note expressing your appreciation for the opportunity and offering to provide more content in the future.

• *Add the editor/contact to your (or your firm's) mailing list to receive additional information in the future.* This might include, for example, seminar invitations, newsletters or client advisories provided by your practice group or department.

B. Disseminating Your Work

To maximize the investment of your time, you should look for opportunities to disseminate the article or publication as widely as possible. Unless you have retained the copyright, this requires obtaining reprint permission (which should be discussed before submitting your work). You certainly want to have the opportunity to use your publication in your marketing efforts.

> *To maximize the investment of your time, you should look for opportunities to disseminate the article or publication as widely as possible.*

Should permission be granted, consider the following steps:

• *If possible, have a reprint done professionally or purchase copies through the publisher.* This will allow you to remove adjacent advertising, format the article under the publication banner, etc.

• *Mail or e-mail copies to clients and others in related industries (e.g., consultants or environmental engineers) who may be interested.* Send your work along with a personal note that says, "Thought you might be interested . . ." and highlights the topic or the gist of your advice.

- *Send copies to other media contacts who cover the industry or area of focus.* This will position you as a source or resource for future coverage of the topic. Depending on the timeliness, magnitude or relevance of the subject, you could highlight the key issue(s) and offer to explain in more detail how the publication's readers are or could be affected.

- *Talk to your firm's marketing department or Webmaster about adding the article to the firm's Web site.*

- *Distribute your article internally.* Forward it to other lawyers in the firm, particularly those who may have clients who would be interested, or ask the marketing department to add it to the firm's intranet, if one exists. Take the time to highlight the focus of the article and its implications for firm clients.

- *Use copies of the article in your future marketing efforts.* For example, include the article in proposals for new business or letters to prospective clients, insert it in your firm's marketing materials, and bring it to speeches you give.

- *Put copies in your office or the firm lobby for both internal and external visitors to take.*

C. Leveraging the Information and Opportunity

If possible, you should explore ways to leverage the article into other marketing activities. If you retain the copyright, you may be able to use the material more broadly; if not, you still may be able to revise or refocus it for another use or another audience. Some thoughts:

- *Send a copy to a related industry association and offer to give a presentation at a future meeting.* For example, if your article appeared in your firm's construction industry newsletter, you can contact the program chair of the Associated General Contractors (AGC) with a copy and a note suggesting you would be happy to address the topic at a future meeting of the group.

• *Update your work.* Consider whether you can write a follow-up piece or an update for a future issue of the same publication.

• *Rework the article.* Perhaps it can be used for a different publication or audience (e.g., a magazine for environmental engineers).

• *Send the final work to other publications.* Offer to let them reprint all or selected portions (again, if you retain the copyright).

D. Augmenting Your Credentials

Finally, since one of the primary benefits of publishing is to enhance your professional credibility, you should be sure to update your printed bio, your bio on the firm's Web site and other lists of firm publications to include appropriate references to your published work.

V. OTHER CONSIDERATIONS AND TIPS FOR WRITING FOR PUBLICATION

The following are some additional ideas for successful writing:

• *Write with a specific person in mind.* Warren Buffett once said he wrote his analyses for his sisters; while they were very smart women, they were not financial experts. Whether you are writing for personal injury victims or chief financial officers, think of a particular individual as you write.

> *Whether you are writing for personal injury victims or chief financial officers, think of a particular individual as you write.*

• *Start with a bang.* A great introduction will help to ensure that people read your work and ultimately receive your important message.

• *Meet your deadline!* Being timely with your submission can present opportunities. One law firm was competing with a number of its competitors to place articles in a statewide journal for the commercial real estate development industry. The firm's lawyers were so good about submitting their articles on time, and the other firms were frequently so late, that the editor ultimately offered the timely firm an exclusive column. Conversely, being late may cause you to lose the trust of the publisher, potentially lose that publishing opportunity and perhaps even lose your chance to be a future resource.

• *Remember that the editor may change your submission to fit the publication's style or layout considerations.* While some editors may give you a chance to approve changes, others may not.

• *Don't submit the same work to different publications without their knowledge.* Publishers will assume the submission is exclusive unless you have informed them otherwise.

• *Include relevant credentials in your "author's bio."* Identify the firm and provide information about why you are qualified to write the work, such as experience in that industry, expertise with that topic or involvement with that case.

• *Give the readers information.* Some people suggest that articles should just be "teasers," requiring readers to call for more detailed information. Actually, the converse is true; the more you help people with your writing, the more likely they will be to call. Writing something that doesn't have value to the audience ultimately will not provide a return to you either.

Checklist for Writing

• *Audience.* Who are you trying to reach?

• *Message.* What information are you trying to convey? How timely does it need to be?

• *Vehicle.* What type of work (e.g., chapter, book, article, blog, etc.) will provide the best vehicle for communicating your message to your target audience?

• *Media.* What media, publishers or other opportunities exist for this work?

• *Work.* Can you make your topic interesting, relevant and readable?

• *Follow up.* How can you leverage your effort to get the best return?

Ideas/Notes: Writing for Publication

My personal challenge(s) or obstacle(s) in this area:

_____

_____

_____

_____

_____

My goal(s) or objective(s) in this area:

_____

_____

_____

_____

_____

What I need to do to get started:

(1) _____

_____

(2) _____

_____

(3) _____

_____

(4) _____

_____

(5) _____

_____

3
Public Speaking

I. INTRODUCTION

Public speaking is a good way to establish credibility and position a lawyer in front of target audiences. Many potential clients, particularly in-house counsel, assert that hearing a lawyer speak is one of the most effective ways for them to determine if someone is knowledgeable about a particular subject area.

There are numerous opportunities for lawyers to speak, including:

> *Many potential clients ... assert that hearing a lawyer speak is one of the most effective ways for them to determine if someone is knowledgeable about a particular subject area.*

- Firm-organized seminars and roundtables
- Seminars and continuing legal education programs sponsored by outside organizations
- Client-specific workshops or programs
- Teaching at colleges or universities

Aside from establishing credibility, an additional benefit of speaking is that many programs will afford you an opportunity to interact with the audience, through question/answer sessions, luncheons, cocktail parties or follow-up activities. These chances for personal contact have the potential to turn a speaking engagement from a passive to an active marketing exercise.

Unfortunately, public speaking is a common fear. And even lawyers who aren't nervous giving presentations don't necessarily make effective speakers. This Chapter provides some ideas to help you prepare and present in a way that gets you noticed by your audience.

II. SELECTING AN APPROPRIATE FORUM

Depending on your practice, an appropriate audience could include other lawyers, law students, referral sources, prospective clients or existing clients. The first mistake many lawyers make is simply responding to requests to speak without adequately analyzing the sponsoring organization and the topic being requested in terms of the potential to generate interest or inquiries.

For example, some estate planning lawyers spend enormous amounts of time and effort delivering generic presentations to general audiences, i.e., speaking in forums such as rotary club meetings or community education classes on things like the importance of having an estate plan. While this may qualify as community service in terms of educating the public, it has a much more remote chance of generating business than speaking to the key clients of a top-producing insurance agent about tax-saving strategies in business succession planning.

As another example, teaching a college course can be a huge time commitment. In some cases, it can pay off, however, through the prestige it brings to your résumé or by generating future business. For instance, many tax lawyers have found teaching to be an effective technique for generating referrals from former students.

In some cases, you may seek speaking opportunities, even submitting a proposal in response to a "Call for Presenters." In other cases, you may be called and asked to participate in a program.

A. Seeking Speaking Engagements

If you are trying to work your way onto a program panel, the first step is to select an appealing topic. In order to choose a relevant and timely topic, consider the following:

• *Talk to some clients or other contacts in the industry or area to get some input into potential subjects.* Review previous years' programs to get a sense of the issues of interest, the format of the programs or the other speakers involved.

- *Speak to a member of the selection committee.* If you know someone who will be involved in reviewing the proposals (or even if you don't), call to discuss ideas you are considering. You may get feedback that will help you present your concept better by making the topic more attractive or refining your format. The members of the selection committee should have a good idea about what topics need to be addressed and what the audience wants to hear. They may even have a specific topic in mind for you to cover.

- *Use your knowledge of the industry.* If possible, include phrases, "buzz words" or hot topics in the description of your presentation to demonstrate your knowledge of the field.

- *Consider alternative formats for your proposed session.* For example, would a panel of industry representatives complement your presentation? Can you team up with a client in the field to lend credibility to your proposal and provide the practical approach that attendees might enjoy? Some groups might be wary of giving an entire session to a "vendor" and more inclined to consider your proposal if it includes association members or other lay people.

- *Incorporate the conference theme.* Every program has a theme; make certain your session supports what the conference organizers are trying to do. In fact, in your pitch or proposal, you should state specifically how your topic relates to the conference theme.

> *Every program has a theme; make certain your session supports what the conference organizers are trying to do.*

If you are asked to submit a formal proposal to present, you need to do a good job of describing your ideas to the conference selection committee. Winning papers usually focus on both substance and form. The substance is key, of course, in ensuring that the audience will be interested in your topic. But form is also important for the members of the selection committee as they wade through proposals. Think about the following:

- *Follow the proposal format.* If the conference materials provide a form, fill it out completely. If they include an outline that you are to follow, follow it to the letter. Your job is to make it easy for the committee members to find the information they seek.

- *Attach a cover letter.* In it you should:

  - *Describe your goals.* What do you hope attendees will gain from your session? Most conference sponsors would like presenters to articulate two or three specific objectives (e.g., "Attendees will learn the five most important clauses to include in their vendor agreements").

  - *Link your presentation to the conference theme.* As previously noted, you will want to show how your proposal supports what the conference organizers are trying to do.

  - *Summarize your presentation.*

- *Make your outline interesting.* If your outline isn't compelling, the committee might infer that your presentation won't be either. In addition, be sure your proposal is well-written and professional in appearance.

B. Responding to Invitations to Speak

Before seeking or accepting any speaking engagements, you should ask about and evaluate the following:

- *What is the composition of the audience?* For example, what positions do the attendees hold, what types of organizations do they represent, and how are they involved with the subject matter you plan to address? Ideally, you will be speaking to people in a position to refer business or make decisions about hiring legal counsel some day.

> *A small number of attendees doesn't necessarily mean the engagement isn't a good one, as it may be more effective for you to speak to a dozen high-level executives than 300 advertising account executives.*

- *How many people are likely to attend?* A small number of attendees doesn't necessarily mean the engagement isn't a good one, as it may be more effective for you to speak to a dozen high-level executives than 300 advertising account executives. Still, knowing the projected attendance may help you determine whether the opportunity will be worth your investment in preparation and presentation time, which can be considerable, or at a minimum help you select a more effective format for the session.

• *What is the topic?* If possible, you should have a hand in determining your topic, or at least the focus of the session. The most effective topics will be timely and relevant to the audience, like "what Sarbanes-Oxley means to private businesses," as opposed to static presentation content, such as "forms of business entity" (unless, of course, the latter is intended for start-up businesses).

> *Find out as much as you can about the people who will attend your presentation, such as their positions and the organizations they represent.*

• *What is the time slot and how many programs will be running concurrently?* You may be scheduled as the last program on the final day of a meeting in a resort location; in that case, the "no show" ratio is likely to be very high. Or you may be placed in a time slot that pits you against one of the more popular programs at the meeting. In many cases, you may be able to request a particular time or day. In addition, you will want to know the amount of time allotted for your speech so you can plan your presentation accordingly.

Once you have accepted a speaking engagement, you can move on to the task of creating a memorable presentation.

III. GIVING A MEMORABLE PRESENTATION

There are two parts of every presentation: the content and the delivery. Your audience will use both to draw conclusions about your professionalism and your expertise.

A. Preparation

The first step is to plan a presentation that will meet the information needs of the audience. In this regard, you need to:

(1) *Know your audience.* Find out as much as you can about the people who will attend your presentation, such as their positions and the

organizations they represent. For example, you don't want to focus on issues facing large companies if the bulk of the audience represents small, family-owned businesses. The attendees' positions and organizations should clue you in to their information needs and level of sophistication. Are they looking for practical tips or recent rulings and case law?

You also want to "speak their language" as much as possible. Whether the audience members represent the construction industry or the telecommunications industry, you need to demonstrate knowledge of their issues and jargon. Knowing your audience will help you determine what information will be most valued.

(2) *Learn about the sponsoring organization.* If the program is being offered by an organization, such as a trade or professional association, learn about the group. What kind of presenters does the organization typically have? What have been some recent topics presented to the group? You want to be sure your comments are not duplicative. Also, what format is generally used for meetings? What are the sponsor's objectives for the program or conference?

(3) *Select a good topic.* If you have the opportunity, based on what you know about the audience and the organization, select a topic that is timely and relevant. If you have time, you may want to poll some representative clients or companies to get their input. You can offer a few topics and get reactions or ask people to identify the three most pressing issues they are currently facing in areas related to your practice. You can always ask your contact at the group for suggestions as well.

B. Presentation Content

Once you have learned about the audience and identified your topic, there are many ways to ensure that your program captures your audience's attention. Keep in mind that most audiences attend programs for substantive information; they are not expecting lawyers to be entertainers or motivational speakers. Therefore, you should give a lot of thought to how you can make your presentation practical and helpful.

The following techniques will help you communicate your material effectively to audiences:

(1) *Use case studies.* Most people want to know how others like them have handled particular issues or problems. You can incorporate one or more examples of companies (real or invented) or, if appropriate, include a client as a co-presenter to bring a "front line" perspective to the table.

(2) *Incorporate practical tips.* Attendees like to walk out of a presentation having learned something that applies to their situation. As part of your session, you can incorporate "Frequently Asked Questions" or "Top Ten Tips" that position you as a solution-oriented lawyer.

> *[Y]ou can incorporate "Frequently Asked Questions" or "Top Ten Tips" that position you as a solution-oriented lawyer.*

(3) *Build in a question and answer session.* If the format allows, a question and answer session will help ensure that you address the issues foremost in attendees' minds and make you appear accessible. Repeat questions that are asked, so everyone can benefit from the response. If you find that no one asks a question, be prepared with some of your own. You can break the silence with a statement like, "One of the questions my clients often ask is . . . ." Invariably, the audience will be engaged and more comfortable posing follow-up questions.

(4) *Write an accurate description.* Make sure your presentation description matches your content. Audiences get upset when a program is not as billed.

(5) *Coordinate with other speakers.* If you will share the program with other presenters or if your topics are similar, contact them to make sure the sessions are not duplicative and that they support each other.

C. Presentation Materials

In addition, you should be certain your presentation materials (e.g., handouts, slides, etc.) are well thought out and add value to your speech. Your materials could include visual aids, like PowerPoint slides or video clips, as well as your written handouts.

(1) *Visual aids.* In preparing your visual aids, remember that their purpose is to reinforce your presentation. Lawyers frequently misuse

PowerPoint slides by including slide after slide of every point or sentence from the presentation in an unreadable font. Slides should highlight the key points of the speech. In addition, remember that video, color charts, cartoons and pictures maintain interest and attention.

(2) *Written materials.* Your written materials should be as comprehensive as possible. Having inadequate handout materials makes your

Tips for Using Visual Aids

PowerPoint and other visual aids can enhance your presentation. Many people retain more information when it is presented visually in addition to orally. However, visual aids can also be misused. Here are some tips for improving the use of visuals in your presentations:

• Visual aids shouldn't include your whole presentation. Limit the information on your slides to key points, bullets and graphics that reinforce your remarks.

• Slides or materials must be legible to every member of the audience, not just those in the front. Generally what you see when you are standing six feet from your computer screen is what the audience will see projected on a large screen in a meeting room.

• PowerPoint slides should contain no more than six to eight words per line, and six or fewer lines per slide.

• Use bold fonts and easy to read colors, like black on a light background.

• Charts and graphs, in lieu of text, will convey your information or data even more effectively.

• Pictures or other visuals, with few words, will often make audiences sit up. They will be curious about the relevance.

• Be familiar with your slides so you don't have to turn toward the screen when you talk.

• Don't read your slides to the audience. They should be used primarily to reinforce major points.

audience think you "held back" or are unprepared. In addition, audience members may become frustrated at having to take detailed notes. Include a fleshed-out outline or your PowerPoint slides as well as supplemental materials, such as articles, lists of relevant Web sites or bibliographies.

You should also give careful consideration to the biographical sketch or résumé that you include with your materials.[1]

> *Having inadequate handout materials makes your audience think you "held back" or are unprepared.*

Audience members will look at this information to evaluate your expertise, and it should also help them find you later should they have follow-up questions or, better yet, be seeking counsel. When preparing your résumé for use with presentation materials, consider the following:

- If possible, limit your biographical sketch to one page

- Highlight things that the audience will be interested in or find compelling, such as relevant articles you've written or professional activities in a field related to theirs or the topic being addressed

- Use subheadings on your résumé to draw attention to key aspects of your background and experience, such as "Education," "Representative Matters," or "Presentations"

- Include a picture, if possible

- Include your name, firm name, address, telephone number, e-mail address, Web site address and other important contact information on the résumé

- Don't forget to bring your business cards

D. Execution and Delivery

Studies have shown that more than half of the impact a speaker makes on an audience is determined by body language. Here are some tips to be more effective in delivering your presentation:

---

[1] See Chapter 5, Section IV *infra* for additional information on preparing effective biographies.

(1) *Make eye contact.* Your eyes are your most important speaking tool. People judge your conviction and sincerity by your eye contact. First, and most important, don't read your speeches; give yourself enough time to practice so you know your material. If you have a small audience, try to make eye contact with each person, but for just a few seconds at a time so you don't make anyone feel uncomfortable. If you have a large audience, move your eyes from section to section to acknowledge the crowd. Speakers often find that they predominantly address just one side of a room until they focus on this technique.

> *Your eyes are your most important speaking tool. People judge your conviction and sincerity by your eye contact.*

(2) *Stand squarely and use gestures for emphasis.* Be conscious of the way you stand and hold your arms. For example, avoid crossing your arms; you will look defensive. If you place your hands on your hips, you will appear to be nervous. Swaying from side to side is distracting to the audience, and crossing your ankles looks unprofessional. Keep your hands out of your pockets (this will also keep you from jangling the coins in them). Instead, you should stand with your feet slightly apart for good balance, with your arms falling freely at your side.

Gestures and hand movements can add or distract from your presentation. Making the same gesture repeatedly, such as pointing, will become annoying to the audience. Clinging to the podium makes you look insecure. You should aim for natural, open gestures, and even exaggerate them in front of large groups.

If the room and equipment allow, get out from behind a podium. You will have an easier time connecting with the audience if you approach it and walk more freely.

(3) *Try to look confident.* Your face should be in sync with your comments. If you are reporting on an unfortunate incident, your face should reflect concern. Smile if appropriate to your content; this will warm up the audience and also make you look more confident. Rehearsing is probably the best way to give you confidence in your

delivery. You might even practice in front of a mirror or videotape yourself to see if you have any obvious deficiencies to correct.

Minimizing Anxiety

If you get nervous before presentations, here are some thoughts to help you reduce your anxiety:

(1) *Prepare and practice.* Organize your presentation well, review your notes, practice your speech out loud, and even videotape yourself speaking. The better you know your material, the more confident you will be and the better you will present it.

(2) *Help yourself with a good outline.* Use a large font to make sure you can read your notes. Highlight key points for yourself. And staple your notes together so you don't lose your place.

(3) *Visualize.* Some people find it helpful to get to the room early, stand at the podium, and imagine the room filled with an audience.

(4) *Give yourself sufficient time to arrive and set up.* Avoid being rushed. You want to appear calm and prepared.

(5) *Include a lot of information.* Audiences are most interested in learning something from you, so the more helpful and practical your speech, the less concerned they will be about your delivery.

(6) *Personalize.* As people enter the room, make eye contact, smile and, if the setting allows, greet them. This will help you see them more as friends than strangers.

(7) *Be selective.* Start speaking in front of small groups or audiences with whom you are comfortable (e.g., giving presentations to other firm lawyers or at CLE programs). As presenting becomes more routine, you can move on to larger or less familiar audiences.

(8) *Breathe.* When speakers are nervous, they often fail to breathe in a normal pattern. If you feel anxious, pause and take a deep breath.

IV. FOLLOWING UP ON YOUR PRESENTATION

One of the complaints that lawyers often voice is that "no one called me" after the presentation. It's important to remember that, with marketing efforts like giving speeches, there is often little "cause and effect." That is because:

- *Everyone in the audience, if not represented by you, has another lawyer.* It is not that easy for people to change relationships.
- *Timing is everything.* The audience members may not have a need in the area that you are capable of filling. It may be years before they do. However, with proper follow-up efforts, time and timing, you may turn audience members into clients.

Direct contact with seminar attendees (if they are not clients) can be tricky. For example, if they were sitting passively in a hotel ballroom filled with hundreds of audience members, you probably didn't have a chance to build any relationship or rapport; as a result, it would be awkward and potentially in violation of the Rules of Professional Conduct to call on them. But there are numerous other ways to facilitate or encourage follow up after presentations and speeches:

- During the course of your presentation, offer something of value, e.g., to send an article or to put attendees on the firm's database for a relevant mailing (e.g., the firm's environmental law newsletter). However, don't shortchange the attendees in terms of your presentation and materials just to have a reason to follow-up; the pretense will be obvious.
- Offer to provide members of the audience with a more customized follow-up activity, such as an in-house workshop on the same topic or a free review of something (e.g., technology contracts) if the number of potential takers would be manageable
- Suggest that people monitor future developments on the topic about which you spoke through your firm's Web site or suggest that they e-mail or call you with questions following the seminar
- Obtain the list of attendees. You can make obtaining the list a prerequisite of your agreeing to speak. Then you can add the names to your

personal contact list in order to send out items that may be of interest to the attendees in the future. (Before doing so, check the Rules of Professional Conduct in your jurisdiction.)

- Offer to monitor an important case or issue in which the audience and/or the organization may be interested, and then provide updates or let them know the result

- Ask the sponsoring organization to provide an evaluation form for attendees that includes an area

> *If you do get an inquiry from a member of the audience, respond promptly. Although answering questions may involve nonbillable time. . . . [Y]our prospect will be judging you on the substance of your response as well as your prompt and effective service.*

where they can request follow-up information. Be certain to ask the sponsor for copies of your evaluation forms. (Audience members' comments will help you determine ways to improve your presentation skills.)

- Create a customized update just for the audience (e.g., the HR Update for Contractors); even if it's only sent once a year, it will give you a reason to contact the audience members

- Turn your presentation into another marketing tool, such as an article for your firm's newsletter or an in-house CLE presentation

- If you do get an inquiry from a member of the audience, respond promptly. Although answering questions may involve nonbillable time, your prospect will be judging you on the substance of your response as well as your prompt and effective service.

V. OTHER CONSIDERATIONS AND TIPS FOR PUBLIC SPEAKING

Here are some final thoughts on effective speaking:

- *Select a topic that is very timely and quite specific.* People will be more likely to call you if they associate you with a particular area of expertise.

- *If possible, negotiate your place on the program.* In a multi-day meeting, it is usually preferable to speak earlier in the conference rather than later; at a full-day program, it can be a challenge to speak right after lunch.

- *Attend social gatherings following your presentation.* If there is a social activity following your presentation (e.g., a luncheon or a cocktail party), be certain to attend. These types of activities may present an opportunity for someone to ask a question more privately or for you to meet members of the audience personally.

- *Provide a highlighted résumé.* Bring a copy of your résumé to your presentation, highlighting the areas or qualities you would like to have mentioned in your introduction. Many times, the program moderator will ask at the last minute what to highlight or will pick and choose facts. Providing a highlighted résumé will allow you to decide what information you would like brought to the attention of the audience.

- *Look for PR opportunities.* For example, you could seek out journalists who cover the topic or area of your speech and offer to provide the content.

- *Make sure to add your presentations to your personal résumé.* Your résumé should contain a section listing your speaking engagements and the articles you have written.

- *Instead of reacting to requests to speak, become proactive.* Identify organizations that have audiences before which you would like to position yourself, and make contact. Send a list of potential topics you could cover along with any relevant supporting material, such as articles you have written or press coverage you have obtained.

Public speaking remains an excellent way to create a perception of expertise and establish relationships with clients and nonclients. However, as with most marketing activities, the quality of your preparation, execution and follow-up will determine your results.

Ideas/Notes: Public Speaking

My personal challenge(s) or obstacle(s) in this area:

_____

_____

_____

_____

_____

My goal(s) or objective(s) in this area:

_____

_____

_____

_____

_____

What I need to do to get started:

   (1) _____

       _____

   (2) _____

       _____

   (3) _____

       _____

   (4) _____

       _____

   (5) _____

       _____

4

Dealing with the Media

I. INTRODUCTION

Whether or not your firm has a formal media relations program, employs a public relations professional or makes other institutional media relations efforts, most interviews involve a lawyer. Your opportunities to be a media contact or serve as a spokesperson may result from your law firm's cases or activities. You may also find yourself dealing with the media as a result of your outside activities, for example, as a section chair of the local bar association.

Depending on the situation, being quoted in the media can bring you and your firm tremendous publicity or unwanted exposure. In some cases, you can seek opportunities for positive coverage and have somewhat more control over the content. In other cases, you may become a target of the media because of something negative, such as a client's involvement in a scandal, an unfortunate firm event or a bad result in a case. In any event, your preparation and execution can make a huge difference in how you are perceived or how the story is ultimately told. While the media cannot be controlled, there are many steps you can take to influence and/or balance a story.

II. RESPONDING TO THE MEDIA

It is important to remember that a reporter's perspective is very different from yours. First, reporters are often under tremendous time pressures to file their stories, and their deadlines may not jibe with your schedule or your desire to prepare. Second, the media's interest in the subject area is likely very different from yours. This could be just one of many stories on which they are working, or the only one they've handled dealing with legal issues. Finally, except in rare instances, they will not have the same level of expertise about the subject as you have, particularly when the subject matter deals with legal or technical issues.

> *It is important to remember that a reporter's perspective is very different from yours. By putting yourself in the reporter's shoes, you might start to understand how best to handle the interview and frame your responses.*

By putting yourself in the reporter's shoes, you might start to understand how best to handle the interview and frame your responses.

A. Responding to the Contact

When you first get contacted by a reporter, keep the following in mind:

(1) *Be accessible.* If you are not available when the reporter calls, return the call as soon as possible. The media contact could be an opportunity. If you don't return the call promptly, the reporter may go to another source, or may not understand all the issues involved and present them in a less than positive or inaccurate light. In a situation with negative ramifications, if you don't return the call, this will likely be noted in the resulting story—"(Name) did not return our calls."

(2) *Be mindful of client confidentiality.* Inquiries involving a client matter require your client's input. (See the Rules of Professional Conduct for your jurisdiction.)

(3) *Follow the firm's policy, if one exists, for routing reporter contacts.* In many cases, firms will designate one lawyer or nonlawyer contact as the firm's spokesperson.

(4) *Find out the reporter's deadline.* Time is critical for many reporters, particularly if they are working on a breaking story. If the interview isn't needed immediately, you can ask to arrange it at a later time so you can prepare.

(5) *Ask questions about the nature or subject of the story.* In addition to the reporter's deadline, find out who else is being interviewed and what the gist of the story will be. You should also try to establish parameters for the length of the interview.

(6) *Seek the advice of your firm's marketing or public relations professionals.* Even if you are the appropriate person to deal with the media on the story at hand, if you have access to a marketing or public relations professional, take the time to solicit some advice.

B. Preparing for a Scheduled Interview

If you have the luxury of planning for an interview, your preparation can be extremely beneficial. For example:

(1) *Try to learn about the interviewer or the medium.* If you have time to review some of the reporter's previous work, you might be able to determine his or her possible perspective. Similarly, if you are not familiar with the medium, you should try to learn about the target audience or readership and the kind of information that would be of interest to the readers. Normally if you contact the medium, someone can send you information on readers/viewers. At a minimum, you can buy or request a current copy of the publication in which your interview will appear or listen to (or watch) the station, especially the program, on which your interview will be heard (or seen).

> *It is always a good idea to create a list of the primary points you want to make in an interview and codify the key issues involved.*

(2) *Review appropriate material.* If the subject matter involves technical issues, you may want to review case details or other background information to brief yourself before the interview.

(3) *Anticipate potential questions and prepare some answers in advance.* It is always a good idea to create a list of the primary points you want to make in an interview and codify the key issues involved. This process will also give you the opportunity to think of interesting quotes you might provide. Depending on the relationship you develop

57

with the reporter, you could offer to make your notes available following the interview.

(4) *Practice.* If you don't have a lot of experience giving interviews, you should try some of your quotes out loud. In addition, if you will be interviewing with a reporter for a written publication, put your thoughts in writing. Sometimes lawyers are surprised to see that their quotes do not adequately convey their perspective once the inflection or body language is removed.

(5) *If the interview will be in person, arrange to have it at your office, if possible.* You probably will be more comfortable there. This also gives you the opportunity to have a colleague present, if desired or appropriate, or to reference facts or materials.

(6) *Dress conservatively.* If you will be on television, avoid wearing clothing with patterns, contrasting colors or checks, none of which show up well on camera. A light colored shirt is preferable to white. Makeup and jewelry should be worn simply and sparingly.

(7) *Don't keep the reporter waiting.*

C. Being Interviewed

When you are being interviewed, keep the following points in mind:

(1) *Avoid legal jargon.* Present your views or information in a positive way, and make sure what you say is understandable.

(2) *Tape the interview.* If appropriate, tape the interview as a way to avoid being misquoted and to critique your performance later.

(3) *Rephrase questions.* While you don't want to appear evasive, you can rephrase questions that you don't understand or would rather not answer in their present form.

(4) *Avoid speaking "off the record."* First, looking at the interview from the reporter's point of view, if information can't be used in the story, it isn't very valuable. In addition, many experts will tell you that there is no such thing as "off the record," unless you have a very close relationship with the reporter.

(5) *Avoid saying "No comment."* A "no comment" reply often makes a reporter suspicious. There are ways not to comment without using that exact phrase. For example, "I'm sorry but I can't discuss that issue for ethical reasons." Or, "I'm sorry I can't comment on that issue, but let me give you the name of another good source." Such replies make it seem as if you would like to help but can't.

(6) *Respond strongly to accusations.* Without confirming or denying an accusation, you could say, "We are taking the allegations very seriously and will do the right thing."

(7) *Try to guide the interview.* If you have not been able to talk about the key points you want to emphasize, look for ways to transition the interview to your preferred topics. For example, "You mentioned industry trends earlier, and I think that . . . ." You can also initiate a new thought that hasn't been covered by saying something like, "One thing that we haven't addressed is . . . ."

> *A "no comment" reply often makes a reporter suspicious. There are ways not to comment without using that exact phrase . . . [and] make it seem as if you would like to help but can't.*

(8) *Be energetic.* You should project enthusiasm and excitement through your comments, expressions and demeanor.

III. OTHER CONSIDERATIONS AND TIPS FOR DEALING WITH THE MEDIA

The following are some additional thoughts about media relations:

• *Proactively seek opportunities for media coverage.* Meet with an editor when he or she isn't on a deadline to discuss the types of stories being sought. Plant the seeds of a story with reporters; they are always looking for a new topic or angle. For example, you might send a client alert to a reporter along with a personal note stating that the information might be of interest to the publication's readers, and offering to discuss it in more detail. Or you might call a business publication and mention a case result or pending legislation that would have an impact on readers, and offer to provide information.

• *Educate reporters.* Many times reporters cover a variety of topics. and usually lack a law degree. Take the time to provide background information, answer their questions and explain legal issues or terms.

• *If you don't like what was written or aired, be cautious with your response.* Keep in mind that the reporter and/or editor will always control the way your interview is presented. Even if you felt you did a good job of communicating with the reporter, the reporter usually has an editor. That means that the article, tape or video is being edited by someone

> *You don't start your role as a media source by talking to reporters from* **The Wall Street Journal.**

Getting Caught Off Guard

There may be occasions when you are called by a reporter unexpectedly. In those instances, it still pays to appear cooperative and responsive. Not returning a reporter's call or responding "No comment" sends up red flags to a reporter. In a story on a failure of a law firm to disclose witnesses to the opposing side, the offending lawyers were named in the article in the following way:

"The partners involved in the case, (name) and (name), did not return calls Friday."

At a minimum, you can call a reporter back to say you cannot respond. For example:

"I haven't had a chance to review the complaint, so I'm unable to answer your questions right now."

However, in many instances when there is the potential for bad publicity involving a prominent client or the firm itself, it is possible to anticipate media inquiry. In those instances, the firm should develop a written position that is shared with all the key contact persons in the office (including, for example, the receptionist and all attorneys involved in the matter).

at least one step removed from the interview. If you feel that information was wrong or that the facts were distorted or presented in a misleading way, you are probably justified in contacting or writing a letter to the editor, in a reasoned tone, to set the record straight.

• *Accept all invitations.* You don't start your role as a media source by talking to reporters from *The Wall Street Journal.* Interview with reporters from small papers; in addition to getting practice, you may find the resulting article picked up by other publications.

• *Be prepared.* Your advanced preparation and your skilled execution during the interview can have a big impact on a reporter's willingness to present your views.

Ideas/Notes: Dealing with the Media

My personal challenge(s) or obstacle(s) in this area:

_____

_____

_____

_____

_____

My goal(s) or objective(s) in this area:

_____

_____

_____

_____

_____

What I need to do to get started:

(1) _____

_____

(2) _____

_____

(3) _____

_____

(4) _____

_____

(5) _____

_____

Preparing Written Marketing Materials

I. INTRODUCTION

Lawyer marketing efforts frequently include use of written materials. These may take the form of promotional information, such as practice descriptions or direct mail letters, or substantive items, like newsletters or client alerts. [See Chapter 14 for a discussion of written proposals for business.]

Well-written materials can enhance your marketing and business development efforts. A letter that "sells" something—even if it's you—is different than most of the writing that lawyers do. This Chapter focuses on how to write client-oriented materials.

II. GENERAL WRITING TIPS

There are several techniques that will improve the quality and effectiveness of any type of marketing communication. These include the following:

(1) *Focus your writing on the reader.* Write with a specific target reader in mind. Anything you write should focus on things that are important or of interest to the readers, not simply to you or your firm's lawyers. For example, while lawyers might be interested in complex substantive discussions and case citations, nonlawyer managers are more interested in business implications.

n addition, you should include the word "you" frequently in your written communications. In fact, you might count the number of times you refer to the reader (or "you") versus the number of times you refer to the firm (or "we").

Compare the following sentences about a seminar being offered by a law firm, and consider their ability to attract a reader's attention:

> *The Anderson Law Firm is pleased to announce a seminar on corporate governance issues. Our lawyers will present the latest information on issues affecting boards, directors and internal policies.*

> Versus: *Is your company concerned about corporate governance issues? If so, plan to attend The Anderson Law Firm seminar, where you will receive the latest information on issues that affect your board, directors and internal policies.*

(2) *Write in language your readers understand.* Avoid legal buzzwords and jargon. For example, instead of using the term "labor and employment," talk about "human resources" and avoid stilted terms like "wheretofore" or "albeit."

> *People are inundated with mailings, e-mails and other messages each day; yours must capture their attention quickly.*

(3) *Have a strategy.* Reduce to one sentence the primary benefits you want to convey in your materials. Develop a key selling point and make that your focus.

(4) *Keep your writing brief and to the point.* People are inundated with mailings, e-mails and other messages each day; yours must capture their attention quickly. Eliminate unnecessary information, then unnecessary words and phrases.

(5) *Follow the journalistic pyramid.* Provide the most important information up front, so busy people can get the basics of your message immediately. Subsequent paragraphs (or pages) can expand on the details. This is particularly important for e-mail communications.

(6) *Write in the active voice, with strong verbs.*

> Instead of saying: *This seminar is intended to provide health care organizations with up-to-date information on regulatory issues.*

Say: *This seminar will help you ensure that your organization's policies and procedures comply with health care regulations.*

(7) *Make it easy for readers to skim and find information.* You need to help recipients get to the information they are seeking. In a newsletter or article, include a table of contents and clear headings. For bios and practice descriptions, use subheadings and bulleted lists instead of full sentences.

(8) *Proofread!* Your material should be free of errors. Run a spell check and grammar check before sending out materials. Be certain to spell check the subject line in e-mail messages as well.

(9) *Get critiqued.* Think about asking someone to critique your materials. Select someone who fits the profile of your target audience, like a good client, and share your résumé, letter, newsletter or attachments. Ask your contact if the package is clear and compelling or what changes he or she would suggest in order to make your materials more effective.

III. WRITING DIRECT MAIL OR E-MAIL MATERIALS

Many law firms communicate marketing messages through mailings or e-mails. These communications range from promotional messages, such as invitations to seminars or special mailings about services, to more substantive materials, like newsletters or alerts. In addition, some innovative lawyers are developing ancillary products or services to complement their practices. For example, a labor and employment practice group might offer an online training program for supervisors. In instances like these, to sell their offerings successfully, firms need to adopt marketing techniques traditionally not practiced by law firms, like direct mail and product advertising. (You should consult the Rules of Professional Conduct before engaging in these techniques.)

The first issue to address when writing is the purpose of the communication. There are many potential objectives that you could be trying to accomplish with the marketing materials, including:

- Providing an educational service or "added value" for clients
- Increasing the visibility or awareness of the firm, a practice or a product

- Generating inquiries or new business
- Staying "top of mind" with members of a target market, in the event they have legal problems

It's important to identify your objectives because different objectives may require use of a different form or format. For example, if your primary objective is to stay "top of mind" with clients and prospective clients, a regular substantive vehicle, like a newsletter, is often a great idea. If, however, you are more interested in generating inquiries or questions, a one-topic, timely "alert" will be more likely to produce results.

Once you have clearly identified the purpose of the communication, you should focus on capturing the attention of your target audience. There are many tips and techniques that will improve the effectiveness of a direct mail piece. Consider the following:

(1) *State your purpose right away.* Get to the point of your letter or e-mail in the first sentence. For example, "Do you have trouble keeping up with the ever-changing laws and regulations facing insurance companies?" If you are using a letter, you might consider including a "RE:" line above the body of your text to outline your objective immediately. If you are contacting people by e-mail, the subject line needs to grab attention quickly while avoiding having the appearance of spam.

> *Don't leave it up to readers to figure out why they should be interested in your materials or use your services, or to determine what makes your program or service different from other options.*

(2) *Clearly state the benefits of your program or service.* Every recipient is thinking, "What's in it for me?" Don't leave it up to readers to figure out why they should be interested in your materials or use your services, or to determine what makes your program or service different from other options.

To illustrate benefits, use examples to which recipients can relate. Describe a situation in which your firm's products or services can help avoid a problem. For example:

> *"As a subscriber to our electronic update, you will learn immediately about new legal developments that may affect your company's*

relationships with franchisees. You'll have the information you need to anticipate and deal with issues before they become problems."

(3) *Describe the target client or customer in the mailing.* Be sure to note for whom the program or service is designed. For example, "As a general counsel, you will benefit from this ongoing CLE forum in the following ways . . . ."

(4) *Personalize.* The more expensive the product or service, the more important it is to personalize your correspondence to the recipient. Take the time and effort to have your letter addressed to each individual. Run envelopes through the laser printer; don't use labels, which look impersonal. Use first-class postage, not bulk rate. Have someone sign each letter. If your correspondence looks like "junk mail," it will be dealt with as such.

(5) *Keep your letters or e-mails short.* In most cases, one page, or three or four paragraphs, will be sufficient. The shorter a communication is, the more likely it will be read. Additional information can be outlined in accompanying materials, attachments or links.

Once your letter is written, take a red pen and eliminate everything that isn't necessary. Reduce sentences to phrases or bullets. For example:

This service helps your company save time and money by:
  • *Enabling you to respond quickly when the government imposes new regulations.*
  • *Providing boilerplate forms and language that you can easily adapt to your particular case.*

(6) *Use compelling words.* Studies have shown that certain words in headlines or key sentences are likely to provoke a positive response. These include:

  • You/your
  • Money
  • Results
  • How to

- Save

- New

- Benefit

- Now

Can you work any of these into the first sentence of your message?

(7) *Make the mailing itself valuable.* You will increase the attention paid to the mailing, as well as the value of your firm, if your letter or e-mail includes something of interest to the recipient—some valuable bit of information or advice. For example, if it's a direct mail letter to market a product or service, you could include a salient case study or a form or checklist. With an e-mail invitation to a seminar, you could include a link to a recent related article or some research or statistics that might be of interest to the reader. Even if recipients decline your invitation or service, they will feel the mailing had value.

> *You will increase the attention paid to the mailing . . . if your letter or e-mail includes something of interest to the recipient. . . . Even if recipients decline your invitation or service, they will feel the mailing had value.*

(8) *Make the material visually attractive.* If possible, make your materials interesting to look at, through the use of mastheads, color, pictures or graphs. One caveat: If your communication comes via e-mail, don't make it so graphically intense that it takes too long to load, is difficult to open or might be blocked by recipients' anti-spamming systems.

(9) *Keep in mind e-mail issues and protocols.* If you are using e-mail to communicate (e.g., a seminar invitation, an electronic newsletter), here are some specific tips:

- Give readers an option of having information in the body of the e-mail. Some companies' systems will automatically block attachments.

- Send your e-mails at the optimum times. Studies have shown that the best time to send e-mails is between 11:00 a.m. and 3:00 p.m., on Tuesday through Thursday.

(10) *Include a call to action or a next step in the process.* What should the recipient do—return a postcard to indicate interest in receiving more information? Call the firm for further information? Expect your phone call within a few weeks?

(11) *Make it easy for recipients to respond.* Amazingly, many invitations or pitches that go out fail to include an easy response vehicle. Give readers or recipients a phone number (toll-free, if possible), a fax number for returning an interest form, an e-mail or Web site address, and a contact person. If the response vehicle is a written form, include a postage-paid envelope as well.

(12) *Build your credibility.* If recipients may be unfamiliar with you or the firm, include information to make them feel more comfortable. This could include a description of your industry expertise, lists of representative clients or other credentials. (See Section IV *infra.*) Other ways to build credibility include client testimonials, endorsements (e.g., from a local manufacturers' association) or co-sponsorships (e.g., hosting a CLE course with the local chapter of the Association of Corporate Counsel). (Before using these techniques, check the Rules of Professional Conduct for your jurisdiction.)

(13) *Reduce risk.* Finally, think about ways to make it easier for recipients to sample your offering. For example, if you are selling subscriptions to a firm newsletter, you might offer three free trial issues or money back for unsatisfied subscribers.

IV. PREPARING EFFECTIVE BIOS AND PRACTICE DESCRIPTIONS

When talking to a lawyer, prospective clients or referral sources often will ask for some information about the lawyer or the firm's practice. Providing such material will support your personal selling efforts.

When you are writing materials to describe your practice, keep in mind that clients and prospective clients are most interested in learning what you have done for other clients. For example, if you are a real estate lawyer, instead of telling people what you do (e.g., eminent domain, zoning, etc.), identify what you have accomplished (i.e., your results). Instead of focusing on "features" (such as how many lawyers are in a practice group), focus on whom you have worked for.

There are several ways you can get your message across to people in written form. In descriptions of your practice or on your individual résumé, consider including:

(1) *Lists of projects.* If you can obtain client permission, consider putting together a list of projects, deals or litigation matters in which you have been involved. For example, "Served as lead counsel for ABC Corporation in patent litigation involving laser technology."

(2) *Representative case studies.* Often, lacking client permission, you can still create a list of representative matters or unidentified descriptions of matters, such as "Assisted a major developer in acquiring property for a regional shopping mall."

(3) *Lists of representative clients.* Again, after obtaining client permission, it is very effective to give prospective clients a list of the people who have used your services in the past who can be called for references.

(4) *Aggregate numbers.* If it works to your advantage, develop some aggregate numbers to show the depth and breadth of your experience. For litigators, this might include the number of former clerks or prosecutors in the firm, or the aggregate dollars at stake in lawsuits involving a certain type of litigation (e.g., comparing the total value of the original offers and demands with the total value of the final settlements or judgments). Other lawyers could include the number of transactions (e.g., private placements) handled or the firm's market share in a particular industry (e.g., renewable fuels).

(5) *Credentials.* Anything that sets you or your firm apart from other law firms should be included. This could be membership in a prestigious organization (like a "College" of lawyers), recognition by an objective party (like the Chambers directory) or unique qualifications (e.g., LLMs).

In addition, although bios and practice descriptions are, by nature, focused on the firm or individual lawyer, try to make them as interesting as possible by varying your sentence structure.

Instead of: *Steve Stein joined Jones & Smith law firm in 1990. He is a partner and leads the firm's corporate department. Steve serves as counsel to many private and family-owned businesses. Steve speaks frequently on issues of interest to closely held businesses.*

Say: *For more than 15 years, private and family-owned businesses have turned to Steve Stein for counsel and advice. As a partner and the Chair of the firm's corporate department, Steve frequently speaks on topics of interest to closely held businesses.*

V. OTHER CONSIDERATIONS AND TIPS WHEN PREPARING WRITTEN MARKETING MATERIALS

Finally, here are some additional thoughts when preparing written marketing materials:

• *Before you start, look at your competitors' materials.* If you're putting together a practice description or bio, review the materials prepared by your key competitors (or people with whom you would like to compete) to see how they are distinguishing themselves or capturing attention. If you are writing a newsletter or e-alert, find out if other law firms or organizations already offer something similar. If so, you may want to consider an alternative format or at least a different focus.

• *Consider alerts or bulletins.* One of the most valuable marketing tools for nearly every type of clientele, and particularly for busy clients, is a client bulletin or alert. Generally these will involve one topic that could have an impact on the recipients. A bulletin should be short (one page), very timely (sent immediately, even by fax or e-mail), and carefully targeted (i.e., only sent to those who have an interest in the topic). A good bulletin or alert also will be written in plain English and contain practical recommendations.

> *One of the most valuable marketing tools for nearly every type of clientele . . . is a client bulletin or alert.*

• *Thank the recipient.* If the person to whom you are sending the materials requested them, thank your contact for the invitation.

• *Follow up.* One mailing will not be enough. You should plan on promoting your services or products several times to the same recipients in order to produce results.

WIIFM: The Key to Effective Correspondence

Every recipient of your correspondence is wondering "What's in it for me?"—or WIIFM, as it is known among professional communicators. The more quickly you can identify the benefit of you, your firm or your services, the more likely your material will be read.

What are the benefits? At their most basic, they could include:

- Saving them time
- Saving them money
- Getting them out of trouble
- Keeping them out of trouble
- Making them look good
- Making a problem go away

Ideas/Notes: Preparing Written Marketing Materials

My personal challenge(s) or obstacle(s) in this area:

_____

_____

_____

_____

_____

My goal(s) or objective(s) in this area:

_____

_____

_____

_____

_____

What I need to do to get started:

(1) _____

_____

(2) _____

_____

(3) _____

_____

(4) _____

_____

(5) _____

_____

6

Organizational Involvement

I. INTRODUCTION

One of the best ways for a lawyer to build a practice is to get involved in appropriate organizations. Depending on the nature of your practice, your interests, your community and your age, an "appropriate" organization could range from the Young Lawyers Association to the Intellectual Property Owners Association to the Heart Association.

The benefits of outside activity are many, including:

(1) *Providing opportunities to meet and build relationships with potential clients, referral sources and others related to the association.* You will have the chance to network and expand your circle of contacts through your attendance at the organization's functions and other activities.

(2) *Positioning yourself in a particular area.* For example, serving as the Chair of your state bar's Tax Section reinforces your expertise in tax to the members as well as others who see this honor on your résumé.

(3) *Making you more valuable to clients.* By being actively involved in a client's industry association, for example, you will be up to date on trends and issues of importance to the client. In addition, you will have opportunities to learn about other related resources, such as consultants or vendors, which may be of interest to clients.

(4) *Identifying further marketing opportunities.* Your activity in a group may lead to opportunities to speak at educational meetings or write for the organization's publication, enhancing your credibility and visibility.

(5) *Enabling you to make a contribution to an important issue or cause.* It is critical that you select an organization that means something to you. Then, as you become more active, you will find personal satisfaction in the work that you do.

There are myriad places in which you can achieve some or all of the benefits outlined above, ranging from civic and community groups to professional or industry associations. The kinds of organizations include:

• Professional associations, such as the American Bar Association (ABA), local bar associations or the associations of other professionals, such as the Association of Independent Certified Public Accountants (AICPA)

• Industry/trade associations (There are thousands of trade and industry groups, from the Associated General Contractors to the Auto Dealers Association.)

• Civic organizations, such as your state or local Chamber of Commerce

• Cultural organizations, like an art museum or symphony

• Social organizations, such as country clubs or networking groups

• Fraternal organizations, like the Rotary or Lions Club

• Charitable organizations (Not-for-profit groups always welcome lawyer involvement, from the Big Brothers to the Red Cross to the United Way.)

• Religious groups (Your church, mosque or synagogue may be an organization in which you want to make a difference.)

• Political organizations or political party activities

• Private entities (e.g., serving on a company's board of directors)

• Community organizations, such as your local library or Parent-Teacher Association

• Educational-related organizations, like a law school alumni association or a CLE provider

II. IDENTIFYING APPROPRIATE ORGANIZATIONS

There are a number of factors that should go into selecting the organization(s) in which you should get involved. Effective activity requires commitment and time; being a "member" in name only will do nothing for you or for the organization. As a result, you need to ensure you are spending

> *Effective activity requires commitment and time; being a "member" in name only will do nothing for you or for the organization.*

your time, energy and, in some cases, resources in places where they will generate the greatest impact.

One logical consideration is whether the organization will contribute to the development of business. Often business can result from the contacts and relationships a lawyer develops through outside activities.

However, for your efforts to be truly worthwhile, you need to have a personal interest in the issues and mission of the group. In addition to, or even in lieu of, considering business development opportunities, many lawyers use their organizational activities to build their reputations as leaders and as contributors—people who make a difference.

What factors might you investigate when seeking the appropriate organization for your investment?

A. Composition of the Group

If you are interested in using your organizational involvement to further your practice or business development goals, then you need to answer the questions below:

(1) *Who makes decisions about, or passes out, the legal work you ultimately are trying to obtain?* A lawyer targeting CFOs of hospitals and other health care organizations for corporate transactions, for example, might investigate activity in the Healthcare Financial Management Association.

(2) *In which organizations do the people you are targeting network?* And from which groups do your targets receive continuing education? A products liability lawyer will find the Defense Research Institute's

Products Liability Section invaluable for networking with other litigators from around the country who often serve as national or regional coordinating counsel and hire local counsel. A sole practitioner may find a broad range of potential helpful contacts in a local Rotary Club.

Another factor to consider is the membership composition of the organization. For example:

• *Age of members.* Ideally, you will be interacting with people who are close in age or experience to your peer group. If you join an organization with members who are much more senior, for example, you typically will find that they already have developed a close circle of contacts and referral sources and it can be difficult to break into their networks. If you are a younger lawyer, through your activity and involvement in an association with peers, you will be able to build your base of contacts as people grow in their professions and levels of responsibility.

• *Number of members.* You should be sure the organization will provide you with adequate opportunities to meet people and network. One construction litigator described how delighted she was to find a local chapter of an organization called Women in Construction only to attend a meeting and find out, in her admittedly flip words, "There are no women in construction!"

> *Without a sincere interest in the group's issues or discussions, you will be less likely to attend meetings, get actively involved and make a substantial impact on the group.*

B. Personal Interest

As mentioned earlier, you need to care about the organization's objective(s) or area(s) of focus. Without a sincere interest in the group's issues or discussions, you will be less likely to attend meetings, get actively involved and make a substantial impact on the group.

C. Ability to Participate and Contribute

You should inquire about the frequency and format of the organization's meetings to determine whether there are adequate opportunities to interact with other members or participate in the way that interests you. Some organizations, particularly trade or industry groups, limit the role that lawyers or other professionals can play, offering "associate" or other categories of membership. In that case, you may want to determine whether the limited exposure will be worth it. Finally, some groups, such as the Young Presidents Organization (YPO), may only permit lawyers to attend meetings if they are accompanied by a member client.

III. BECOMING ACTIVE IN AN ORGANIZATION

Simply being a member of an organization has limited value; the real value—to you and the organization—comes with activity. Once you have determined that a group is one in which you want to become involved, you should begin to investigate ways to raise your profile and increase your contribution.

Frequently, lawyers find opportunities to increase their activity by serving on boards, committees or sections of the association. Often, other activities, such as speaking or writing, also exist. When making your decision about getting more involved, you should examine a number of factors as well as the potential roles you might play.

A. Decision Factors

As you explore a specific activity within an association, consider the following:

(1) *Your interests.* Some lawyers like to find a role that utilizes their legal skills and training. If that is your desire, you could volunteer to handle some *pro bono* assignments, such as drafting vendor contracts, or to present an educational program. In other cases, lawyers like to use their outside activities to do something completely different or to build a new set of skills. If this is your wish, your activity could range from serving on a group's finance committee to helping with the group's marketing plan.

(2) *The organization's needs.* Obviously, your activity should benefit the association. You could evaluate the existing committees or activities to determine if any are languishing from a lack of activity or leadership. Perhaps the association's newsletter could benefit from a new editor. Similarly, you might propose a new activity or committee if you feel it

would be of value. Perhaps you could offer to spearhead a member survey or form a new substantive discussion group.

(3) *The composition of the committee or subgroup.* One of the benefits of getting involved in a committee or smaller group of an association is the opportunity to build relationships with the other people involved. Therefore, you should evaluate if your targeted group is comprised of the type of people you would like to get to know better. For example, if lawyers from other firms dominate certain committees or activities, that may reduce your potential impact or your ability to interact with the nonlawyer members.

> *One of the benefits of getting involved in a committee or smaller group of an association is the opportunity to build relationships with the other people involved.*

(4) *The time requirement.* You need to be realistic about the amount of time you can commit to the group, and the way the time is spent. Does the group meet during breakfast or in the evening? How often does it meet? And for how long? Once you know the extent of commitment required, you can determine if it will fit into the demands of your personal and professional lives.

(5) *The financial requirement.* Some organizations, particularly many desirable ones in which high-profile lawyers would like to be involved, have expectations that board members will make personal financial contributions, help with fundraising or do both.

B. Potential Activities

Most groups offer opportunities for members to serve in the following roles, all of which can be very effective in terms of both contributing to the organization and providing the lawyer with business development potential. Using the factors outlined above, you could investigate:

(1) *Boards of Directors.* Ultimately, to receive the maximum exposure and prestige, many lawyers set their sights on serving on an organization's board. However, becoming a board member generally requires that you first "pay your dues" in other ways, such as leading key committees.

(2) *Committees*. There are many committees that offer excellent networking and business development opportunities while contributing to the organization. Among the most effective are:

- *Program or education committee*. Members of the program committee usually plan the content for CLE programs or association meetings. This allows you to communicate with members to ascertain the issues or topics of most interest, and to contact high-profile speakers. You also might have the opportunity to speak, get one of your colleagues involved, or at least introduce speakers, providing visibility for your firm.

- *Membership committee*. The membership committee spreads the word about the association and identifies new members. Involvement on this committee will give you a reason to contact decision-makers—to get them involved in the group—and position you with new members, who will likely seek you out at meetings (as one of few people they know).

- *Fundraising committee*. Virtually every not-for-profit organization needs help raising money. Not only is this among the most important contributions you can make to an organization, it will help you get more comfortable with "sales calls" and give you a reason to contact leaders in the community. If you think about it, every major community or business leader actively, and in many cases visibly, raises money for some cause.

> *Not only is [fundraising] among the most important contributions you can make to an organization, it will help you get more comfortable with "sales calls" and give you a reason to contact leaders in the community.*

- *Special projects or events*. Another good way to make a visible and often tangible impact on a group is by helping to organize a special event, like a charity ball or golf outing. These projects have a definite conclusion, usually raise funds, and allow you to showcase your organizational skills.

(3) *Legal/pro bono work*. Most organizations need help with legal issues, from leasing space to preparing articles of incorporation. You can volunteer your skills and time in this capacity.

(4) *Editorial board.* Another way to keep abreast of the issues facing the members of the organization and maintain a high profile is to serve on the editorial board for the organization's newsletter or publication. In this capacity, you can contact people to submit articles, position your colleagues, write articles yourself or review editorial content.

(5) *Presenter.* Whether or not you serve on the program committee, you may be able to identify opportunities to speak to the membership at conferences, educational programs or seminars.

(6) *Sponsorship.* Another potential opportunity for exposure is to serve as a sponsor of the organization. Depending on the group and its activities, you could "buy a hole" at a golf outing, host a cocktail party at a networking gathering, place a half-page congratulatory ad in the ball program, buy a table at the annual meeting or even staff a booth at a trade show. Associations are always grateful for sponsors.

IV. OTHER CONSIDERATIONS AND TIPS FOR ORGANIZATIONAL INVOLVEMENT

Here are some additional thoughts as you begin your efforts to identify and get involved in outside organizations:

• *Be visible in the organization.* Woody Allen once said, "Eighty percent of sucess is showing up." When it comes to organizations, he's right. Participate in telephone conferences. Contribute to member listservers. Attend meetings and social events. (If you're uncomfortable with social functions, see Chapter 8 *infra* for some ways to improve your confidence level.)

• *"Own" the organization.* A "firm" membership in an organization is not effective; each membership requires one or more consistent and active individuals who become the "face" of the firm. The more personally invested you are in the organization, the greater your return on your investment.

• *Follow through.* Don't sign up for something if you can't or won't follow through. While this is a corollary to the first point, it is worth noting here. If you are elected to a board, you must attend its meetings.

If you volunteer to raise money, you must make your phone calls. It is far worse to make a commitment to the organization and not carry through than to promise nothing at all.

> *It is far worse to make a commitment to the organization and not carry through than to promise nothing at all.*

- *Be a big fish in a small pond.* You can often gain prominence and make contacts more quickly through a very targeted organization. For example, a young labor and employment lawyer will probably find more benefit through participation in the local Society for Human Resources Management chapter than at the national level of the ABA Labor and Employment Law Section.

- *Pass the torch.* If you have outgrown a worthwhile organization, are winding down your term on a board or need to move on, bring in another firm lawyer. You can often pave the way for another person to fill your seat on the board or an important committee. Having someone you helped or another member of your firm in an important position is always a good thing.

- *Don't spread yourself too thin.* Some lawyers make the mistake of getting involved in too many outside activities. As a result, they are unable to commit the time and attention required to do a good job and raise their profile.

- *Express your interests.* If you would like to get on a committee, seek out the committee's chair and let him or her know of your interest. If you would like to get on a board, find out what the usual path is to that role and start to communicate your desire to the appropriate people.

- *Be patient.* This point goes hand in hand with the preceding one. While you should let people know about your interests, you need to take a long-term view of your activity in an organization and your career as a whole. For example, if you are interested in becoming a member of the American College of Trusts and Estates Lawyers, an invitation-only group, your quest may take fifteen to twenty years to accomplish. You will have to begin with activity at your local or state bar level, and work to gain prominence nationally. However, if you don't start now, you may never get there.

Having Trouble Locating an Organization that Would Be Effective for You?

If you are willing to join an organization but don't know where to start, here are some ideas:

• Ask clients or other contacts in the field (e.g., other advisors) which organizations they belong to and which ones they find most valuable.

• Ask clients or professional contacts if you can accompany them to a meeting of an organization in which they are involved. This will give you a chance to check out a group while positioning yourself with your contact.

• Check your firm's policies and procedures. Many firms will provide funds for membership in selected organizations or attendance at their meetings. Conversely, some firms have prohibitions on certain activities, such as membership on a private company board of directors.

• There are many informal opportunities that exist, like breakfast clubs or networking groups. Many times, such clubs or groups will limit membership to one or two of a given type of professional (e.g., lawyer). The entrée to these groups is usually provided through an existing member.

• If you don't see something that interests you, form an organization! One franchising lawyer started a roundtable discussion group for franchisers, which subsequently held meetings at his firm. Another law firm's associates started a chapter of the Toastmasters with counterparts in a client bank, a large accounting firm and several client entities.

Ideas/Notes: Organizational Involvement

My personal challenge(s) or obstacle(s) in this area:

_____

_____

_____

_____

_____

My goal(s) or objective(s) in this area:

_____

_____

_____

_____

_____

What I need to do to get started:

(1) _____

_____

(2) _____

_____

(3) _____

_____

(4) _____

_____

(5) _____

_____

PART III:

DEVELOPING BUSINESS

Overview: Developing Relationships and Generating Business

I. INTRODUCTION

While Part II of this book focused on "positioning," i.e., how you can build credibility and make people aware of you and your practice, Part III focuses on developing relationships that can lead to business.

Most lawyers understand that developing business is important for them personally and for the firm. Yet, although many lawyers engage in "marketing" activities, typically only a small percentage of lawyers in any given firm generate the bulk of the firm's revenue.

Why is developing business so difficult? There are many good reasons. First, most lawyers have not received any training in this area and are quite uncomfortable with it. It's not unusual to hear lawyers say they went into the legal profession because they didn't want to go into sales. Many lawyers dislike the term "sales," finding it an anathema. Having to sell their services runs counter to their ideas about the legal profession. In addition, there are many times lawyers don't generate business because they fail to express an interest in getting the work.

Perhaps it will be of some comfort to know that typical sales techniques usually cannot be applied successfully to legal business. For

> *[T]ypical sales techniques usually cannot be applied successfully to legal business.*

most legal practices, generating business isn't about making cold calls or begging for files. Trying to obtain business from companies or business executives usually involves a risky or high ticket "sale" (i.e., there is a lot at stake, financially or otherwise), the decision-makers are often quite sophisticated and will resist traditional high pressure techniques, and actually getting the business generally requires a very long sales cycle (i.e., an extended decision-making process).

Most legal businesses are built on relationships, whether they are with prospective clients or referral sources. This Chapter provides an overview of networking and the business development process as well as some general tips for building relationships and "adding value" (i.e., enhancing relationships).

II. IMPORTANCE OF BUILDING A NETWORK

To be a successful lawyer, you need a good network. Effective networking is not just a key to generating business; it's important for your practice and your clients. Knowing the right people, for example, can:

• Be useful for your clients (e.g., assisting them in finding a good Realtor or the right expert witness)

• Lead to opportunities for you to market your services (e.g., speaking or writing)

• Provide opportunities for you to network or position yourself in important organizations (e.g., getting an invitation to serve on a board)

So your objectives in the area of networking, in the broadest sense, are two:

(1)   Finding ways to expand your base of contacts (e.g., through organizational involvement, introductions, networking); and

(2)   Working to develop good relationships with, and referrals of business from, your target contacts.

Having a broad network is critical if you want to develop business. The odds of developing business from any given contact are not that great; for example, if you have ten prospects on your list, you may realistically develop business from two or three. There are myriad reasons you will not get work from targets—they may already be satisfied with existing legal counsel or simply not need your services. So you will have to build your network continually in order to experience good results.

III. OVERVIEW OF BUSINESS DEVELOPMENT

Business development can be analyzed on a macro and micro basis. Generally, the following process applies to clients and referral sources when they are making decisions to hire legal counsel:

(1) *Awareness.* The prospect needs to be aware of you or your firm.

Clients consistently cite "expertise" as the most important criterion when hiring legal counsel.

(2) *Perception of expertise.* Prospects need to feel you have expertise in the area in which they are seeking counsel (e.g., class actions, transportation industry defense, the entertainment industry, etc.). Clients consistently cite "expertise" as the most important criterion when hiring legal counsel.

(3) *Relationship.* Generally there will be a relationship that precedes obtaining the business. Either the prospect will connect with you or a third party (e.g., a referral source) will steer the prospect to you.

How business actually is developed, however, is a complicated issue because each practice area gets its work in a different way. For general corporate lawyers, business is often generated through relationships with accountants or other advisors. For litigators, substantial practices can be built on referrals from other lawyers. Commercial real estate lawyers usually see success by targeting prospective clients, such as developers or building owners, directly.

So the first step for most lawyers is to identify who exactly has the business and what their needs are. To understand how business comes to your practice area, you might undertake one or more of the following activities.

(1) *Interview a partner with a book of business (i.e., a good clientele) in the area you are trying to build.* If you are in a large firm, you could ask a successful partner in your practice area for advice. If you don't have an internal resource, you might identify a lawyer in a noncompeting firm (e.g., a lawyer from another state you have met through bar association activities). Ask these resources to share with you:

- How they developed their biggest clients

- Who are the best sources of business for them or the most important contacts for that practice or industry

- Which organizations they find most helpful for learning about the practice area or industry

- Which organizations they find most helpful for networking in the practice area or industry

- Which publications you should be reading religiously to learn more about the practice or industry

(2) *Interview a client or prospective client.* It can be very valuable to talk to someone who typifies your target market. For example, if you practice in the financial services area and are interested in developing additional work, you could ask one or more of your contacts in the banking industry to tell you:

- What they look for when selecting a lawyer or law firm

- What criteria are most important to them when selecting outside counsel

- What kinds of issues lead them to look for an outside lawyer or law firm, i.e., under what circumstances they will think about hiring a new law firm or sending work outside the bank

- Who makes the ultimate decision about hiring outside counsel. For example, does someone else make recommendations? How is the entity organized to handle legal matters?

- What you need to know about the bank or the industry generally to obtain business from these contacts.

- In which organizations they recommend you get involved for purposes of professional development or networking

(3) *Interview an industry contact.* Often people who work in an industry or area can provide very useful intelligence. If you work in the health care area, for example, you could ask an officer or the executive director of the local hospital association to share with you:

• The trends in the industry or area that might affect members' legal needs

• What members look for when they work with lawyers or law firms

• How members' entities tend to be organized to handle legal matters

• How they make decisions about hiring lawyers

• How you might better understand the needs of those working in the industry or area

(4) *Interview another professional service provider.* Similarly, other professionals that serve your target clientele can be very good sources of information. If you want to develop legal work for the hospitality industry, for example, you might invite accountants or other professionals with substantial practices in that area for lunch to ask:

• How they have been successful building their practices

• What organizations they find most helpful for networking in the area or industry

• What thoughts or recommendations they have for you as you seek to build a clientele in the industry

IV. BUSINESS DEVELOPMENT – ONE ON ONE

Over time, your marketing and networking activities should help you identify specific targets for business. On a micro level, there are many questions you need to answer before you will get business from a particular organization or contact:

(1) *Who is the decision-maker?* In some cases, the person you know or with whom you have contact may not be the one who actually decides which lawyer or law firm to use. A bank loan officer may be required to use a lawyer on a list of panel counsel. A human resources manager may be the primary user of legal services, but the company president makes the decision about which law firm to use. In order to get

the business, you will need to identify the process that the target uses to select counsel. And, if your contact isn't the decision-maker, you will need to request an introduction to that person or it is unlikely you will obtain the business.

(2) *What is the current situation with respect to outside legal counsel?* If a prospective client is delighted with present outside counsel or if the current lawyer is a relative of the company president, it will be very difficult to break that bond. Remember, if a contact isn't using your firm, it generally means that he or she doesn't have a need for your services or is using someone else. You need to be realistic about your chances of getting the work.

> *[I]f a contact isn't using your firm, it generally means that he or she doesn't have a need for your services or is using someone else.*

(3) *What obstacles or objections will you face in trying to obtain work?* For example, your firm may have represented an opposing party at some point in time and the executives in the target organization have not forgotten. Perhaps the target thinks your firm is too big or too small. Maybe you look too young to have the requisite experience. Without identifying and addressing the target's objections, you will not get the business.

(4) *Do you understand the prospect's need?* Many of the people you are targeting don't have an immediate need for your services. Even if they do, there may be alternative ways to handle a problem (e.g., with internal staff). Unless you know the right buttons to push, you won't connect with the client.

(5) *Does the prospect or referral source feel comfortable with your experience and capabilities?* Sometimes people know the individual well, but are unfamiliar with his or her expertise. It is your responsibility to educate the target about your qualifications.

(6) *Does the prospect or referral source know you are interested in getting legal work?* Many lawyers diminish their business development chances with inadvertent comments or counterproductive behavior. For example, if you complain about being "swamped," a prospective client may wonder if you can make time for a new project. If you fail to return

an accountant's phone call on a timely basis, he may conclude his clients will receive similar, unresponsive treatment. Finally, it may be necessary for you to actually ask for the business. Many clients expect you to express an interest in their business and may assume you're not interested unless you do.

V. GETTING STARTED

While some lawyers are natural rainmakers, most are not. But that doesn't mean they can't be successful business developers; it just means they require some regimen or process to help focus their efforts.

If you are not a natural rainmaker and want to be more successful in developing business, you will benefit from bringing more structure to the process. To that end, think about undertaking the following activities:

> *If you are not a natural rainmaker and want to be more successful in developing business, you will benefit from bringing more structure to the process.*

(1) *Create a contact list.* Your existing contacts are very important assets for business development. Today's law school friend could be tomorrow's general counsel; maintaining a list of contacts will help you remember people and keep up your relationships as time goes by. Start by developing a list of people with whom you want to stay in touch as well as those you want to get to know better, such as:

- Law school or undergraduate classmates (and possibly deans, professors and advisors)
- Former clients with whom you have worked
- Past referral sources
- Former colleagues
- A client's advisors (e.g., the advertising agency executives who work with your client if you do trademark or copyright law)
- Other lawyers (e.g., co-counsel on matters, friendly opposing counsel, friendly competitors). Remember that in some practices, like bankruptcy or appellate law, most business referrals come from lawyers in the same practice.

- Expert witnesses or vendors who sell to your law firm as well as to client companies

- Other professional service providers (e.g., accountants, bankers, financial advisors, environmental consultants, etc.) who serve the same type of clientele that you do or hope to represent

- Executive directors or officers of organizations in which you are involved or that you are interested in joining

- Fellow members of boards or committees on which you serve

- Prospective clients

(2) *Define your ideal client.* Spend some time thinking about the kind of people with whom you would like to work, classifying them if possible by industry, size, type of matter, position, etc. Because your time is so limited, you should be very clear about the type of prospect on which you want to focus your efforts. For some lawyers, this step might lead them to target people who know these ideal clients. For example, if your goal is to work with wealthy clients on their estate planning needs, it is almost impossible to target them all; instead, you might focus your efforts on high-end insurance executives or financial planners.

(3) *Develop a list of top prospects or referral sources.* Building on your description of your ideal clients, try to identify actual people or companies with whom you would like to work. This will help you target your efforts instead of spreading your efforts too thin or taking a scattershot approach to business development.

> *Because your time is so limited, you should be very clear about the type of prospect on which you want to focus your efforts.*

(4) *Organize a system for your contacts.* Once you have developed your lists, you can determine the frequency and type of contact that will be appropriate for each person. For example, you may have a law school classmate you want to see once a year; a loan officer at a client bank may warrant quarterly contact. As part of this process, you should determine your objectives for each contact. For example, you may want to schedule a lunch with a venture capitalist acquaintance to ask for an introduction to a

client of his that is on your list of top prospects. Or you may want to schedule a meeting with a friendly competitor to educate him about your practice goals and expertise, and to request referrals. Your system should also include a way for you to track your contacts and other useful information about the targets (e.g., personal information, what you last talked about, follow-up ideas, etc.).

VI. OTHER CONSIDERATIONS AND TIPS IN DEVELOPING RELATIONSHIPS AND GENERATING BUSINESS

As you work toward developing your own book of business, keep the following in mind:

• *Continue to be "out there."* Your positioning activities support your business development efforts—they lead to business opportunities, from establishing your perception of expertise to helping you meet the right people.

> *Just because you meet with someone doesn't mean you have advanced the ball in developing the relationship.*

• *Have an objective for every contact you make.* Some lawyers engage in what are commonly called "random acts of lunch." Just because you meet with someone doesn't mean you have advanced the ball in developing the relationship. Each time you contact someone, establish a personal objective or reason for doing so. In other words, what is the purpose of getting together with that contact?[1]

• *Try to be helpful.* By helping people, you will increase your value to your targets and your odds of seeing a return. Keep in mind that just because someone isn't a potential client doesn't mean you shouldn't be professional friends or acquaintances. That accountant may be a good resource for a client that needs specialized expertise in an industry. That broker may be able to help you get a speaking engagement at a high-profile industry seminar. And that prospect who doesn't send you her own legal business may refer other people to you.

---

[1] This is discussed in more detail in Chapter 15 *infra,* Following Up with Targets.

• *Do what is comfortable.* For example, networking doesn't have to be done at parties or large group events. If you hate large gatherings, focus on developing individual relationships; some of the best networkers are those who excel at one-on-one contact.

• *Find a way to build regular contacts into your busy schedule.* For many people, lunch is an effective time to network because most people eat lunch, and it doesn't have to take a lot of time out of your day. It is also a good time to be seen with and by other professionals and business people.

• *Focus on people you like.* Your networking and relationship development efforts will be easiest, most enjoyable and most productive when you are with people you sincerely like. This means that you should seek out people with whom you have something in common—a peer group, a practice area, an industry expertise, a clientele, a hobby, etc.

• *Continually expand your circle of contacts.* Networking requires a certain diligence. Your goal should be to move beyond your existing circle of clients and friends to meet new people on a regular basis.

• *Don't be afraid to ask for help.* Clients, colleagues and friends generally are happy to help you. If you would like introductions, for example, most people are more than willing to make them.

• *Follow up.* Good relationships require cultivation. Your networking will pay off if you build long-term relationships and find a way to bring value to your target contacts.[2]

• *Improve your business development skills.* If you are not particularly comfortable with your skills, take it upon yourself to learn as much as possible about how business is developed. Read books from outside the legal industry, take a Dale Carnegie class, or attend seminars and workshops on business development or networking.

• *Be realistic.* You will not get business from every good prospect or referrals from every good target. In fact, you may periodically want to

---

[2] *Id.*

assess your progress and results to determine whether to "cut bait" on certain activities or with certain contacts.

• *Be patient.* Developing business is a time-consuming venture. Success requires investing in relationships, which take time to cultivate.

Ideas/Notes: Overview: Developing Relationships and Generating Business

My personal challenge(s) or obstacle(s) in this area:

_____

_____

_____

_____

_____

My goal(s) or objective(s) in this area:

_____

_____

_____

_____

_____

What I need to do to get started:

(1) _____

_____

(2) _____

_____

(3) _____

_____

(4) _____

_____

(5) _____

_____

8

Attending Social Events, Meetings and Conferences

I. INTRODUCTION

One of the keys to generating business is developing relationships. And opportunities to build relationships abound, from networking functions to client entertainment events to conferences and seminars.

Some lawyers thrive in social situations; others find them daunting. Despite what people think, even those who are "naturals" at networking

> *[E]ven those who are "naturals" at networking will agree that socializing effectively requires preparation, hard work and follow up.*

will agree that socializing effectively requires preparation, hard work and follow up. Making small talk with strangers is difficult for almost everyone.

Taking advantage of chances to encounter your targets will be an important element in determining your business development success. The following are ways to increase your confidence and improve your networking skills when attending events.

II. MAKING THE MOST OF SOCIAL EVENTS

Depending on your practice, your community and the size of your firm, you might have the following opportunities to network with people:

- Social events, such as parties or networking functions
- Fundraisers
- Meetings of organizations in which you're involved

- Events with tables sponsored by your firm
- Sporting events, especially when seated in a suite, booth or loge
- Golf outings
- Client events or open houses
- Seminar luncheons or cocktail parties

In conjunction with social events, some lawyers' efforts are limited to arriving late, sitting at the first available table, eating and leaving early, not taking advantage of the opportunity to interact with clients, potential clients or referral sources. Generally, most lawyers don't have time to waste; if you don't plan to use your attendance at a meeting or social event effectively, you might as well not go.

There are three parts to capitalizing on networking opportunities: preparation, execution and follow up.

A. Preparing for Social Functions

Oprah Winfrey once said, "Luck is a matter of preparation meeting opportunity." Your preparation before social functions or events will greatly improve your odds that something positive may result.

Here are some steps to take before attending a social event:

(1) *Review the list of attendees.* By thinking about who will be in attendance at the event, you can determine with whom you would like to network, be prepared to greet them, and perhaps recall earlier conversations to follow up on. Before attending a firm-sponsored function, review the RSVPs to see who will be there. Before other groups' functions, look at the membership list or try to remind yourself about people you have run into at previous events or meetings.

Before you go to the event, determine what it is you hope to accomplish.

(2) *Establish your objectives.* You should have an objective for everything you do in marketing; it is the only way to know if your investment of time (and resources) is worthwhile. Before you go to the event, determine what it is you hope to accomplish. Examples of potential objectives are:

- Meet two new people
- Follow up with a consultant you met at a previous meeting
- Introduce a colleague to an existing client
- Sit with a targeted prospect during a luncheon
- Be introduced to a target contact
- Talk to a particular vendor

(3) *Plan some conversations.* As you review the list of people or think about those who might attend the event, you should also consider what you might talk about and be prepared to make small talk. What will your icebreakers or conversation starters be?

There may be some issues of general interest to potential attendees that you've heard about recently, e.g., "I was reading about a new software program that middle-market banks are using to help them cross sell to their customers." There may be particular issues that you can address with individuals based on the last conversation you had, such as, "How was your vacation to Italy?" You can talk about something of local interest such as the previous night's baseball score, or just show an interest in the person or the business, e.g., "So are there any new developments at XYZ Enterprises?" If you know or anticipate that specific clients will be at the event, talk in advance of the meeting to other lawyers in the firm who have relationships with the clients to see if they have any information or leads.

Keep in mind that some settings require you to use good judgment about business versus entertainment. For example, clients who join you for a football game may not want to discuss business issues there. Your top priority is to ensure that the participants enjoy your company and the event.

(4) *Think about what you will need.* First, bring your business cards. At social and networking events, it is expected that you will have and use business cards. You can hand them out as the conversation warrants, or use them to jot down information for the person to whom you are speaking, such as helpful Web sites, names of authors or contacts to make.

You should also bring your calendar or Blackberry. This will allow you to respond to requests or follow-up opportunities immediately.

For example, if your contact says something like, "Let's have breakfast next week to talk about this in more detail," you can go ahead and set up the meeting.

Finally, for cocktail parties or after-hours functions, you might consider setting up a dinner reservation following the event. During the course of the evening, if you would like to spend more time with a small number of people, you can invite them to join you for dinner.

(5) *Consider your attire.* You should try to fit in with the mode of the group. While the members of your office may dress casually on Friday, it's possible the accountants attending a meeting do not. Conversely, you may want to rethink the pinstriped suit for a meeting of general contractors. Your best gauge of the formality or informality of a function is the host; taking his or her lead, it may be appropriate to remove a jacket or loosen a tie.

Other tips to help you prepare for an event:

• *Eat before you go to the function (unless it includes a meal, of course).* Eating interferes with networking by taking time away from socializing (as you stand in a line), disrupting your ability to ask or answer questions, and making it awkward to shake hands.

• *Put five or more business cards in a pocket instead of your wallet or purse.* This will make them more easily accessible.

B. Attending Functions and Events

Adequate preparation is one step in networking; effective execution at the event is another. The following are some thoughts on making the most of your attendance at a function:

(1) *Take stock of the situation.* When you first arrive at the function, determine your course of action. Do not simply sit at a table and wait for lunch to be served. Start by looking around to see if you recognize anyone; you can talk to those you recognize first. If you don't recognize anyone, you might notice that people are standing around a bar; that might be a good place to go mingle.

(2) *Appear confident (even if you are not) and take the offensive.* At receptions or networking events, it is your job to introduce yourself. Before you sit down for lunch or dinner, introduce yourself to the others at your table. If you are attending a small function, be sure to greet everyone in the room. If a new guest arrives at your table or in your circle, introduce yourself.

When you introduce yourself, shake hands. Remember, your handshake will create an impression. A limp handshake implies you are unsure of yourself; a crushing handshake makes you appear insensitive and dominating.

If you have difficulty initiating conversations, you can try the following:

- *Look for people you already know.* They invariably will introduce you to others.

> *Before you sit down for lunch or dinner, introduce yourself to the others at your table.*

- *Introduce yourself to someone else arriving or registering at the same time.* Then you can walk into the event together.

- *Seek out the event's host or sponsor, or the organization's officers or administrative staff, and introduce yourself.* These individuals will appreciate your attendance, and likely will introduce you to others.

- *Look for someone else who is alone.* Usually someone standing by himself or herself will welcome a conversation seeker. That person probably feels equally uncomfortable.

- *If you want to break into a small group that is engaged in conversation, focus on the person who is speaking, and try to make eye contact.* The speaker generally will acknowledge eye contact or smile, which will naturally open up the circle to let you in.

Much of the impression people get of someone is based on nonverbal cues. The more comfortable you appear, the more comfortable you will make everyone else. Smile, look relaxed and confident, and others will find it easier to communicate with you.

(3) *Ask questions.* The best way to start a conversation is to ask good questions. Your goal is to find an area of common interest, such as a

mutual contact, a love of sports, a favorite author or knowledge of an industry. This common interest will provide you with future conversation starters and potential ideas for follow up.

Some topics you can explore with people include:

> *The best way to start a conversation is to ask good questions.*

- *Their occupation.* You can inquire about their jobs, their companies, their roles within their organizations, etc.

- *Their involvement in the group hosting the function.* How long they've been a member of the club, for example, or their experience with the industry association would be natural questions.

- *Their personal interests.* Depending on your relationship and the setting, you might ask about recreational activities or family.

Be sure not to get too personal, however. In particular, disclosing too much information about yourself or asking personal questions can make others uncomfortable or defensive.

If you ask for a business card—which is usually a good idea—spend a moment looking at the card. For most people, a business card reflects at least a portion of their identity. It could be the source of some conversation ideas as well, such as "I didn't realize you were a vice president there" or "That's an interesting logo; what does it signify?"

The key to networking is listening. If you spend 80% of your time asking questions and listening to the responses, and just 20% of your time talking, people will remember you as an interested conversationalist and seek you out in the future.

(4) *Focus on your contact.* When you are talking to contacts, you should give them 100% of your attention. To this end:

- *Focus on the person with whom you are talking.* Looking around the room or appearing distracted is discourteous.

- *Respond to the person with appropriate facial expressions or body language.* This will confirm your interest in what he or she is saying.

- *Face the contact squarely.* Turning away shows a lack of interest.

- *Don't interrupt.* Doing so is very rude.

• *Respect people's space needs.* You should maintain a comfortable amount of space when conversing with someone and avoid touching unless someone is a good friend. If your contact appears to be backing up, you are probably invading the comfort zone.

• *Avoid approaching someone with a plate and fork in your hand.* It is not appealing for someone to carry on a conversation with a person who is eating.

(5) *Remember names.* A lot of people have trouble remembering names, in some instances forgetting them within seconds of having been introduced. The primary reason people forget names is because they are busy thinking about what they're going to say and never hear them in the first place.

To improve your ability to remember names, consider the following tips:

• *Listen.* Don't think ahead to your own introduction.

• *Use the name right away in a conversation or greeting.* For example, "It's nice to meet you, David."

• *Ask a question about the name.* You might inquire, for example, "Do you spell Sarah with an 'h' at the end?"

• *Ask the person to repeat the name.* If you weren't listening properly or didn't hear the name, ask the contact to repeat it, i.e., "I'm sorry, can you tell me your last name again?"

• *Associate the name with something memorable.* This could be someone you already know, an actor, a food, a thing or a characteristic. You might try a rhyme, if it works, such as "Paul is tall" or "Brian from Ryan [Company]."

• *Ask for a business card.* This will ensure you have a record of the person's name. Don't put the card away right away. Keep it in your hand while you talk in the event you forget the name.

(6) *Be strategic.* With a limited amount of time available, effective networkers don't leave things to chance. Target the people with whom you want to spend time and seek them out; don't just stand around and expect people to come to you.

If you are attending a networking event, your goal should be to talk to several people during the course of the function. If you attend with a friend or colleague, split up for a time. Try not to monopolize one per-son too long; remember that other people are expecting to mingle and make contact with a number of people too. After ten minutes or so, move along to someone else in the room. If you have more to discuss, perhaps you should set up a follow-up meeting with the contact to continue the conversation.

> *Try not to monopolize one person too long; remember that other people are expecting to mingle and make contact with a number of people too.*

If you have trouble breaking away from a conversation with someone, there are different tactics you can use. For example, you can suggest the two of you refresh your drinks, and then part ways at the bar. You can say, "My colleague (friend or spouse) is signaling me, so I should really get going." Or you can be up front about the purpose of networking and say, "I'm sure you want to talk to a number of people here, so I should-n't monopolize your time. It was really nice talking to you."

If your function includes a meal, don't sit down without knowing who will be seated at your table. For better or worse, a meal provides an opportunity to talk to a very small number of people (at times, just those to your right and left) for a long period of time. Without planning, you could end up seated next to some unrelated vendors or even competi-tors. As you talk to people, you might suggest you'd like to join them for lunch or invite them to sit with you at dinner.

Other tips for "working" a social event:

• *Carry your drink in your left hand.* This will free up your right to shake hands, and help you avoid giving an icy cold handshake.

• *Drink in moderation, if at all.*

• *If you're in a cold winter location, try to leave your overcoat in the car.* This will help you avoid spending time in the coat check line, which can be considerable for an event of a relatively short duration.

• *Make your name tag prominent.* A name tag is important when you are meeting new people. First, wear it on your right side; as you shake hands it will become more prominent with your extended right shoulder. Second, don't hide it with a scarf or lapel, or clip it to a purse or belt. And if you think your name appears too small, or if it is incorrect or

> *For better or worse, a meal provides an opportunity to talk to a very small number of people ... for a long period of time.*

illegible, turn the tag over and write your name in large, readable letters.

- *Think like a host.* The most effective networkers are those people who go to a function and act like hosts, not guests. If you think about the role of a host, it involves:

  - Arriving first and leaving last (or at least coming early and staying late)
  - Greeting people and introducing yourself
  - Introducing people to each other
  - Offering to get beverages for others
  - Not sitting to eat until others are seated

Engaging in this kind of behavior will make you much more effective in networking functions.

C. Following Up

The third prong in effective networking is follow up. Interacting with contacts after or between events is how you will begin to develop relationships.

If you had the opportunity to meet someone you feel you would like to know better, based on your conversations, look for a way to follow up after the event. For example:

- Send a personal note expressing your interest in getting together for breakfast or lunch
- Forward a copy of an article, a paperback book or something else you think would be of interest
- Call to invite the contact to join you at a sporting or cultural event
- Put the person on your contact list, and sign him or her up for appropriate firm materials or mailings (e.g., newsletters)

• Keep an eye out for news about the person or company, such as a trade article on a new company product, a promotion or relocation. This will give you the opportunity to write a personal note or letter, send a gift or possibly call for a follow-up meeting.

III. ATTENDING PROFESSIONAL, TRADE OR INDUSTRY CONFERENCES

Lawyers frequently have opportunities to attend professional, trade or industry conferences, seminars or CLE programs, some of which are out of town. While the primary purpose of attending the conference or meeting may be educational, these forums can provide numerous marketing opportunities as well.

How Do You Answer the Question, "What Do You Do?"

If you are attending an event that will involve people you don't know, one question you can anticipate is, "What do you do?" This question presents an opportunity to position yourself and your practice, and potentially prompt follow-up questions.

In forming your response:

• Your answer shouldn't sound canned.

• Your response should take into account the person asking the question. If you are an intellectual property lawyer attending a bar association function, it might be sufficient to say, "I handle patent prosecutions for a number of Fortune 500 company clients at Smith & Jones law firm." If you're talking to an entrepreneur, however, you might say, "I'm a patent lawyer who helps companies protect their technology and ideas."

• A good response often will refer to both you and your law firm. For example, "I'm a lawyer who works primarily with private businesses and their owners, but my firm, Smith & Jones, has more than 200 lawyers and handles a wide range of matters for a broad spectrum of clients."

The marketing benefits of attending a conference or professional meeting can include:

• Gathering information (on the group or association, prospective clients, competitors, vendors, the industry, etc.)

• Attending educational sessions

• Networking and prospecting

• Exchanging ideas

• Giving the firm visibility before a targeted audience

A. Preparing for the Conference or Meeting

Before the meeting, you should develop your strategy for the conference. For example, you may want to:

• *Read the conference materials and familiarize yourself with the program.* Review the names of the conference committee members and the group's board of directors. Note the names of the conference sponsors and underwriters.

• *Review the list of attendees.* Circle or jot down the names of a few attendees you would like to make a special effort to meet.

• *Plan your days.* Develop your personal agenda of sessions you would like to attend, times to visit the exhibit area, social events, etc.

• *Sign up for the social activities.* These will likely provide you with the best opportunities to meet people.

• *Set some objectives for yourself.* In other words, what would you like to accomplish by the time you leave the conference? Examples could be: Meet all the other attendees from my city; talk to five prospective clients; find out how I can get active in the association; etc.

• *Pack a supply of business cards.* If available, bring along some informational material on your firm's services related to the conference or meeting topic.

B. Attending the Conference or Meeting

While you're at the conference, be sure to:

• *Attend educational sessions or workshops.* Sit near the front of the room. Ask good questions but don't dominate the discussion.

> *Introduce yourself to vendors or consultants with products or services related to your practice or your clients. Knowing the key players will help your firm in developing its marketing strategy and may come in handy when making referrals for clients.*

• *Go through the exhibit area.* Introduce yourself to vendors or consultants with products or services related to your practice or your clients. Pick up their materials and ask questions about their work with clients like yours. Explain your own or your firm's experience in the area. Thank those who have contributed to or sponsored events at the meeting. Knowing the key players will help your firm in developing its marketing strategy and may come in handy when making referrals for clients.

• *Arrive at sessions or meals a little early and introduce yourself to people sitting nearby.* Try to sit with different people at each event (unless you have a good prospect you want to talk to further).

• *Conduct some "intelligence."* Make note of competitors who are prominent in the organization, as leaders or speakers.

• *Exchange business cards with attendees and vendors you meet.*

• *At the end of each session or day, make a few notes as reminders about the people you met.* Write something on their business cards or on the master list of attendees that indicates the nature of the discussion you had, personal information you learned or your ideas for follow up.

C. Following Up After the Conference or Meeting

The activities you undertake after the conference will impact whether attending the conference or meeting is a success from a marketing perspective. Think about the following:

• *Organize a follow-up plan.* On your trip home or when you're back in your office, develop a list of prospects, vendors or other contacts with whom you would like to follow up, and how you intend to do so. Keep in mind that the more substantive the follow up, the more effective. In other words, sending someone an update on how a proposed regulation will affect his or her business will generate much more attention and goodwill than sending a "nice to meet you" letter.

> *The . . . more people you know, the more enjoyable it is to attend events.*

• *Prepare a brief report for other lawyers in your firm.* In it, summarize the gist of the conference, the value of the organization, what you learned or accomplished while you were there, and your recommended follow-up steps.

• *Think about whether any of the conference materials* would be appropriate for clients or other contacts. If so, make copies and send them along with a letter explaining your involvement in the conference.

• *Add your new contacts to your mailing list.* If appropriate, they can receive future newsletters, mailings or holiday cards.

• *If the conference was worthwhile, plan to attend each year.*

By taking these steps, you will maximize your firm's investment in the conference as well as your future networking and business development opportunities.

IV. CONCLUDING THOUGHTS

Remember, networking or "working a room" isn't easy for anyone. Even lawyers who are good at it find it tiring and hard work. The simple fact is that the more people you know, the more enjoyable it is to attend events. You can expand the number of contacts by becoming a good networker and getting actively involved in the group.

Business Dining Etiquette

If your networking activities include meals, here are some tips for business dining:

- Be ready to order. You don't want to hold up the rest of the table while looking indecisive.
- Order foods that are easy to eat. That means avoiding messy meals like barbequed ribs, some pastas and juicy sandwiches.
- Put your napkin in your lap, not in your shirt or belt. And your napkin shouldn't return to the table until you are done with your meal.
- Don't fight over the check. Whoever issued the invitation should be the host and pay the bill.

Ideas/Notes: Attending Social Events, Meetings and Conferences

My personal challenge(s) or obstacle(s) in this area:

_____

_____

_____

_____

_____

My goal(s) or objective(s) in this area:

_____

_____

_____

_____

_____

What I need to do to get started:

(1) _____

_____

(2) _____

_____

(3) _____

_____

(4) _____

_____

(5) _____

_____

Satisfying Clients and Building Loyalty

I. INTRODUCTION

One of the most basic principles in marketing is that your efforts should begin with existing clients. There are many reasons why this makes sense:

- Clients can serve as sources of future business—both in terms of additional work of their own and referrals.

- It costs up to five times more to develop a new client than to keep an existing client. The time and resources required to develop business can be considerable.

- Client retention impacts profitability. A study reported in the Harvard Business Review showed that firms that retain 98% of their clients/customers from year to year can be twice as profitable as firms that retain an impressive 94% of their clients.[1]

- Dissatisfied clients tell others. Depending on the study you read, if someone is dissatisfied, he or she, on average, will tell between eleven and seventeen other people.

---

[1] Reichheld and Teal, *The Loyalty Effect: The Hidden Force Behind Growth, Profits and Lasting Value* (Harvard Business School Press 1996).

You should not simply expect that clients will be satisfied. More important, you should make it a real goal to instill client loyalty. Loyalty and satisfaction are two different things. In a remarkable finding reported in *The Loyalty Effect: The Hidden Force Behind Growth, Profits and Lasting Value*, the authors found that between 65% and 85% of people who had defected from a particular service provider said they were actually satisfied or very satisfied with the services performed by the firm.[2] Simply meeting expectations was not enough to keep the client; clients want more, whether it is remarkable results, a great relationship or "added value."

> *Loyalty and satisfaction are two different things.*

Law firm clients may be even less loyal. The BTI Consulting Group polled 170 corporate counsel from Fortune 1000 companies.[3] The results revealed that only about 25% of the clients were satisfied with their outside law firms; in addition, the respondents planned to reduce the number of their core outside law firms by half.

So the initial steps in any good marketing program are to build client satisfaction and loyalty. This Chapter provides tips and techniques on building good client relationships, from basic communication skills to ways to add value.

II. BUILDING STRONG RELATIONSHIPS WITH CLIENTS

There are two aspects to the relationship between a lawyer and a client: the substantive legal services to be performed (e.g., a divorce, property settlement or sale of real estate), and how that service is provided (e.g., the lawyer's attentiveness, dedication, skill and finesse). Lawyers often fail to understand that, in many cases, how the service is provided is as important to clients as the service itself. First, clients often assume that they will receive quality legal services; clients hire a lawyer

---

[2] *Id.*

[3] Rynowecer, *The Strategic Review and Outlook for the Legal Service Industry* (The BTI Consulting Group 2004).

with the expectation that he or she will be able to execute the work. Second, clients often have difficulty judging the quality of the legal services. How will an estate planning client ever know if the assets transfer smoothly and in accordance with his wishes or if the estate taxes are, in fact, minimized?

> *Lawyers often fail to understand that, in many cases, how the service is provided is as important to clients as the service itself.*

So service is a critical aspect of building a satisfied and loyal clientele. This section focuses on some of the basic principles in creating a strong client relationship. While many of these principles may seem like common sense, most clients will agree that there can be vast improvement in how lawyers execute these techniques.

A. Identifying and Meeting Expectations

One of the most important steps toward building a satisfied and loyal client base is to identify what clients expect in terms of your performance. Many a relationship has been derailed because of a lawyer's failure to meet a client's expectation.

Clients also differ in terms of the type and frequency of contact they expect from their lawyers. For every client who wants a formal, monthly status report there is a client who wants a weekly "check in" telephone call. If you give the latter client a formal status report, he or she will think you are producing unnecessary work and probably charging too much to boot.

Here are two stories that illustrate how not understanding the client's expectations can offset even good intentions. At one litigation boutique firm, the lawyers prided themselves on their cost-effective approach to client cases. They staffed their matters very leanly, they didn't conduct what they felt was unnecessary discovery, and they paid utmost attention to the bottom line. A very disappointed client, however, interpreted the firm's efforts as not being aggressive enough. The client wanted "no stone unturned" on his case, and felt the low bills signaled that the litigators were not giving the matter adequate time and attention.

A client of another firm complained about the detailed billing entries the firm was sending him—something nearly every other client demanded.

As a contractor with a closely held business, he was upset that his company's bookkeeper was privy to all the legal problems that he was facing and he wanted just a vague description of "services rendered."

Without knowing the client's expectations, your likelihood of disappointing the client goes up dramatically. The best way to identify expectations, of course, is simply to talk to your clients. In addition to eliciting important information from your clients, this will show your willingness to listen and be flexible, and establish good two-way communication from the start.

> *Without knowing the client's expectations, your likelihood of disappointing the client goes up dramatically.*

The following are some questions you might ask to understand better the kind of relationship the client is seeking:

• What is the most effective or desirable way to communicate with you?

• What type of status reporting would you like—in what form, and how often?

• Do you prefer having a "quarterback"—a client manager who will be your contact and coordinate matters for you at the firm—or would you rather go directly to the "specialists" in various substantive areas?

• How, or how often, would you like to be contacted outside of our day-to-day business dealings (e.g., socially)? What activities do you enjoy?

• In what format would you prefer to receive your invoices? How much detail would you like?

• What else do you expect from an outside lawyer who works for your company?

You should also have conversations with clients about their expectations when you receive new matters or assignments from them. Inquire about:

• *The scope of the project.* Is this a project of strategic importance for the company, a nuisance matter or an idea in a very preliminary stage?

- *The client's objectives for hiring you.* For example, many companies will turn to outside counsel when they have "overflow work," i.e., work that is typically handled in-house but for which they have no capacity at the time. In these cases, the client's goal typically will be to get the projects done quickly and cost-effectively, as the organization is not accustomed to having to pay outside lawyers for the work.

- *The client's time frame.* By talking about the timetable, you will have the opportunity to address any unrealistic expectations on the part of the client.

- *Who will do the work.* Some clients will hire you expecting you to do the work; others will wonder why you didn't delegate it to a lower-cost person in your firm.

- *What role the client wants to play, if any.* You should try to ascertain how the client wants to be involved. This could range from a total hands-off approach to wanting to participate in a trial.

- *The anticipated cost.* Of course, all clients want to know how much you think the project will cost.[4]

- *The work product or deliverable.* If the client is expecting a two-page document and gets a twenty-page document, more than likely he will think it cost too much.

- *How the work product will be delivered (i.e., overnight, by mail, hand delivered, etc.).* As basic as this seems, it will show clients your concern for their timing needs and for their budget. For example, one client may want a document delivered in time for a Wednesday breakfast meeting of the board of directors; another may say to send it via mail because it doesn't need to be received that quickly.

Remember too that clients cannot always judge the quality of your work. For example, the "quality" of a contract may be judged only when problems arise or problems are avoided due to the contract's existence. So keep the following in mind:

---

[4] See Section II.H *infra.*

• *Let the client know if you are pleased with a result.* In many cases, clients may not be able to determine whether the resolution was a good one.

• *Don't be afraid to "toot your own horn," and that of your firm.* Talk about your colleagues, their activities and their accomplishments, or good results obtained for other clients.

B. Improving Communications and Responsiveness

Clients hire a lawyer to accomplish something—draft a contract, finalize a lease, defend them in a lawsuit. However, most clients assume that the lawyer will accomplish the legal task or service well; the factors on which they often judge a lawyer's performance relate to the delivery of the service—communications, status reporting, building rapport. In fact, most malpractice claims arise because of poor communications or misunderstandings with clients, not poor work quality *per se.*

The Association of Corporate Counsel (formerly American Corporate Counsel Association or ACCA) conducted a study in conjunction with Altman Weil about why general counsel sever relationships with law firms. According to that study, the number one reason is lack of responsiveness, cited by nearly one-third of the respondents.[5]

> *[T]he number one reason [general counsel sever relationships with law firms] is lack of responsiveness.*

Providing excellent communication and service are other keys to satisfied and loyal clients. All of the recommendations below are presented with the caveat that you should find out whether that is what the client wants;[6] however, clients generally will be pleased with these efforts.

The telephone is the primary point of contact for most clients when dealing with their lawyer. Here are some thoughts on good telephone habits:

• *Return clients' telephone calls within a few hours.* Studies have

---

[5] *2004 Chief Legal Officer Survey* (Association of Corporate Counsel and Altman Weil, Inc. 2004).

[6] See Section II.A *supra.*

shown that clients expect their calls returned within half a day; if they call in the morning, they expect a return call by noon.

- *Check your voice mail frequently.*

- *If you know you cannot return calls quickly, manage the clients' expectations.* For example, update your outgoing voicemail message so clients know that you are out of the office. While this takes discipline, it can inform the client immediately when to expect a return call, e.g., "On Tuesday, October 20, I am scheduled to be in court all day. If your call requires immediate attention, please dial 0 and ask for my secretary, Karen Kelly. Otherwise, please leave a message and I will get back to you no later than tomorrow morning."

- *Give clients your direct dial number.*

- *Don't use your secretary to screen calls.* Place your own calls, and don't have your secretary screen incoming calls.

- *Answer your telephone when you are at your desk.* Clients are impressed when lawyers actually pick up the phone! Clients will gain confidence that, if you are available, you will take calls. Then they will also be more tolerant when you are not there.

- *Use the speakerphone only when necessary.* If you are planning to use the speakerphone, tell clients why (e.g., you need to take notes, another lawyer is sitting in your office), and advise them you are closing the door.

- *If you need to block out time to work on a matter, put your telephone on Do Not Disturb.* This will help eliminate some rings before your client reaches your secretary. There are things you can do to make clients feel that you are still accessible. One is to ask your secretary to advise all clients that you are unavailable but will be returning calls at a particular time. Another option is to return calls as you are moving from one task (e.g., reading) to another (e.g., drafting). Advise your secretary if there are calls you need to take; this way, when taking the message, he or she can say, "Oh, Mr. Smith, he asked me to interrupt him if you called."

- *Don't call clients back during the lunch hour.* Unless that is the only time you are available, clients know you probably don't expect them to be there.

• *Set up telephone appointments.* If you have a hectic schedule or clients that are difficult to track down, ask your secretary to schedule a time you will call the client.

• *Hold for clients.* If the person you are calling is on another line, ask if you can hold. This will show clients your effort to reach them. You can put your phone on speakerphone while you wait and tend to other matters, like opening mail or checking e-mail.

• *Call clients at home, if necessary.* Clients will appreciate your efforts to get back to them.

• *Make yourself available outside the office.* Leave your cell phone or car phone number with selected clients. And if you have major matters in progress, you should give clients your home phone number or cell phone number for emergencies.

Other communications are also important in creating satisfied and loyal clients. Remember, a lack of communication often creates the perception that you are too busy for more work. For example:

• *Keep clients informed.* Regular status reporting is extremely important to clients. Send copies of correspondence or documents, such as deposition summaries or research memoranda to clients so they can see the status of their work and progress being made. Or develop a regular status reporting procedure. Let the client dictate the form and frequency of the

> *[A] lack of communication often creates the perception that you are too busy for more work.*

status reporting. Depending on client preferences and the volume of matters, reporting may range from a weekly telephone call to a quarterly written summary.

• *Check and respond to your e-mail frequently.* In contrast to getting a voicemail message that indicates you are out of the office, clients have no idea whether or not you are in your office when they send an e-mail. If you will be gone for an extended period, consider putting an auto-reply message on the e-mail, advising clients of your status or what to do in your absence. Use a Blackberry or other device to check e-mail when out of the office.

- *Schedule regular reviews or meetings with major clients.* Meeting with the client on a quarterly or semiannual basis will help you pinpoint potential problems, eliminate misunderstandings, provide status reports, and maybe even anticipate new assignments.[7]

- *Speak and write in plain English.* Clients don't like legal jargon.

- *Call clients before they have to call you, especially if there's a problem.* Clients hate surprises. If you anticipate a problem, such as an unexpectedly large bill, a cancelled deposition, a delay in the report or a missed deadline, let the client know as soon as possible.

> **Clients hate surprises.**

- *Call the client after key events to "check in."* For example, after a day of meetings for your client, leave a message about how you felt things went.

- *Deal with client problems or disputes quickly and in a straightforward manner.* If there is a problem, the most effective way to deal with it is face-to-face. The second choice should be the telephone (in writing is least effective).[8]

- *Make it easy to work with you.* Try to learn the communication preferences of the client. For example, if your client is a financial person, you may want to provide more statistics or data.

- *Create a client team, including staff.* Let your team know about the client's issue and needs, and meet periodically to keep team members up to date on any situations.[9]

- *Get clients involved in the firm and build more relationships.* Ask the client to sit in on a client team meeting or to address a practice group, for example.

- *Be honest.* If you don't know an answer to a client's question, for example, admit it and say you will get back to him or her on the matter.

---

[7] See Chapter 11, Section IV.D *infra* for further information on client relationship meetings.

[8] See Chapter 12, Section IV *infra* on dealing with an angry client.

[9] See Chapter 11 *infra* on managing client relationships.

Then get the answer to the client as quickly as possible. You should be most interested in building credibility with a client, not trying to look good.

• *Use engagement letters.* Engagement letters can be used to clarify the scope of the relationship and the client's expectations.

• *Indicate a contact person in your absence.* If you are going to be out of the office, let clients know in advance and let them know who they should contact in your absence.

• *Express appreciation for their business.* Say thanks!

• *Send them articles or other information in which they may be interested.* For example, you might want to send a client a link to an industry-related Web site you discover or alerts on laws that affect the client's business.

• *If a new person joins a client company, be proactive in making contact.* Send a welcome note or gift (if appropriate). Ask to set up a face-to-face meeting or lunch to make the transition easy. Bring a list of files in progress, your team organizational chart and other pertinent information.

• *Follow up.* After a matter is completed, check in to see how things turned out. If a client has been inactive, follow up to say hello and find out how things are going.

C. Working with Staff

The practice of law today has resulted in a very different relationship between the lawyer and his or her staff member(s). For example, many lawyers now draft their own legal documents and send things to clients directly via e-mail. As a result, the secretary or administrative assistant may be in the dark about the status of client matters.

> *In order to provide good client communications, you need to work closely with your secretary, assistant, paralegal or other staff members.*

In addition, many law firms have increased the ratio of lawyers to staff. While partners typically used to have a full-time, dedicated secretary or assistant, today's lawyers may share a staff member with two or even three other people. The secretaries have many more projects or clients to manage.

In order to provide good client communications, you need to work closely with your secretary, assistant, paralegal or other staff members. A helpful and empathetic secretary, for example, will make clients more comfortable in your absence.

The following activities will help you provide better service and, in turn, make clients happier:

• *Get your staff involved with clients.* If you observe the lawyers who are the best at building client relationships—and business generally— they typically make their staff members a vital part of the effort.

• *Introduce staff to clients when they visit the office.*

• *Send a letter to new clients introducing your secretary. Invite clients to call him or her with questions.*

• *Take your staff with you to visit an important client.*

• *Explain your projects to the members of the staff.* You should cover what the matter entails, key deadlines, what's important to the client, and what staff member roles will be. Keep staff members apprised as things change so they can answer clients' questions (e.g., was something filed?).

• *Give staff members the authority to return clients' calls.* For example, the secretary can advise the client when you will be able to return the client's call.

• *Let staff members know what they should do if you are out of the office.* Should they call your cell phone, e-mail your Blackberry or get another lawyer in the office to contact the client?

• *Advise staff members what they should do with important calls if you are out.* One such option is to forward calls to your cell phone.

• *Provide parameters for staff members.* Make sure they know their options, like giving out your cell phone number or home phone number to a client.

• *Keep members of the staff apprised of your schedule.* Give them access to your calendar. Let them know when you are expected back in the office so they can answer clients' questions. If your schedule changes, let your staff members know as soon as possible. For example, if a deposition you thought would last two hours extends into a full day, call so your secretary can update clients who have left messages and manage the expectations of those who have not yet called.

• *Consider allowing your secretary to check your e-mails if you are often unavailable or unable to access them.*

• *Appreciate the staff's conflicting priorities and demands.* When a staff member works for more than one lawyer, keep in mind that each may want things handled in a different way or expect the staff member to play a different role. The more you can communicate your expectations and involve staff members in your client relationships, the greater priority they will place on your client matters.

> *Let [members of the staff] know when you are expected back in the office so they can answer clients' questions.*

D. Meeting with Clients

Because so much of a client's contact with a law firm today is done by telephone, mail and e-mail, in-person meetings have become extremely important in shaping a client's perceptions of the firm. Meetings provide an opportunity for lawyers to build rapport and a relationship with a client, and to leave a lasting impression.

In arranging and conducting your client meetings, think about the following:

• *Be on time.* If you are going to be late, inform the receptionist and your secretary so they can make the client comfortable by providing access to a telephone or getting a beverage.

• *Be prepared.* Anticipate files, forms or other materials that will be needed. Create an agenda so the client feels more engaged in the meeting. Have a conference room available, if necessary. Review your notes from the last meeting to remind yourself of business or personal details that were discussed. And clear your meeting space so only the client's files or materials are in front of you.

• *Inform staff members about the meeting.* The receptionist can greet the client by name, and the secretary can make sure everything is ready.

In addition, the staff can help with special arrangements, such as ordering lunch or having a notary available.

- *Greet clients when they arrive.* Shake hands, and walk them to the office or conference room. If you are not available, ask your secretary to greet clients and take them to the conference room (but not your empty office).

> *Meetings provide an opportunity for lawyers to build rapport and a relationship with a client, and to leave a lasting impression.*

- *Don't take phone calls.* The client should be the focus of your attention. Ask your secretary to take messages so you are not interrupted.

- *Build rapport.* Take some time to make small talk about the client's business, a recent vacation or the latest score of the home team.

- *Be a good listener.* Take notes. Make eye contact. Paraphrase and acknowledge comments.

- *Consider meeting at the client's home or office.* While it is often to the lawyer's advantage (and sometimes necessary) to meet at the law firm, consider meeting at the client's home or place of business.

- *Introduce the client to other people in the firm.* Stop to say hello to your secretary, or greet other lawyers in the firm.

E. Learning the Client's Business, Situation and Needs

Clients want their lawyers to help them accomplish their goals. In order to be effective in this regard, you must understand the client's business, industry, customers, competitors, distributors, vendors and other professionals.

There are many things you can do to learn more about the client and anticipate issues or problems:

- *Visit the client's place of business.* Ask if you can take a tour. Consider bringing along other lawyers or staff members from the firm who will be working on the client's matters. While there, ask to meet people from various functional areas, such as HR or operations. Meet the plant manager.

- *Offer to spend some time on site.* You could volunteer to spend a day at the client's office (perhaps at no charge) to better understand the client's processes, or to work on site a few days a month to get closer to the managers.

• *Have regular "house calls" or meetings.* For example, one successful lawyer has a breakfast meeting with each of his business owner clients once a month to discuss their businesses.

• *Learn about the company's mission, products or services and operations.* Try to understand its jargon.

• *Follow the client's industry activities.* Attend meetings of related trade or industry groups, and subscribe to related publications.

> **The client understands the business better than you ever will.**

• *Listen to the client's perspective.* The client understands the business better than you ever will.

• *Be a counselor.* Present alternatives, and point out the best solution to a problem, given the company's risk tolerance level, personnel, finances, etc.

• *Visit the client company's Web site on a regular basis.*

• *Attend the client's annual meetings.*

• *Attend client board meetings.*

• *Ask to be added to the client's in-house newsletter distribution list.* Alternatively, inquire whether you can have access to the company intranet.

• *Read the company's materials.* This includes marketing brochures, product descriptions, annual reports, etc.

• *Review media coverage of the client's activities.*

• *Get your clients involved with your firm.* Ask clients to address your practice group or partner meeting to discuss trends in their industry, their use of law firms or their relationship with your firm.

In addition, when you have opportunities to talk with a client, ask good questions—questions that will enable you to learn more about the client and demonstrate your interest. If you don't know the answers to the following questions, for example, you'll be able to get them from the client:

- Who are your main competitors? How do they differentiate themselves from you?
- What is your typical customer like?
- What has the financial climate been for your entity?
- Are there any uncertainties affecting your business, or changes of any sort, that have particularly concerned you in the last few months?
- How would you characterize the organization's leadership style?
- What do you want your organization to look like in one year, two years or five years?
- Do your plans involve new offices, facilities, plants, personnel or locations?
- Will you be developing important new products/services, or making major changes in your product/service lines?
- Is there an in-house legal department at your entity? If so, how is it organized?
- How do decisions get made about whether to use outside counsel versus handle a matter in-house?
- How do decisions get made about which outside counsel to use?
- Are there any trends or changes in your industry that will have an impact on your future relationship with our law firm?
- What are the company's plans related to acquisitions, divestitures or mergers over the next few years?
- What is the most significant issue your company has faced in the last three to five years? What particular challenges resulted from that issue?
- What do you see as the most pressing legal problems you will be facing in the next two or three years?
- What do you see as the biggest risk to your business?
- Which business issues keep you up at night?

F. Adding Value

Adding value is a marketing term that represents an important concept—in short, what does a client get from a law firm in addition to getting the legal work done? A client's perception of "added value" often comes down to three things: a great relationship, a great result or "extras."

[W]hat does a client get from a law firm in addition to getting the legal work done?

The "extras" you might provide a client include the following kinds of activities:

• *Sending personal notes to let clients know you are thinking of them.* Acknowledge a referral with a hand-written thank-you note. Send a congratulatory note or bouquet acknowledging a client's promotion or a new building. Send notes of condolence.

• *Giving small but meaningful gifts.* (Be sure that the client's company allows employees to accept gifts.) There are a number of things that you can use to provide mementos to clients, such as:

• Gifts that remind the client about a good result or project success, such as a pen from a document signing, a laminated miniature patent or a framed tombstone of a securities offering

• Gifts that recognize special events in the client's organization or life, such as a Founder's Day plaque, an anniversary cake or a bottle of champagne for opening a new facility

• Gifts that recognize the individual's preferences, such as a pound of a special flavor of coffee, tickets to a sporting event, golf balls or a new book by a favorite author. (By looking around client offices, you often see indications of what is important to them, e.g., pictures of kids, a replica of a sailboat, golf trophies, etc.)

• *Helping clients on a personal level.* Get them involved in appropriate networks (e.g., professional or trade meetings, social networks). Recommend a good chiropractor. Offer to get a client on a board or sponsor his or her membership in a country club.

• *Offering workshops.* Conduct in-house or on-site workshops (e.g., on avoiding sexual harassment claims) to address areas of concern or to train client employees.

• *Using technology to improve the relationship (e.g., set up a client extranet).*

- *Looking for creative ways to solve problems or save the client money, even without being asked to do so.* For example, provide a template for client professionals to use in preparing documents for the firm, or suggest a more efficient process for communicating with the firm.

- *Making clients look good.* Send a letter acknowledging the contribution of a client's staff counsel to his or her supervisor. Honor clients by entering them in awards programs or through other types of recognition.

- *Helping them find personnel.* Volunteer to help find a new in-house counsel or CFO, for example.

- *Referring clients to other people who can help them.* For example, you may want to help them find accountants, venture capital companies, financial planners or consultants or to identify potential vendors, customers or distributors. Look for opportunities to introduce two clients with mutually beneficial businesses.

- *Sending materials of interest.* Examples might include flyers on conferences in which one of the client's employees may be interested or articles on competitors.

- *Offering firm resources, such as the use of a conference room or the firm's marketing director.*

- *Promoting client products and services and publicizing news within the firm.* If the client is a winery, host a tasting for the lawyers or other firm clients. If the client is a car dealer, circulate a note to everyone in the firm encouraging them to shop at the client's dealership if looking for that make of car. If the client is a printing company, get its name on the short list for consideration for firm projects.

Finally, you should treat your most important clients as though they are the most important.[10]

---

[10] See Chapter 11 *infra* on managing client relationships.

G. Entertaining Clients

Clients want to do business with people they like. As one client said, "The legal business is about relationships and people." One way to build personal relationships is through social activity.

(1) *Entertaining Clients*

Many clients enjoy spending time in a more relaxed setting with their lawyers. This allows everyone to become more comfortable on a personal level and build mutual experiences. The range of activities is virtually unlimited, including:

- Breakfasts, lunches or dinners (working or nonworking)
- Events with spouses
- Events with families (e.g., Disney on Ice)
- Entertaining at home
- Sponsoring get-togethers at the firm's offices
- Sporting events (including seating in firm-leased suites)
- Cultural or arts events, such as the theater
- Professional or industry events (e.g., attending an ABA Section meeting or association cocktail party together)
- Open houses

Entertaining must be done with a few things in mind:

- *You should take into account the client's interests.* Not every client likes baseball and some don't like the opera.
- *You should consider whether spouses/significant others or even families should be involved.* By including them, the client isn't always forced to choose between work and home.
- *You should consider the dynamics of your relationship.* It may be difficult or even awkward for a thirty-year-old female lawyer to invite a sixty-year-old male client to dinner. Instead, you might opt for a "working lunch."
- Some clients don't want to spend time "off the clock" with their

lawyers. So you should try to determine if the client would even like to get together periodically outside the office.

Finally, there are occasions when a personal relationship can come between a lawyer and a client. For example, one young partner went out for drinks with a client. As time wore on, the client had a lot to drink and provided many details about the company and its situation. While the lawyer thought this gave him additional insights, the client was embarrassed by his behavior and having divulged too much information. He opted to hire another law firm.

> *If the client begins talking about things that make you uncomfortable, change the subject.*

If the client begins talking about things that make you uncomfortable, change the subject. You never want to put yourself in a position where you do, say or learn something that causes the client to question the efficacy of the relationship.

(2) *Building Relationships When You Can't Entertain*

Increasingly, companies are implementing policies that can inhibit a lawyer's ability to entertain and potentially develop relationships with employees. They may not allow "vendors" to pay for lunch, may forbid gifts to employees or may require their staff members to pay their own way to sporting events.

While these policies certainly restrict what you can do, they do not prevent you from building or maintaining close relationships. In most cases, there are still a number of effective activities that don't violate policy, for example:

• *In most cases, you can still have lunch if you conduct business.* Set up a lunch meeting to discuss the status of a case or, as an alternative, establish a regular meeting schedule (monthly or quarterly) to review all the files in progress.

• *Offer to provide in-house seminars or training at the client's place of business.* This will give you a reason to go on site and have the "face time" you are seeking while providing the client with a valuable service.

135

- *Invite the client's representatives to CLE programs or seminars sponsored by the firm.*

- *Make arrangements to sit together at an industry lunch or professional meeting.*

- *Ask for the opportunity to come in and conduct an annual "relationship" meeting.* You (and other lawyers from your firm, if appropriate) can meet with relevant members of the client organization to discuss the previous year's matters, how things are going and ways to improve the relationship.

- *If allowed, send gifts to the whole office or to the staff specifically.* For example, you might send candy or cookies for Secretaries' Day.

- *Don't forget the value of telephone contact, particularly without a specific work-related reason.* Make it a habit to "check in" with clients by phone according to whatever schedule makes sense for your relationship.

H. Discussing Fees and Invoicing

Unless you are doing *pro bono* work, the lawyer-client relationship is also a relationship in which money is exchanged. Many lawyers do an extremely poor job of discussing fees with clients and then billing for their time. When that happens, the financial aspect of the relationship can cloud the good services that have been provided.

(1) *Discussing Fees*

There have been many studies of clients and their preferences regarding fee discussions. The research indicates that the vast majority of clients would like the lawyer to:

- Discuss fees at the first meeting;
- Initiate the discussion about fees; and
- Provide a detailed explanation about how fees are determined.

If you want to develop good relationships with clients and reduce future collection problems, initiate the discussion about fees with phrases such as these:

- "I'm sure you're wondering what it will cost you to incorporate your business."

- "Before we wrap up the meeting, I'd like to tell you how I charge for my services and see if you have any questions about my fees."

- "I'm delighted to be working with you on this matter. Before we get started, we should discuss fees."

- "I find that many clients want to start their relationships with our firm by talking about how our fees are determined."

> *If you want to develop good relationships with clients and reduce future collection problems, initiate the discussion about fees.*

- "I like to make it a practice to discuss fees at the beginning of the client relationship to make sure there are no concerns or misunderstandings."

Other tips when discussing fees with clients:

- If you plan to provide a free service, let your client know. For example, "I asked Jerry to sit in on the meeting in case any potential tax issues come up in the future; you won't be billed for his time today."

- Be clear about what is and what is not included in your fee, and how charges are determined. For example, inform clients about how you charge for travel time. This often will prevent complaints from arising in the first place.

- Explore alternative fee arrangements, such as contingency fees, flat or fixed fees, or results-oriented fees. Clients appreciate your willingness to be flexible, even if they resort to the hourly rate.

- Learn how to budget or estimate for clients. Analyze your past projects to see if you can determine the range of fees for projects fitting certain parameters, such as negotiating and/or drafting real estate leases, handling commercial finance deals or even conducting depositions. Clients want to know what something will cost.

Finally, once a client relationship has been established, you should inform clients of rate increases before they take effect. If clients notice a fee increase and nothing has been said, they may feel you have tried to "sneak" something past them, and may be more likely to scrutinize future bills. Whether you meet with clients, call them or send a letter, you should try to incorporate the following ideas:

• *Justify the increase.* Explain why it is necessary (e.g., rising salaries for top associates). This way you can avoid having clients invent their own reasons.

• *Build the perception of value for the firm.* Explain what clients get in return for the fee increase (e.g., top-notch people to support certain areas of expertise, new technology that allows the firm to be more responsive, etc.).

• *Open the lines of communication.* Invite clients to call or talk to you about the rate increase or the firm generally. This will reinforce to them the value you place on your relationship with them.

(2) *Invoicing*

Even if the client knows what the service will cost or how you determine your fees, you still need to ensure that the invoices are clear, timely and accurate. Invoices are more important than you might think. They arrive frequently, and often are used by clients to judge the progress of their matters.

With respect to invoices, think about employing the following techniques:

• *Be flexible in how you bill clients.* Some clients like fees broken out by project or business unit; some like tremendous detail. Ask clients about their billing preferences, including the frequency, form and detail to include. Find out if it matters what day of the month the bills arrive or to whom the invoice should be sent. A "client-friendly" bill will match the client's way of doing business.

• *Unless told otherwise, provide detail so clients can understand what they are paying for.* Instead of just billing for a telephone conference, indicate which parties were involved and what was discussed.

- *Send regular bills.* Clients will be apprised of the status of their matter, and will have a better sense of the aggregate cost of the work being done.

- *Get your bills out promptly.* Study after study shows that the sooner an invoice is rendered after the service is received, the more likely it is to be paid. In addition, if bills arrive too late, it is easy for clients to forget what you did for them or perceive the work as less important or less valuable.

> *Cover letters . . . give clients comfort that you have actually reviewed the bill.*

- *Use cover letters.* The cover letter can be used to explain unanticipated costs, extra value or terrific results. Cover letters also give clients comfort that you have actually reviewed the bill. You can also use a cover letter to thank clients for their business.

- *Be careful with the language you use.* There are many phrases that commonly appear in legal bills that are considered objectionable or raise "red flags" with clients. These include:

  - *Inter-office conferences.* Clients don't like to pay for you to talk to a colleague.

  - *Reviewing files.* They often feel this does not add value to the matter and only occurs because you have taken off too much time since last working on a matter.

  - *Research.* Unless approved in advance, many clients don't like paying for research; they feel they are hiring you for your expertise.

  - *"Nickel and dime" items.* Many times lawyers charge for small things that add up to big concerns for a client, from five-minute phone calls to a fee for incoming faxes.

If clients see too many small or objectionable entries, they may call into question the cost of the larger, more expensive entries.

- *Use active, not passive, descriptions of your time.* For example, "Consideration of tax issues" should be replaced by "Analyzed tax issue in proposed structure of merger." Use the invoice to show clients what has been accomplished.

• *Scour the bills for errors.* The number of billing errors that reach clients is astounding. These range from addressing the bill to the wrong person to errors in arithmetic. For example, it is quite common for two lawyers who attended the same meeting to bill for different periods of time, and this obviously raises concerns about your efforts to be a good steward of the client's money.

> *If clients see too many small or objectionable entries, they may call into question the cost of the larger, more expensive entries.*

• *Be careful with the amount of time recorded.* Clients with a lot of legal work have a general idea of how much things should cost. They may look at the actual time spent on projects or the number of people involved. This is particularly true if clients work with multiple law firms. In those instances, your invoices will be compared to those of other law firms.

• *Discuss irregularities in advance of billing them.* The worst thing you can do is send a bill with unexpected amounts or work. While issues frequently arise that may change the scope and cost of a legal matter, you should communicate with the client about these changes before billing for them.

• *If a client has issued billing guidelines, follow them closely.* For example, billing a client for secretarial overtime when that is expressly forbidden will generate ire.

• *If you are writing something off a bill, such as excessive research time or time spent preparing for an in-house client seminar, let the client know you have done so.* Include a sentence in the cover letter noting the value received or include the time on the bill with a "No charge" notation. Similarly, if you have discounted a client's invoice, include the original rate and the discounted rate, to reinforce the value of your work.

• *Use good judgment.* You don't want to bill a client $50,000 and then tack on a $2 incoming fax charge.

• *Send the work product before billing for it.* For example, you should attempt to send the deposition summary before billing for the deposition.

• *Be careful with disbursements.* While they often represent just 10% or less of a bill, clients understand them better and often scrutinize them more. They may not know whether they received value from a $25,000 invoice for legal services, but they know if they needed a document delivered for $14.

• *Let clients know how to resolve a billing dispute or question.* Tell clients you are always open to hearing from them if there are questions or concerns about the bill. Work with your firm's accounts receivable people to understand red flags and deal quickly with problems.

> *[Clients] may not know whether they received value from a $25,000 invoice for legal services, but they know if they needed a document delivered for $14.*

III. CONCLUDING THOUGHTS

The Harvard Business School article cited earlier provides justification for your efforts to move clients from simply satisfied to loyal.[11] According to the research, "totally satisfied" customers are six times more likely to repurchase the company's products or services than customers who rated themselves as merely "satisfied." The "totally satisfied" customers are also more likely to refer other clients to your firm. Good client relationship skills aren't just a good idea, they can assure the success of your practice.

---

[11] Reichheld and Teal, *The Loyalty Effect: The Hidden Force Behind Growth, Profits and Lasting Value* (Harvard Business School Press 1996).

Avoiding Miscues with Clients

There are many nonverbal or inadvertent communications that can create unintended perceptions on the part of clients. Here are some to avoid:

- *Not returning phone calls promptly.* How quickly you return clients' phone calls is the factor clients use most often to determine how important they are to you.
- *Making clients wait in the reception area.* If a client shows up for a 10:00 a.m. appointment and isn't shown into a conference room or your office promptly, this will communicate that the client's time isn't as valuable as yours or that you are not very organized.
- *Not meeting deadlines.* Lawyers often forget that, in many cases, if they miss a deadline, the client misses a deadline. Being late (particularly without giving the client a "heads up") communicates more than a lack of respect for the client's deadline; it also tells the client you are too busy to take on more work.
- *Belittling your capabilities.* When a client gives you a compliment, don't downplay it, e.g., "Oh, it was nothing." First, this minimizes the client's perception, which is never a good idea; second, clients want lawyers who exude confidence.
- *Not proofing or running spell check on documents.* Clients use the tangible products of your work to evaluate your concern and quality. Sending documents with errors tells clients that you're too busy to review their work, that their matters are not very important, or worse, that you are careless or ignorant. In contrast, putting client documents on quality paper and using nice presentation materials can create the perception that the substantive content is of high quality as well.
- *Saying you've handled "hundreds" of similar cases or that the matter is "routine."* While lawyers may feel this approach builds the perception of their capabilities or even gives clients a measure of

comfort, most clients believe their matter is important and unique. Saying a matter is routine makes clients feel they will not be given a customized solution.

- *Badmouthing colleagues.* If a conference room isn't available or you're late for a lunch, don't blame receptionists or secretaries, no matter who is at fault. Just apologize for the mix up and move on. Clients want to think that everyone in the firm works together as a team on their behalf.

- *Excusing colleagues.* One client complained to his primary lawyer that another firm lawyer didn't return his calls for days. The primary lawyer replied, "Oh, he doesn't return anyone's calls." The client was left wondering why the firm would tolerate such behavior. A more appropriate response would be, "I'm sorry to hear that," or "Would you like me to look into the problem for you?"

- *Taking calls during a client meeting.* This indicates to the client that something or someone else is more important. If you know in advance that you will need to be interrupted, advise the client at the beginning of the meeting and apologize for the inconvenience.

Ideas/Notes: Satisfying Clients and Building Loyalty

My personal challenge(s) or obstacle(s) in this area:

_____

_____

_____

_____

_____

My goal(s) or objective(s) in this area:

_____

_____

_____

_____

_____

What I need to do to get started:

(1) _____

_____

(2) _____

_____

(3) _____

_____

(4) _____

_____

(5) _____

_____

10

Cross Selling and Expanding Client Relationships

I. INTRODUCTION

It is widely known that existing clients are a firm's best source of future business. Expanding an existing client's relationship into new areas—substantive or geographic—is easier and more profitable for a law firm than obtaining new business.

Cross selling or cross marketing is the term that most people use to describe the process of introducing additional services to existing clients, and expanding the client relationship. Some people prefer to call it cross servicing, which connotes an effort to help clients with additional needs. The truth is, you are doing a service for clients when you advise them of areas in which you can be of assistance or about services you are not currently providing.

> [Y]ou are doing a service for clients when you advise them of areas in which you can be of assistance or about services you are not currently providing.

There are a couple of fundamental tenets of cross selling. Understanding these will greatly improve your odds of success.

First, cross selling is most effectively done one client at a time. The "firm" cannot cross sell. There are institutional activities that will lay the groundwork for cross selling, like a Web site, a brochure or a series of seminars, but it is the responsibility of the lawyers working with a particular client to spot areas of need and let the client know the firm can help.

Second, the more you customize your approach to a specific client, the more effective you will be at generating new business. Instead of telling every client about all of your firm's capabilities, you need to target your message. In other words, tell one client about a specific service from which he or she will benefit, such as the intellectual property practice or an office in China.

Third, most cross selling fails because the lawyers do not make the client comfortable with the person they are proposing to do the new work. You have to remember that if the client has legal work in an area you aren't handling, it usually means the client is using another law firm. The law business is a relationship business; rather than relying on institutional or passive descriptions of your capabilities, like lawyer résumés, you need to make a connection between the client and the lawyer in your firm who would do the work. (This assumes you are able to obtain the cooperation of your colleagues.)

Unfortunately, there are many obstacles to cross selling in law firms. Some firms' compensation systems provide disincentives for lawyers either to share their clients with colleagues or, conversely, to work on other lawyers' client matters. For example, in a firm with a compensation system that rewards the originating lawyer with lifetime credit for all new matters received from a client, other lawyers may feel their time is best spent working to develop their own books of business. In some cases, lawyers have been known to refer business (which the firm is capable of handling) outside their own firm so they can maintain referral relationships that result in new business to them.

> *[I]n large or decentralized client organizations . . . dealing with the new contact can be akin to approaching a prospective client.*

There can also be issues of trust. If a lawyer isn't confident that the client will have a good result or a good experience with a colleague, he or she may not want to risk the potential damage to his or her own relationship with the client.

In addition, in large or decentralized client organizations, decisions about hiring counsel for various types of legal matters may be spread throughout the company. In that instance, having a relationship with the tax executive may not help you in obtaining business in the litigation area. Similarly, a law firm handling defense work for an insurance company must understand that the decisions made about corporate or real estate work are handled by a completely different set of executives. In these cases, the existing client contact may be able to facilitate introductions within the company, but dealing with the new contact can be akin to approaching a prospective client.

Finally, cross selling is not even an option if the client is dissatisfied with the existing service being provided. If the client feels the firm is not responsive with existing matters, for example, he will be reluctant to send any more work your way.

Assuming a client is satisfied, however, you can look for ways to expand the relationship. Effective cross selling requires three basic steps:

- Understanding the client's needs
- Understanding the firm's capabilities
- Presenting the information to the client

The following sections discuss these steps in detail.

II. LEARNING ABOUT ADDITIONAL CLIENT NEEDS

A. Identifying Targets for Cross Selling

The first step in cross selling is to identify clients with additional needs that the firm might fill. A quick analysis of key client relationships can often reveal where the firm is providing assistance and where it is not.

Table 10 shows an example of a cross selling chart. This type of analysis can make it easier to determine if there are opportunities with clients.

(Please see page 148 for Table 10.)

For example, looking at the clients in Table 10, if you know ABC Corporation has 150 employees, you should be trying to determine who currently handles the labor and employment work and why the work doesn't come to your firm. Perhaps you handled a major litigation matter for Jane Doe with a very good result. You should be asking

TABLE 10
CROSS SELLING CHART
2005 FEES

Client	Billing Attorney	Date Open	Total	Labor	Tax	Finance	General Litigation	Corporate
ABC Corporation	AAA	Jun-04	$547,000		21%		33%	46%
XYZ Corporation	BBB	Apr-05	$200,000	36%	14%		9%	41%
Jane Doe	CCC	Sept-04	$319,000				100%	

yourself whether she would benefit from an estate plan now that she received a large settlement.

Generally, to determine if you have opportunities to expand a client relationship, you need to know about:

(1) *The client's business.*

- What does the company or business do?
- How many employees does it have?
- What is its annual revenue?
- Where are its locations or regions?
- What are its subsidiaries or divisions?

(2) *The key players.*

- Who are the key players or executives at the company?
- Who are the outside advisors?
- Is there in-house counsel?
- Who is involved in deciding who will handle legal services in the new area(s)?
- What are the criteria for choosing counsel (e.g., turnaround time, results, industry expertise)?

(3) *Legal issues and relationships.*

- Who is the current outside counsel in the area(s) being targeted? Without knowing who has the work now, it will be difficult to position yourself as a better alternative.
- What kinds of matters do existing outside counsel handle for the company?
- What other relationships does the company have with outside counsel? For example, is a lawyer on the company's board?
- Have noteworthy legal issues arisen lately that provide an opportunity to discuss the new area for representation?

(4) *The firm's relationship with the client.*

- What has been the firm's relationship with the company?

- Do you have any conflicts—real or perceived—in the new area(s)?

- Do you or any of your colleagues have relationships with decision-makers in the new area(s)? If so, how strong are they?

- Does the firm have the capabilities to handle the work in the new area(s)?

When attempting to expand relationships with clients, it's important to be honest about your odds and abilities. For example, if you work in a mid-sized regional law firm and your client is currently using a major New York firm for its international work, it will probably be difficult to convince the client that you are a better alternative in this area.

Most clients will not be inclined to change counsel without a compelling reason to do so.

It is also important to appreciate that there is a reason for the client's existing relationship with the other law firm. Most clients will not be inclined to change counsel without a compelling reason to do so.

In addition, you need to recognize that clients are taking a risk when moving more business to you. They may have had a bad past experience with one of your firm's litigators and are reluctant to use your firm again. They may worry about having all their "eggs in one basket." They may not be convinced that you have the manpower to handle a certain type of matter or question whether you have the specialized expertise in a certain niche. They may think you are already too busy to handle additional business. You need to understand and factor in all of these issues if you want to be successful in expanding client relationships.

How can you find information that will help you uncover additional client needs? There are good sources within and outside your firm. For example:

(1) *Research resources.*

- Run a cross selling analysis through the firm's time and billing system

- Check the company's Web site for information

- Do an analysis of company operations, locations, etc., through online services like Hoover's

- Run a search for recent articles on or media coverage of the client

- Conduct some research on court filings

- Review industry or other related reports and publications for trends and issues in the client's lines of business

(2) *Talk to others who have material information. This might include:*

- Colleagues with relationships at the company

- Advisors (e.g., the client's accountant)

(3) *Talk with the client.* Obviously, talking with the client is the best way to discover unfilled needs.

B. Talking with Clients About Their Needs

The most important skill that good cross marketers possess is listening. By asking intelligent and informed questions and demonstrating good listening skills, you should be able not only to uncover client issues and needs, but to position your firm to help with them.

When talking with clients, you should employ the following techniques:

(1) *Use active listening skills.*

Active listening skills show clients you are interested in what they are saying. When meeting with clients, you should:

- Nod

- Make good eye contact

> *The most important skill that good cross marketers possess is listening.*

- Paraphrase or summarize

what the client has said (e.g., "So the board is interested in exploring ways to prevent lawsuits?")

- Express empathy (e.g., "I can understand why you are frustrated.")

- Lean forward to demonstrate that you're engaged

(2) *Ask open-ended, informed questions.*

Good questions can reveal issues the client is facing and help you spot opportunities. Many times, you will find new opportunities by asking follow-up questions about an existing situation or a recently completed project.

For example, if you worked with a company on an acquisition, you might ask the client contact:

"Now that you've acquired the business, what plans do you have for managing its legal affairs?"

You may discover that the client has considered centralizing certain aspects of the decision-making for legal counsel, which could benefit you. After a litigation matter is resolved, you might ask:

"Now that the antitrust issue is behind us, have you thought about implementing any strategies to stem potential problems in the future?"

In other cases, regular discussions with open-ended questions often reveal opportunities for future work. For example:

"Looking at your areas of operation, it occurred to me that you probably have real estate leasing issues in our state. How do you handle those matters now?"

"What are the company's plans related to acquisitions, divestitures or mergers over the next few years?"

"How do you think your response to product liability claims will change in the future?"

"We want to be sure we're positioned to be of the greatest value to you in the future. How can we add more benefit for you? What can we do to be more valuable to your business?"

In the end, your objective for cross selling should be to find an area where you can clearly satisfy a client's need.

III. KNOWING THE FIRM'S CAPABILITIES

Effective cross selling requires a lot of internal effort to understand the firm's collective capabilities. It is important for each lawyer to know the other practices and locations of the firm well enough to talk about them with clients.

To be an effective cross seller, you need to understand:

• *Who does what in the firm.* In other words, what practices exist and who provides the services.

You never know when it will be useful to highlight a colleague's alma mater or prior experience in an industry.

• *Background and experience of colleagues.* The best cross sellers learn as much as they can about everyone with whom they work. You never know when it will be useful to highlight a colleague's alma mater or prior experience in an industry.

• *How to describe each practice to clients.* This means understanding what benefits a particular practice brings to a client. Instead of just saying that the firm has a bonding practice, you should be able to highlight how this practice has benefitted clients, whether helping them raise money or helping them achieve a goal.

• *Recent activities.* You should be able to mention specific transactions, notable happenings or good results that the firm has provided for other clients in the area of interest.

There are many activities that can help you understand the firm's capabilities better or to help your colleagues know more about your practice and spot opportunities for you. Here are some ideas:

(1) *Target colleagues in areas related to your practice or the industries of your clients.* For example, if you represent closely held businesses, target the estate planning lawyers. If you work with technology companies, get to know your firm's immigration lawyers.

(2) *Study the materials related to your colleagues' practices.* This will allow you to see who in your firm is handling certain types of matters or who has expertise with respect to particular issues. For example:

• Read practice area brochures
• Review lists of clients or representative matters

- Read the new matters listings carefully
- Read firm newsletters, client alerts and white papers
- Look at firm seminar invitations
- Visit the firm Web site or intranet regularly

(3) *Treat your colleagues like targets or prospective clients.* Set up appointments or take them to lunch, and ask about:

- Their clients' businesses and industries
- Recent successes or results they've attained
- Their best sources of business
- Hot button issues in their area(s) of practice
- Recent changes to the law in their area(s)
- Trends in their practice(s)
- Ways to describe their practice(s) (i.e., how would you describe what they do in fifty words or fewer to an interested client?)

(4) *Plan inter-group (e.g., inter-department) activities to foster discussion of mutual opportunities.* For example:

- Participate in your firm's other practice groups' meetings occasionally to listen to their discussions of recent client matters
- Invite members of other groups to participate in your practice group or department meetings to talk about recent client projects or other matters that would be of interest to your group (e.g., proposed legislation affecting an industry)
- Ask if you can make presentations or provide updates on your area of law for other practice groups

(5) *Use firm meetings or social activities to interact with lawyers with whom you do not normally work.*[1]

The bottom line is that it is your responsibility to know about the firm's capabilities. Once you have a command of your firm's other practice

---

[1] See Section V.C *infra* for additional ideas on networking with colleagues.

areas, it becomes easy to talk to clients about them, and you will also be better equipped to recognize opportunities to help clients in new areas.

IV. PRESENTING YOUR CAPABILITIES

In some cases, your cross selling opportunity requires immediate action. If a client expresses interest in knowing more about your firm's services—specifically or generally—you should be prepared to respond immediately with information.

Some lawyers, when asked if their firms can handle a new area of law, will answer "I think so" or, worse yet, "I don't know. I'll check and get back to you." These are not very compelling pitches and certainly do not create a perception of strength in the mind of the client. The best reply will provide evidence of the firm's capabilities and show your enthusiasm for your colleagues, such as: "Yes, we do a lot of work in the hospitality industry. In fact, one of my partners recently wrote an article on the impact of food-borne illnesses on restaurants."

> *Some lawyers, when asked if their firms can handle a new area of law, will answer "I think so" or, worse yet, "I don't know. I'll check and get back to you." These are not very compelling pitches.*

In other cases, however, your approach will be more intentional. After you recognize an opportunity—such as a planned new facility, a need for intellectual property protection, required changes to distribution agreements, etc.—you are in a position to present your capabilities to clients and request the chance to help. The first step is to contact the client to discuss the new area.

A. Making Contact with the Client

Whether the client contact is someone with whom you have a personal relationship or someone newly introduced to you, you first need to let the client know you are interested in talking about a new area of work. In a telephone call to set up a meeting or discussion, you should be very clear that you are hoping to talk about a new business opportunity. The following are several approaches you might consider:

"Now that we're done getting the leases reviewed, if you're open to it, I'd like to introduce you to my colleague, Jim, who is the head of our firm's tax section. He might be able to help you structure future transactions in a way that will reduce your tax liabilities."

"We recently helped another client develop procedures to protect Internet communications. I'd like to talk to you about the kinds of issues you may want to look at now that you're doing Web-based marketing and selling."

"The members of our San Diego office recently handled some litigation for another construction company. I'd like to talk to you about some of the services they offer clients in your industry."

"I just helped another client develop a program to reduce the number of violations of employment agreements by sales people. I immediately thought of you and how this type of program might benefit your company."

If the person with whom you have been talking is not the ultimate decision-maker but is happy with the work you have done, you can ask for help. For example, if the contact is an HR person and you can make a case for your firm's capabilities in the international area, ask your contact if she would be willing to introduce you to the company's general counsel. Ask if a meeting could be set up with the three of you or, at a minimum, see if your HR contact would put in a good word about your firm. In this instance, if you do ultimately get an opportunity to talk with the general counsel, be sure to acknowledge the existing legal relationship when making contact. For example:

"From my conversations with Susan, I know you currently work with Smith & Jones on your cross-border projects, but I was hoping to get a chance to let you know about our firm's capabilities in that area should you need additional help or conflicts arise."

If you're not comfortable with a telephone call, you can begin the process with a letter explaining your purpose and suggesting that you will call to set up a meeting. But it's imperative that you make that call— and do it promptly (e.g., within a week of sending your letter). This will ensure that the subject is fresh in the mind of the client and will show your enthusiasm for handling the new work.

In some cases, these meetings will be quite informal, and may involve only you and the client contact. In other cases, they may involve a team of lawyers and a formal presentation.

Before meeting with the client, you should develop a solid strategy for presenting the firm's capabilities. Chapter 14, Section III, presents a summary of the issues that are typically involved in developing a pitch strategy. In particular, when assembling the pitch team, be certain to select colleagues who will be a good fit with the client, based on personality, prior experience, age or background. In addition, prep these people about the client, including its business, industry, needs, key players and methods of operation, and share any additional information you were able to uncover.

B. Meeting with the Client

Hopefully the contact you make will result in the chance to discuss expanding the relationship with the client. When meeting to discuss a new business opportunity, keep the following in mind:

- *Thank the client for his or her time.*

- *Introduce the players.* If you bring along lawyers from your firm's other offices or practice areas, be sure to explain why they are there.

- *State the purpose of the meeting.* For example:

   "We've been looking forward to this meeting and the chance to tell you about the nature of the work we've been doing for other technology clients."

- *Show, don't tell.* Minimize the risk in moving additional business to your firm by bringing along a list of recent successful results or transactions, or a list of client references to prove a precedent.

- *Assemble appropriate materials.* Consider bringing along:

   - Copies of articles related to the new area of law or geographic area

- Bios or other information on the personnel you are proposing to handle matters

- Information about the legal or geographic area in which you are proposing to do the work

Obviously, it will be very important to bring the right people to the meeting so you connect on a personal as well as a professional level.

> *[I]t will be very important to bring the right people to the meeting so you connect on a personal as well as a professional level.*

When you are discussing the opportunity, be certain to talk about the benefits to the client of using the firm in the new area and to anticipate any objections the client might have. For example, perhaps you handle a company's litigation needs in your local area; the company uses other counsel throughout the region, and you would like to position your firm to handle the litigation statewide. You should outline the benefits of consolidating the work in your firm, such as your familiarity with the issues, efficiencies, good results, etc. You will also need to anticipate and be prepared to address potential issues or objections like billing for travel time, familiarity with local players (e.g., judges), etc.

V. OTHER CONSIDERATIONS AND TIPS FOR CROSS SELLING AND EXPANDING CLIENT RELATIONSHIPS

A. Handling the Work

If you are fortunate enough to get an assignment from an existing client in a new legal or geographic area, you need to approach the new matter very carefully. How you handle that first matter will determine the client's (and possibly your colleagues') willingness to send you additional work in the future.

When you get the first file in a new area, you should discuss with all parties on the client's team how this client likes to do business. For example:

- What things are most important to the client?

• What kind of communication does the client prefer (e.g., phone calls, formal status reports, etc.), and how often?

• What reporting or billing guidelines does the client have that must be followed?

> *How you handle that first matter will determine the client's (and possibly your colleagues') willingness to send you additional work in the future.*

• What quirks or specific needs does the client have?

• What should everyone know about the client's business, issues, products, operations, procedures or industry in order to provide effective representation?

B. Following Up

In some cases, you will not be successful at expanding the relationship. The clients may already have a very good relationship with another firm that has served them well and, as a result, you will never wrestle the work away. In that situation, it's important to remain positive and not take the rejection personally. Your response may be to position yourself as counsel in the case of conflicts or overflow work.

But even if the client is amenable to expanding the relationship, the odds that he will have a piece of litigation or will be ready to tackle an estate plan when first meeting with you are slim. Often, the work will come, but it will take time. As a result, your follow-up efforts will determine your ultimate success.

There are many activities that will allow you to remind clients about the new area(s) of practice. Often, it is just a matter of you being more effective and calculating when organizing or implementing activities. For example:

• Set up seminars for existing clients to showcase firm lawyers and their capabilities, and to begin to establish face-to-face client/lawyer relationships with other members of your firm

• Host small group roundtables with existing clients to allow an exchange of ideas and information with other lawyers in the firm

• Tell clients when a new lawyer in an area of interest joins the firm.

That way the new lawyer won't be a stranger when first arriving to work on a client's matter

• Offer to provide clients with in-house training or programs in other areas of law, such as an environmental compliance audit

• Set up visits to key clients to introduce different colleagues face to face and let them learn about the client's business

• Consider carefully who will be included in client entertainment or at events. For example, you might have one of your litigators attend a baseball game to introduce him to the client.

• Offer to have colleagues in other practice areas sit in on client meetings or telephone conferences at no charge to the client

• Be certain to invite the client to any of the firm's events and seminars dealing with potential areas of need

• Proactively introduce a "team" of lawyers to the client[2]

• Try to get clients into the firm's offices whenever possible (e.g., extend an invitation for them to use conference rooms if they are from out of town and visiting your city)

• Add clients to mailing lists to receive relevant communications, such as newsletters or alerts, to showcase colleagues' accomplishments or present substantive updates

• Talk positively, and continuously, about colleagues, to build their perceived strengths and demonstrate your enthusiasm. Use your colleagues' activities, such as awards or speeches, as your entrée.

> *Talk positively, and continuously, about colleagues, to build their perceived strengths and demonstrate your enthusiasm.*

• Introduce clients to colleagues whenever they visit the firm. Ask your colleagues to stop into your office or visit the conference room, or take a client on a tour and stop in your colleagues' offices. The greater the breadth and depth of a client-firm relationship, the more secure it is.

---

[2] See Chapter 11, Section IV.B *infra* on developing a client service team.

If you are trying to cross sell the capabilities of a lawyer or an office in another geographic area, it can be difficult to get a client together with a colleague. However, there are still steps you can take to make clients comfortable with your firm's other capabilities. For example:

• *Share work product.* Send a client a copy of a skillful cross-examination conducted by a colleague on a tough expert witness from the client's industry or share a copy of a lawyer's particularly impressive brief (redacted as necessary).

• *Look for opportunities to get your colleagues involved in the client's location.* If your client is involved in a lawsuit near another one of your office locations, for example, you might send a colleague from the nearby office to take a deposition that other firms would take over the telephone.

• *Look for chances to get lawyers from other offices to meet clients in the context of their legal projects.* For example, when working on a major transaction for a client, you could suggest that your firm's top real estate lawyer, who is located in another office, participate in the meeting via conference call, at no charge to the client.

• *Whenever you have opportunities to establish face-to-face contact between clients and colleagues, do so.* For example, if your firm holds an all-lawyer or partner meeting in your location, ask selected colleagues if they would schedule a little extra time around the meeting to go visit clients with you. Or look for social activities, such as ball games, that might provide a chance for out-of-town lawyers to interact with your clients in a comfortable way.

• *Position your out-of-town colleagues as experts before the client.* You can do this by forwarding copies of articles they have written or inviting them to be speakers at local seminars sponsored by the firm or other organizations.

Keep in mind that once lawyers in other substantive or geographic areas have been introduced to the client, they should be encouraged to follow up directly to develop their own relationships. Your colleagues will need to find appropriate ways to stay in touch with the client so the firm stays top of mind in the area.

Finally, remember that you must make regular attempts to educate clients about the services, offices or personnel that are most relevant to them. Clients may not pay much attention to the information until it's important to them.

C. Networking with Colleagues

As previously noted, networking with colleagues is a crucial ingredient in successful cross selling. Here are some additional ideas for networking inside the firm:

• *Take the initiative to meet new people in your firm.* For example, at each meal at a firm retreat, sit at a table with someone you haven't met or don't know well. At internal workshops or meeting sessions, sit with colleagues from other practice areas or locations. At the firm's summer outing, ask the event coordinator to put you in a golf foursome with lawyers from another office.

• *Focus on your peers.* Presumably they will be moving up the ranks with you.

• *Follow up with colleagues.* Send an e-mail after meeting a lawyer from one of the firm's other offices. Try to become an out-of-town colleague's major contact when visiting the city. Introduce these colleagues to other lawyers in your firm.

• *Visit other firm offices whenever you have a chance.* Call ahead to let people know you're coming. Introduce yourself to the office administrator and receptionist. Make the rounds to say hello.

• *Be the champion of other offices or practice groups.* When your department or practice group discusses clients, matters or issues, mention things you've learned from colleagues in other areas. Suggest those lawyers participate in meetings or conference calls, or get copied on correspondence, if appropriate.

Advice to Lawyers Wanting to Be "Cross Sold"

There are many times when lawyers are hoping to be introduced to colleagues' clients. In such cases, it is important to recognize that your target is the colleague, and it will be necessary to demonstrate the benefit or reduce the risk before that contact lawyer will be willing to introduce you to his or her client.

When you want to be cross sold to other lawyers' clients or contacts, there are many things you should consider. For example:

(1) *Attempt to target lawyers with natural ties to your practice area.* For example, if you know a lot about Internet-related legal issues and want to target firm clients, you may want to start by visiting the Web sites of the firm's top fifty clients. Then you can determine which lawyers are responsible for those clients. These lawyers should become your target audience.

(2) *Show your targeted colleagues how you can be of benefit to their clients.* Your message needs to center on how you can help your colleague and their clients—not how they can help you. Focus on how you have helped clients avoid problems or save money through protecting their Internet communications or marks. Demonstrate why it's in their best interest and the best interest of their clients to meet you.

(3) *Educate your colleagues about your area of practice/expertise, so they can talk to their clients about it.* Provide the targeted lawyers with enough information so they can describe your services and experience. Educate them about trends or buzzwords in this area, and give them insights into other key issues, such as timing, which might help or hinder their cross selling efforts. And use what you've done for one client to explain what you can do for others.

(4) *Make your colleagues comfortable with your capabilities.* Build your internal credibility and demonstrate your capabilities by putting together a list of client matters or a résumé of your professional activities (e.g., professional associations, articles, etc.).

(5) *Make it easy for your colleagues to sell you to their clients.* For example:

- Offer to set up a conference call with a client and the primary lawyer at no charge
- Ask if you can drop in on a meeting when the client is visiting so you can meet face to face
- Offer to visit the client or attend a lunch to discuss the practice area at no charge to the client
- Offer to present an informative workshop on the topic, internally or for a client

Once you are ready, you can set up meetings with your colleagues in groups or individually to express your interest and request their cooperation. If you target selected colleagues with these principles in mind, your odds of being cross sold will grow dramatically.

Finally, if you are successful in your efforts to be cross sold and have the opportunity to work with another lawyer's client, you should treat your colleague like a client too. For example:

(1) Thank your colleague. Express your appreciation for the confidence in you and provide assurance that you will do whatever you can to make sure the client is satisfied.

(2) Ask what role your colleague would like to play. For example:

- How would he or she like to be kept apprised of the status of the client's matter?
- What information would he or she like to have about the issue?
- How should communication with the client be handled?
- What else can you do to ensure a smooth transition?

Ideas/Notes: Cross Selling and Expanding Client Relationships

My personal challenge(s) or obstacle(s) in this area:

_____

_____

_____

_____

_____

My goal(s) or objective(s) in this area:

_____

_____

_____

_____

_____

What I need to do to get started:

(1) _____

_____

(2) _____

_____

(3) _____

_____

(4) _____

_____

(5) _____

_____

11
Managing Relationships with Significant Clients

I.   INTRODUCTION

Many client relationships are episodic or temporary. An out-of-state company hires you as local counsel to litigate a matter and isn't likely to have other matters for you to handle. A client sells its business to another company, which plans to consolidate decision-making and legal services, so the client is lost. An individual goes through a divorce and needs help from a family lawyer, hoping never to hire a lawyer again.

However, if you are fortunate to have clients—companies or individuals—with an ongoing stream of legal work, you need to manage these relationships. Many law firms have introduced a system similar to "account managers," which may be called "Client Service Managers," "Client Relationship Partners," or even "Responsible Lawyers." The overriding responsibility of these lawyers is to manage the client relationship in order to create a satisfied and loyal client, and to identify new opportunities to help the client. A client management system affixes accountability for important client relationships.

> *The overriding responsibility of [a Client Service Manager] is to manage the client relationship in order to create a satisfied and loyal client, and to identify new opportunities to help the client.*

This Chapter focuses on the roles that a Client Service Manager can play and provides tips and techniques for managing client relationships. In an ideal world, lawyers would take this approach in every client relationship; in reality, however, this approach should at least be taken with the largest or most significant clients.

II. THE ROLE OF THE CLIENT SERVICE MANAGER

Whether your firm has a formal client management program or not, any lawyer with primary responsibility for a significant client relationship should have the following goals:

(1) Understand the client and the client's needs

(2) Ensure client satisfaction through excellent service, improved coordination and communication, and a better understanding of the client's business and/or industry

(3) Manage the client's work and expenses at the firm

If done properly, the result of these efforts often will be:

- A more loyal client (i.e., less likely to defect)

- Increased revenues and flow of work

- An enhanced relationship (i.e., better relations between client and firm representatives)

To be effective, the Client Service Manager will need to commit time and be devoted to the client. Specific areas of responsibility for the Client Service Manager would be as follows:

- Take overall responsibility for the relationship with the client and the client's satisfaction with the firm

- Have an in-depth understanding of the client: legal needs, business, industry, other preferences (e.g., how the client does business), the politics of the company, the chemistry of the people, etc.

- Be aware of all significant developments, legal or nonlegal, that affect the client

- Be the "point person" for client work—coordinate the client's services in all practice areas, be informed on the current status of all matters being handled for the client, assign the most appropriate lawyers (based on expertise or other factors) to work on the client's matters, and ensure the client's work is properly managed and delegated within the firm

• Build a close relationship with the individual client or key representatives of the client entity, and spend time with the client on a nonbusiness basis

• Be available to the client—be accessible, promptly return phone calls, ask and encourage questions, and respond to any complaints and concerns

• Make certain that all your lawyers and staff members working for the client are apprised of the client's needs, business, quirks, guidelines, etc., and coordinate and communicate developments internally—providing consistency and continuity for the client

• Understand the firm's capabilities and identify new opportunities to serve the client or ways to expand the relationship

• Manage the client's expectations and be responsible for client fees and billing arrangements

• Look for ways to add value to the client's relationship with the firm

III. GETTING OFF TO A GOOD START

Identifying and meeting—or better yet, exceeding—client expectations is a key to client satisfaction and loyalty.[1] You can set the tone for a good relationship at the beginning of any new relationship as well as any new, significant matter with a few simple activities.

A. New Client Welcome Letter

> *[T]he [new client] welcome letter is an easy and excellent way to start the relationship on a positive note.*

While most law firms are quick to send engagement letters, few send a "welcome" or thank-you letter. However, the welcome letter is an easy and excellent way to start the relationship on a positive note.

Your welcome letter can be used to:

---

[1] See Chapter 9, Section II.A *supra*.

- Thank the client for selecting you or the firm

- Indicate your enthusiasm for the project or your assurance that you will provide your best effort

- Provide information that will help the client contact the firm, such as names and phone numbers of assigned staff, the file number(s), etc.

- Include a map of the office

- Provide materials on the firm and the assigned lawyers (e.g., a brochure, résumés of the lawyers, etc.)

B. New Client Relationship Checklist

There are myriad details that need to be discussed with new clients to ensure that you understand their substantive and service needs—everything from staffing to how documents will be delivered. If you have developed what will likely become an ongoing, financially significant client for the firm, you should think about reviewing the checklist presented below with the client at the onset of the relationship.

Having a discussion about these issues should help you identify the client's expectations as well as plot a strategy for keeping the client happy. For example, when discussing preferences for status reporting and meetings, every client is different; some clients will appreciate weekly breakfast meetings while others prefer more formal quarterly meetings.

New Client Checklist

Staffing Issue

☐ Discuss the client's team (i.e., which lawyers and staff will be assigned to client matters, actual or anticipated), including who will be the "lead" lawyer and who will serve as the backup in that lawyer's absence[2]

---

[2] See Section IV.B *infra* for further discussion of the client team.

☐ Provide the client with a directory or organizational chart of the team (including direct dial numbers and e-mail addresses) or biographies of the team members

☐ Determine how the client would like to work with the firm (e.g., funnel work through the primary lawyer or interact with the substantive "specialists" directly)

☐ Introduce the client to secretaries, paralegals and other lawyers on the team. (This can be done in person or on a conference call.)

☐ Ask for the names of key staff members or representatives of the client and their roles (including assistants or secretaries to company executives). If appropriate, ask for an organizational chart.

Procedures

☐ Discuss with the client on what issues he or she wishes to provide feedback or input (e.g., staffing changes) or give prior approval

☐ Determine what role client representatives want to play in the relationship

☐ Advise the client how the firm plans to proceed with the matter

Client Information/Client Profile

☐ Research the client[3]

☐ Visit the client's offices, plants or facilities to learn about the company's culture and methods of doing business

☐ Obtain a copy of the client's annual reports, 10K reports, and strategic and business plans

☐ Obtain the client's company or product brochures

☐ Visit the company's Web site

Technology

☐ Obtain the client representatives' e-mail addresses

☐ Determine client software and other systems for exchanging documents and information

---

[3] See Chapter 9, Section II.E *supra* for a list of appropriate questions.

□ Obtain the client's telephone, cell phone and facsimile numbers

□ Discuss developing an extranet for the client

Communications and Preferences

□ Determine client preferences or obtain client guidelines or policies regarding:

  □ Status reporting

  □ Meeting frequency, times and locations

  □ Delivery services

  □ Receiving work product or projects in progress

  □ Billing

  □ Entertainment

□ Discuss client invoicing preferences (e.g., does the client prefer one consolidated bill or invoices for separate matters)

□ Determine client information needs (e.g., seminar topics of interest, desire to receive firm newsletters)

□ Provide the firm's marketing materials

□ Provide a list of other resources related to the client's issue that might be helpful (e.g., agencies, consultants, departments)

□ Introduce client representatives to others in the firm who may be of assistance in the future

C. New Matter Letter

Another important point in a client relationship is when you receive a significant new assignment. Let's say your client is a financial institution, and you handle a lot of real estate loan documentation. However, the client has called to ask your firm to handle a major litigation matter involving environmental issues related to a property.

After your discussions with the client, think about preparing a summary letter establishing your understanding of the project and the client's needs. This could include a description of:

- The legal issue. Why the client hired you or the firm.

- The objectives. What you hope to accomplish for the client.

- The anticipated schedule. Estimated timetable or deadlines for the project. In this area, you can identify important court dates or other imposed deadlines, as well as your starting date.

- The budget. Estimated fees, hours, expenses and total costs for the project.

- The client's role. Client responsibilities (e.g., providing personnel, support, etc.).

- Status reporting plans. How the client will be kept apprised about the matter (e.g., monthly status reports, weekly telephone conferences, etc.).

- Other case- or client-specific issues.

IV. EFFECTIVELY MANAGING THE RELATIONSHIP

Happily, some client relationships grow over time. The client may consolidate more and more work in the firm, using lawyers from many practice areas or offices. In some cases, the client entity grows and, consequently, so does the need for legal services.

Lawyers with primary responsibility for large and complex client relationships should think very strategically about how they manage and cultivate these key accounts. The following are some effective activities for Client Service Managers.

A. Understanding the Client's Relationship

If you are assuming the Client Service Manager role for an existing client of the firm, you should start by educating yourself about the client's business and its relationship with the firm. This might include:

- Learning about the client's history with the firm (e.g., when did the relationship begin? Who generated the client?)

- Identifying all the services the firm is currently providing to the client as well as work performed over the past three to five years, including major matters handled

• Identifying the relationships that exist between firm lawyers and representatives of the client, work-related and other (e.g., college friends, neighbors, etc.)

• Learning about services being provided by other law firms—in what substantive areas, and which firms, for example

• Conducting research into the client's business, such as three to five years of sales, profit or stock information, media coverage, etc.

• Identifying the entity's structure, including, if appropriate, business and product lines, subsidiaries or affiliate companies, distributors, important clients, etc.

• Identifying the major players at the client, including board members, directors, in-house legal staff, etc.

B. Developing a Client Service Team

How you staff their matters is very important to clients. One step you can take to demonstrate to clients that you are managing their work effectively is to develop a client service "team." This team should include lawyers and staff who will be assigned to the client's matters.

When selecting the team members, you obviously need to identify the strengths and skills of firm lawyers and staff to match the substantive requirements of the client. In addition, however, you might think about other factors that will enhance the relationship, including personalities, diversity and even potential or future needs. For example, if you have a client who is using the firm for many corporate transactions at this time, you may ask a litigator to serve on the team to become familiar with the client should disputes arise in the future. As another example, you may want to include a team member from an office location where the client has a facility but has not used the firm.

> *One step you can take to demonstrate to clients that you are managing their work effectively is to develop a client service "team."*

You need to find members who are team players, and demonstrate a willingness to learn about the client, its business and its industry. They also should be willing to attend team meetings and communicate client-related information to other team members.

Once you have your team, consider the following steps:

(1) *Develop a directory or organizational chart of the team and provide it to the client.* See Table 11.1 on page 177 for an example of a client team organizational chart. Many clients like this concept because it assures them that the firm is communicating their objectives to those involved, and that they are not paying to "train" new people about their issues. Directories and organizational charts also make it easy for clients to contact people in the firm. In addition to the lawyers on the team, the chart could include support staff members (and contact information), as well as other people in the firm who might be of interest, from the IT Director, for questions about the extranet, to the Billing Coordinator, for questions about invoices. You also should consider including direct dial numbers, e-mail addresses, fax numbers and even home telephone numbers.

(2) *Make introductions.* You should introduce the client contact(s) to team lawyers, secretaries and paralegals, if not in person then through a conference call. When clients visit the office, take every opportunity to introduce them to members of the staff or lawyers in areas in which services are not yet needed. If possible, invite your colleagues to attend a relevant portion of a client meeting (possibly at no charge) or to join you for lunch. In addition, try to meet as many client representatives as necessary, through an on-site visit (and consider bringing others along) or through conference calls.

(3) *Educate the team about the client's needs.* You should notify the members of the team about client expectations (e.g., how frequently and in what form status reports are to be provided, billing guidelines, etc.) and client policies (e.g., entertainment). They should also be made aware of important client staff members or representatives and their roles (including assistants or secretaries to company executives).

(4) *Meet as a team periodically.* The team should discuss:

- Work in progress, to coordinate client matters
- Client guidelines regarding billing, reporting, staffing, etc.

175

- Personnel changes (on either side of the relationship)

- Client business developments (e.g., a new product launch) or personal developments (e.g., a client representative having a baby)

- Marketing efforts (for example, you don't want two separate team lawyers calling independently on the same client representative for lunch)

You should consider including staff members in some or all of these team meetings. Secretaries and paralegals benefit from learning about the "big picture" and goings on at the company, as well as specific issues to which they should be attuned (e.g., changes in billing or status reporting procedures).

(5) *Encourage the team to build relationships with client contacts.* Lawyers and staff, if appropriate, should develop relationships with their peers at the client entity; this will build a strong, institutional bond with the firm. However, as the Client Service Manager, you need to be informed of these efforts so they are properly coordinated.

> *Lawyers and staff, if appropriate, should develop relationships with their peers at the client entity; this will build a strong, institutional bond with the firm.*

One caveat to the Client Service Team: There are occasions when clients may hear the word "team" and think "overlawyering." You need to assure clients that your intention is not to have multiple people working on their matters, but rather to provide better coordination and continuity within the firm resulting in increased efficiency and better service. However, for some clients, particularly those who are most concerned about fees, the team approach may be unwise.

The following is an example of a client team organizational chart.

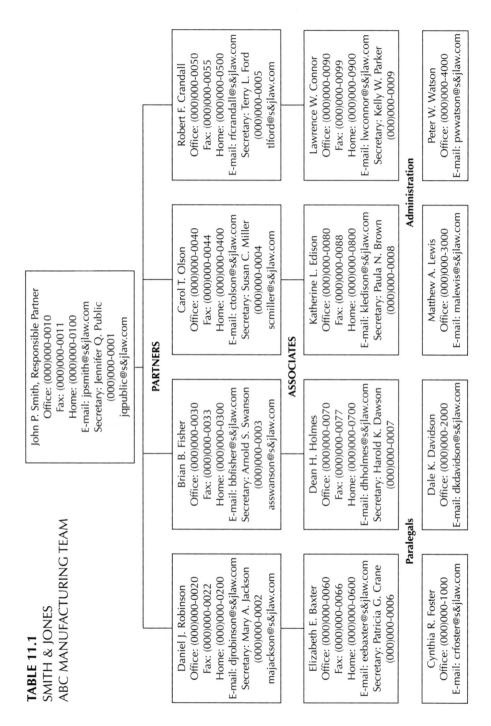

TABLE 11.1
SMITH & JONES
ABC MANUFACTURING TEAM

John P. Smith, Responsible Partner
Office: (000)000-0010
Fax: (000)000-0011
Home: (000)000-0100
E-mail: jpsmith@s&jlaw.com
Secretary: Jennifer Q. Public
(000)000-0001
jqpublic@s&jlaw.com

PARTNERS

Robert F. Crandall
Office: (000)000-0050
Fax: (000)000-0055
Home: (000)000-0500
E-mail: rfcrandall@s&jlaw.com
Secretary: Terry L. Ford
(000)000-0005
tlford@s&jlaw.com

Carol T. Olson
Office: (000)000-0040
Fax: (000)000-0044
Home: (000)000-0400
E-mail: ctolson@s&jlaw.com
Secretary: Susan C. Miller
(000)000-0004
scmiller@s&jlaw.com

Brian B. Fisher
Office: (000)000-0030
Fax: (000)000-0033
Home: (000)000-0300
E-mail: bbfisher@s&jlaw.com
Secretary: Arnold S. Swanson
(000)000-0003
asswanson@s&jlaw.com

Daniel J. Robinson
Office: (000)000-0020
Fax: (000)000-0022
Home: (000)000-0200
E-mail: djrobinson@s&jlaw.com
Secretary: Mary A. Jackson
(000)000-0002
majackson@s&jlaw.com

ASSOCIATES

Lawrence W. Connor
Office: (000)000-0090
Fax: (000)000-0099
Home: (000)000-0900
E-mail: lwconnor@s&jlaw.com
Secretary: Kelly W. Parker
(000)000-0009

Katherine L. Edison
Office: (000)000-0080
Fax: (000)000-0088
Home: (000)000-0800
E-mail: kledison@s&jlaw.com
Secretary: Paula N. Brown
(000)000-0008

Dean H. Holmes
Office: (000)000-0070
Fax: (000)000-0077
Home: (000)000-0700
E-mail: dhholmes@s&jlaw.com
Secretary: Harold K. Dawson
(000)000-0007

Elizabeth E. Baxter
Office: (000)000-0060
Fax: (000)000-0066
Home: (000)000-0600
E-mail: eebaxter@s&jlaw.com
Secretary: Patricia G. Crane
(000)000-0006

Paralegals

Dale K. Davidson
Office: (000)000-2000
E-mail: dkdavidson@s&jlaw.com

Cynthia R. Foster
Office: (000)000-1000
E-mail: crfoster@s&jlaw.com

Administration

Peter W. Watson
Office: (000)000-4000
E-mail: pwwatson@s&jlaw.com

Matthew A. Lewis
Office: (000)000-3000
E-mail: malewis@s&jlaw.com

C. Developing a Client Service Plan

Another useful exercise for the Client Service Manager is to develop a client-specific service plan; in other words, determine the steps you and the team will take in the next year to retain, satisfy, or expand the relationship with this client.

There are many things you might include in your client service plan, such as:

- Setting up a workshop on site for the client on a topic of concern

- Making assignments within the team to cultivate relationships throughout all levels of the client organization, and to arrange regular entertainment of individuals

- Inviting the client to address a team, practice group or partner meeting to discuss its business, industry or needs

- Organizing a client appreciation function for the client with firm representatives (e.g., a dinner party, a golf outing, a client "roast")

- Collaborating with the client on professional development opportunities (e.g., co-sponsoring a seminar, co-authoring an article, etc.)

- Putting client representatives on appropriate invitation and other lists (e.g., newsletters, holiday parties, holiday cards, etc.)

- Looking for ways to recognize the client, such as advertisements in industry or business publications congratulating the company for specific successes (e.g., awards) or growth

- Sending holiday gifts or cards as a "team"

- Taking a tour of the client facilities to learn more about the operations and meet individuals with responsibility for different areas

- Scheduling a "relationship meeting" to discuss candidly how things are going and how the relationship can be improved.[4]

Table 11.2 provides an example of a client service plan.

---

[4] See Section IV.E *infra*.

TABLE 11.2

CLIENT SERVICE PLAN

Client: ABC MANUFACTURING

Goals and Objectives:

This section should include a summary of the team's goals or objectives for the client for the next year. Examples:

- Achieving specific revenue goals
- Introducing the client to a new service area or firm members at another geographic location
- Building closer relationships with members of the client's in-house legal staff
- Instituting a procedure to improve communications (e.g., an extranet, formal status reporting)
- Building personal relationships (e.g., entertaining, a client event)

Action Plan:

Description of Activity/ Procedure/Policy	Targeted Individual or Group	Purpose	Date	Lawyer(s)

D. Developing Client "Annual Reports" and Annual Meetings

One of the most effective ways to educate key clients about the firm's contributions and successes is to provide a client-specific annual report on the relationship. Ideally, this would be presented at a face-to-face meeting (i.e., an "annual meeting") to discuss the relationship.

In a client annual report, you can summarize the matters the firm handled for the client and highlight the value you added to the relationship.

A client annual report might include:

> *In a client annual report, you can summarize the matters the firm handled for the client and highlight the value you added to the relationship.*

(1) *Matters assigned.* In this section, you can review for the client all the active matters assigned to the firm. In addition, you can summarize trends, for example, the number of cases, the nature of the matters, the percentage of matters representing different substantive issues, the number of matters handled for each subsidiary or location, etc.

(2) *Matters resolved.* You can summarize the matters that the firm was able to resolve in the prior year and, depending on the number and nature of the matters, explain the firm's results. For example, for litigation matters, you might indicate the case, the nature of the dispute, the demand, the resolution (e.g., settlement, trial, etc.), and the cost to the client (e.g., fees and verdicts or settlement figures). If the volume of matters is too large for this approach, you may want to consider providing an Executive Summary or somehow highlighting the most important matters.

(3) *Fees and costs to the client.* The annual report can help the client track the cost and value of your firm's services. For example, you can summarize total fees and expenses. Again, depending on the nature of the files, it might be beneficial to create summaries, such as the average fees per matter or cost per file. These numbers can be compared to those of previous years, if such information would be helpful.

(4) *Client benefits.* Your firm undoubtedly provides other benefits to the client, many of which are probably unbillable. These might include: in-house workshops on legal matters; training for client personnel; tracking of cases; conformity with client guidelines or instructions (e.g., installation of software to enhance the firm's billing procedures); etc. Other benefits may accrue to numerous clients but can still be noted, such as firm industry newsletters or substantive seminars.

(5) *Client kudos.* Finally, an annual report is an excellent vehicle for giving the client representatives their due. You can summarize the

important role that in-house legal staff members played in making decisions, or how they contributed to the relationship or the good results.

A client annual report can be particularly effective if presented at an annual relationship meeting. The objectives of a meeting like this can be many, but the primary purpose is to ensure the client's satisfaction with the firm, open the lines of communication, and explore your future relationship.

Specifically, you can use the annual meeting to:

(1) *Review past and present matters (or the "annual report")*. This is an opportunity to review the year and plan for next year's needs.

(2) *Discuss the client's satisfaction*. This should involve both the firm's handling of substantive matters as well as its performance on service factors (e.g., responding to telephone calls).

(3) *Propose improvements to the relationship*. You might come prepared to present an idea for a retainer arrangement or ways to improve communications, for example.

(4) *Discuss future projects and plans of the client*. Here you should address how such plans might affect (or be affected by) legal issues. This could also include a discussion about your firm's role in these future initiatives.

(5) *Answer questions*. Having annual meetings is an excellent way to demonstrate to the client that you are open to discussing ways to improve the relationship.

Before you set up a relationship meeting, you should think carefully about the people you would like to include, both from the client organization as well as from your firm. In addition, you should hold the meeting in a place that is comfortable and conducive to the discussion—probably the client's place of business.

E. Taking Clients' "Temperature"—the Client Interview

Perhaps the most beneficial activity you can undertake as a Client Service Manager is to interview your key clients. A personal interview can be used to determine needs and satisfaction levels, identify problems and opportunities and, in short, obtain client input.

For significant ongoing clients, you might consider conducting an annual client interview. For a significant episodic client (e.g., a legislative assignment or a major litigation case), you might conduct a "post-project" interview to get an evaluation of the firm on that one matter or case.

> *A client interview is a wonderful way to enhance the relationship while gathering in-depth information about the client's needs, experiences and perceptions.*

Generally client interviews are best conducted face to face, although if that proves impossible because of geography or scheduling problems, a telephone interview will suffice.

(1) *Objectives*

A client interview is a wonderful way to enhance the relationship while gathering in-depth information about the client's needs, experiences and perceptions. There are many potential objectives for a client interview, including:

- Assessing the client's needs and satisfaction with the firm
- Determining the characteristics or factors that the client values most, and how the firm is performing on them
- Conveying appreciation for the opportunity to work with the client
- Inviting the client's involvement, ideas and feedback
- Reassuring the client of the firm's dedication to meeting the client's objectives
- Institutionalizing the client, i.e., giving the client a better sense of the "firm"

(2) *Logistics*

Client interviews are best conducted at the client's place of business (where the client is most comfortable) and usually last about an hour. (You could also request a tour of the client facility while you are there.)

(3) *Preparation for the Interview*

The first step is to notify the client about your desire to conduct the interview, and ask for his or her cooperation. For example:

"Since you are one of our firm's most valued clients, I would like to ask if you would be willing to spend about an hour with me—at no charge, of course—to talk about our firm and your level of satisfaction with our services. I would plan to come to your office on a date and at a time convenient for you, and would like to discuss a number of topics, including our level of service, our relationship with you, and how we might better fill your needs."

Once the date and time are agreed upon, send a confirmation letter to the client. You might consider including an outline of the areas about which you plan to inquire. You should also plan to call the client the day before the meeting to confirm.

Before meeting with the client, if necessary, you should learn as much as you can about the client's relationship with the firm, and the client's business and legal situation. For example:

• Ask your accounting department for a copy of the prior two years' billing information to review the type of work that has been done for the client as well as to ascertain who is handling the work within the firm.

• Talk to other lawyers who have worked with the client. Have there been any problems noted recently?

• Obtain information about the client, e.g., company Web site, annual report or other filings, product or company brochures, recent news about the client, etc. (Be sure to get information on the individual(s) being interviewed as well as the entity.)

(4) *Conducting the Interview*
The following are some suggestions for the interview:

• Be on time!

• Introduce the firm's participants, if you bring others along; hand out business cards if people are meeting for the first time.

- State your purpose and thank the client: "We appreciate your business and have a strong interest in working more closely with you to achieve your goals."
- Reiterate your objectives and the process to the client:
    - The meeting should take about an hour
    - We are interested in making sure that we are meeting your goals
    - We are interested in taking a tour of the facilities

There are many questions you can ask and different approaches you can take; you should carefully consider which areas to include in light of the client's relationship and the information you obtained through other lawyers or your background research. Examples include:

Service.

- How satisfied are you with our:
    - Telephone responsiveness?
    - Accessibility?
    - Communications?
    - Status reporting?
    - Follow up after the matter is concluded?
    - Knowledge of your legal requirements?
    - Knowledge of your business?
    - Billing arrangements/invoice formats and frequency?
    - Overall fees?
    - Value provided for fees paid?
    - Overall handling of your needs?
- Are you receiving the level of service you expect or need from our firm?
- What are some specific ways we can provide better service?

Staffing.

- How satisfied are you with the people we have working on your matters?

• Do you have comments about the mix of people—skills or seniority?

• Do you have comments about the continuity of staffing, i.e., are people adequately up-to-speed about your affairs?

• Do you have any other comments about your relationships with people in the firm?

Benefits/Results.

• What do you feel are the major benefits of using our law firm?

• How do you evaluate "results"?

• How satisfied are you with:

   ◆ The results we have obtained on your behalf?

   ◆ Turnaround time?

   ◆ The work product or deliverable you receive?

• What is the thing that we do best, in your estimation, so we make certain we continue doing it?

Opportunities/Future Relationship.

• What else can we do to provide more value to you?

• What work do you send outside to law firms other than ours?

• To which firm(s) does that work go?

• Why did you select that/those firm(s)?

• In which areas of practice do you feel we are particularly strong?

• In which areas of practice do you feel we are weak?

• How can we better help you achieve your objectives?

• Are there any services that the firm might provide for you that it currently does not provide?

(5) *Conducting and Concluding the Interview*
The following are some tips as you conduct your interview:

• *Be a good listener.*

   ◆ Ask a question, and then listen

- ◆ Sit squarely
- ◆ Lean forward; don't cross your arms
- ◆ Take notes
- ◆ Make eye contact
- ◆ React: Nod, paraphrase and acknowledge comments ("Uh-huh")
- ◆ Seek clarification to prevent misunderstandings

- *Probe the client's responses.*

- ◆ Read body language
- ◆ Listen for and follow up incomplete thoughts or uncompleted sentences
- ◆ Draw the client out
- ◆ Don't jump to conclusions

- *Make the meeting as interactive as possible.* Let the client lead.

If the client raises a problem:

- Do not minimize the issue (e.g., "I'm sure he didn't mean that."); your job is to uncover issues, listen and acknowledge comments
- Get a full description of the issue or concern
- Acknowledge the client's feelings ("I can understand why you were angry.")
- Find out the client's original expectations and why they weren't met
- Conduct some joint problem-solving, i.e., what would the client like the firm to do?

Finally, as you conclude the interview:

- Ask if there are any issues you didn't raise that the client would like to discuss
- Summarize the client's situation, problems or requests, and your follow-up steps
- Thank the client for his or her time

(6) *Follow Up*

- After the client interview, you need to follow up internally as well as with the client:

  - Send a thank-you letter to the client

  - Prepare a summary of the meeting as soon as possible

  - Meet with the appropriate lawyers, or the entire client service team, to discuss the client's situation, issues or concerns, including both remedial and long-term responses

  - Follow up with the client to communicate the firm's response, if needed, to problems, issues or opportunities

Some lawyers resist the idea of interviewing clients, saying that they already know what the client thinks, or, in some cases, that they would prefer not to know what the client thinks. However, providing an open and candid forum for clients to discuss their relationship with the firm may be the most important thing you can do to ensure a lasting relationship. Keep in mind, however, that clients will expect you to act on their suggestions and ideas, so your follow-up efforts are paramount to the success of this strategy.

> *[C]lients will expect you to act on their suggestions and ideas, so your follow-up efforts are paramount to the success of this strategy.*

F. Introducing the Firm's Resources

Another important role for a Client Service Manager is to ensure that the client is acquainted with all the firm's resources, in addition to the members of the team. You should regularly:

- Identify issues with respect to which other firm lawyers (or staff) might be of assistance

- Send promotional materials to the client on relevant subjects (e.g., newsletters, seminar invitations, brochures, etc.)

- Be on the lookout for colleagues' accomplishments that you can bring to the attention of the client, such as an article published in a trade journal or an honor bestowed by an industry organization

• Arrange for introductions to other lawyers in the firm

• Arrange for presentations or pitches, if appropriate. For example, you may request an opportunity to make a presentation to the company's board on the firm's expertise in the tax area

VI. OTHER CONSIDERATIONS AND TIPS FOR MANAGING RELATIONSHIPS WITH SIGNIFICANT CLIENTS

There are endless activities that you might consider for important clients, and many more roles a good Client Service Manager might play.

Tips for Effective Interviewing

The following are some tips for conducting effective client interviews:

• Don't assume you know everything about the client; you'd be surprised how much you don't know

• Don't ask leading or loaded questions ("Do you think we try to provide good service?")

• Be specific; avoid ambiguity (e.g., instead of "occasionally," use a specific timeframe like "once a month")

• Start with general questions and get more specific; this will allow you to engage clients in the process

• Keep it simple—discuss one idea or topic at a time; for example, you should group together questions dealing with staffing

• Demonstrate your knowledge of the client in the questions (e.g., "Richard tells me that recently you have increased the volume of environmental matters we are handling for you. How do you evaluate the work we've done for you in that area?")

• Try to capture verbatim comments whenever possible (e.g., references to lawyers or descriptions of the firm)

• Don't sell, but do answer questions about capabilities and probe opportunities (e.g., "What would be the best way for us to bring our experience in other relevant areas to your attention?")

Here are some additional thoughts to consider as you set out to manage significant client relationships:

• *Take every opportunity to talk with the client about the other lawyers' contributions.* Give credit to the litigator who gets a good result or the associate who drafts a contract. Encourage other lawyers to sign letters to the client. Credit the other lawyers at your firm who helped you resolve a question. These efforts will build the client's confidence in the capabilities of the firm as a whole, and will help to develop a stronger bond.

• *Thank those in the firm who help you maintain a positive client relationship.* Be certain their work and their teamwork come to the attention of appropriate leaders of the firm. Consider a "team" activity, like a pizza party, to recognize everyone's contributions.

• *Thank the client for the opportunity to work together.* This could take the form of a letter, a special social event or a tangible memento of the relationship, such as a plaque, a paperweight or a commissioned piece of artwork.

• *Engage the client in the firm.* For example, solicit the client's input into your practice group's business plan.

• *Look for ways you can team up with a client, literally.* For example, perhaps your lawyers and the client representatives could start a Toastmasters chapter, join a softball league or build a house for Habitat for Humanity.

• *Create a repository about the client.* This can take the form of a file, an intranet site or a binder that includes client information: annual reports, company brochures, résumés of key executives, billing guidelines, etc. Require all members of the team to review this information and be sure new team members consult this record before starting to work on the client's projects.

• *Expand your knowledge of the client and its needs.* Learn as much as you can about your client's customers—they ultimately determine what your client wants to do. Visit the company's Web site on a regular basis for news. Ask to be added to the company's mailing list to receive promotions or employee newsletters.

- *Check into whether the company has training programs.* Find out if the company has any regular training programs in which it might make sense for you or someone else from the firm to participate.

- *Find out who the client's other external advisors are.* Such external advisors may include auditors, and bank or industry consultants. If appropriate, meet them.

- *Meet as many people as possible at the client entity.* For example, spend some time with the company's engineers to learn how the technology was developed. Visit with the HR manager, the CFO or other members of the in-house legal staff to learn about their roles in the company and their experiences with legal issues.

- *Communicate about the client internally.* For example, if the client is a computer manufacturer, you should regularly remind lawyers and staff to check out the company's products when shopping for their personal needs.

- *Look for ways to add value to the relationship.* This could range from placing an associate in-house, on a short-term or part-time basis, to developing alternative billing arrangements (e.g., retainers), to recommending other service providers, such as local counsel, accountants, etc.

Ideas/Notes: Managing Relationships with Significant Clients

My personal challenge(s) or obstacle(s) in this area:

_____

_____

_____

_____

_____

My goal(s) or objective(s) in this area:

_____

_____

_____

_____

What I need to do to get started:

(1) _____

_____

(2) _____

_____

(3) _____

_____

(4) _____

_____

(5) _____

_____

12
Handling Difficult Client Situations

The three previous chapters have dealt with the upside of clients—building loyalty, expanding opportunities and better managing client relationships. However, there are times when relationships go sour, or when other issues stymie your attempts to build client relationships. This Chapter addresses a few common scenarios.

I. CLIENTS WHO ARE DIFFICULT

There are clients who are so difficult that they drain lawyers of energy and enjoyment of the practice. Other clients may be difficult because of their "fit" with the firm or their financial situations.

As a result, there are times when lawyers "fire" their clients. Obviously, the Rules of Professional Conduct determine when and how you can withdraw from a client matter, and you must consult them before doing so. However, there are some clients a firm may be better off without. These include:

• A client ethically on the edge, such as one you suspect of "cooking the books"

• A client who is abusive to you or your staff or takes advantage of the relationship

• A client who complains excessively about fees or fails to compensate your firm fairly for its work or for special changes the client necessitates, such as last-minute filings, delivery charges, etc.

• A client who is so demanding that he forces you or your staff to shortchange other clients in service or work product quality

If you are in a position that allows you to withdraw from a difficult client's matter or case, many lawyers find that it actually benefits both the client and the firm to do so. If possible, you might even be able to steer the client to another advisor who is a better fit.

II. PARTNERS WHO DON'T ENCOURAGE RELATIONSHIPS

There are times when the partner with the primary client relationship does not encourage other lawyers to get involved in building client rapport. In some cases, they have the client's best interest in mind; in other cases, they may have insecurities, such as a fear of losing the client to another lawyer. Whatever the motivation, no lawyer should reach out to a client without the responsible partner's approval.

If you are working on a client's matters and the responsible partner has not encouraged you to develop relationships with your counterparts, you might consider the following approaches:

• *Take initiative with the partner.* Ask if you can be introduced to the client. For example, if you know a client representative is planning to visit the office, ask if you can sit in on the meeting (and write off your time) to become more familiar with the client's affairs. At a minimum, you could suggest that the client stop by to say hello.

• *Run a specific client development idea past the partner.* For example, you could ask the partner if it would be okay for you to take your contact at the client company to lunch.

> *[I]f you know a client representative is planning to visit the office, ask if you can sit in on the meeting (and write off your time) to become more familiar with the client's affairs.*

• *Make the partner look good to the client.* If you see something that might be of interest to contacts at the company, such as an article on a competitor or a discussion about a relevant case, send it to the partner with a suggestion that the client might be interested. This will show the partner that you're thinking about the client and are sensitive to the partner's relationship.

• *If all else fails, provide great service by phone, fax or e-mail.* Whatever your existing relationship is with the client contact, make the most of it. If the client representative ever leaves, he or she will remember how you met the company's needs.

III. CLIENTS FACING DIFFICULT TIMES

There may be times when a client relationship can change due to company financial problems or a large drop in the volume of work. Clients remember very well how they are treated by their lawyers during difficult times. One general counsel from an insurance company that had

> *Clients remember very well how they are treated by their lawyers during difficult times.*

implemented a new policy to settle rather than litigate said he was "dropped like a hot potato" by his law firms. Noting that the company's business philosophy was like a pendulum, he added, "I'll remember the lawyers who continued to remember me."

If you have a client in financial crisis, or a formerly large client with little legal work, consider the following:

• *Show concern for the client.* Continue to check in with your contact(s) on a regular basis and ask how things are going. At the same time, be sure to respect the pressure and stress the client is facing; you don't want to be too intrusive.

• *Ask what, if anything, you can do to help.* This may extend well beyond legal work. For example, you might be able to recommend a turnaround consultant or financing alternatives for the company.

• *If appropriate, continue the same type of relationship you had in the past.* If you entertained the contact occasionally, continue to offer the same opportunities. Keep the contact on the list for seminar invitations, holiday cards and other regular activities of the firm.

• *If you continue to do legal work, consider offering credit terms (if necessary and if the client is a good risk, of course).* For a client in financial crisis, this shows that the law firm is willing to make an investment in the company's future success.

By maintaining your contacts and your interest level, you will create a very loyal client if the company survives. If the company doesn't survive, your contacts will probably end up at some other potential client entities, and they undoubtedly will remember how you treated them during difficult times.

IV. ANGRY OR DISAPPOINTED CLIENTS

Unfortunately, there may be occasions when a client is unhappy with the work or the service received from you. Responding effectively to an angry client is crucial to your ability to retain the business.

When you become aware of a difficult situation, whether it is a bad result in litigation or fees that are unexpectedly high, you should deal with the situation immediately. Delivering bad news is never easy, but how you do it can determine your future relationship with the client.

Here are some techniques to consider when you learn of a bad situation:

• *Respond quickly.* Once a client has voiced a complaint or expressed concern, or as soon as you recognize a problem, act quickly and positively. The more serious the problem, the more important it is for the responsible lawyer or senior partner to make the contact.

• *If the client called, thank him or her for calling.* This will make the client feel that you are interested in keeping the lines of communication open and airing concerns.

• *Set up a meeting.* If possible, a face-to-face meeting is preferable when dealing with a problem; the worse the news, the more important it is to meet face-to-face to resolve it.

Responding effectively to an angry client is crucial to your ability to retain the business.

• *Do your homework.* Meet with the lawyers in your firm that handled the matter. Get their perspectives on the situation and their suggestions on how to handle it. Gather up the billing records to familiarize yourself with what has been done to date.

Your actions and reactions when interacting with the client can make or break the relationship. When conducting the meeting with the client, consider the following:

- *Set the stage for the client.* Give a brief overview of your understanding of the issue, and bring the client up to date on what has transpired at the firm.

- *Explain what has happened (the "bad news"), if necessary.* Communicate in plain English, not legal jargon. If there is any good news, deliver that too, and try to help the client put things in perspective, whether in economic terms or in terms of the company's objectives for the matter. At the same time, don't add your own value judgments; the client's perception is what's important.

> *An apology goes a long way and does not have to acknowledge fault.*

- *Let the client vent.* Once you have explained the problem, your job is to listen. Be empathetic. Let the client express concern or frustration. Don't react except to acknowledge the concern or say, "I understand." If you respond to specific issues as they are raised, it will be perceived as a rebuttal and may aggravate the situation. In addition, letting the client vent may ultimately leave him or her more open to hearing solutions.

- *If the client is argumentative or rude, resist the temptation to be the same way.* Whether reacting to a real or perceived problem, the client feels the firm let him or her down.

- *Don't get defensive.* Don't finger point or argue. And don't place blame on colleagues or do anything to imply that the client doesn't understand the situation.

- *Maintain an even tone.* Your tone is extremely important, and should be positive and calm.

- *Summarize.* Once the client is done expressing his or her view of the situation, provide some feedback that demonstrates that you were listening and understand the key points. Use the client's name. And acknowledge that the client has a legitimate concern. Show that you are committed to resolving the issue to the client's satisfaction.

- *Say you're sorry.* An apology goes a long way and does not have to acknowledge fault. You can say you are sorry that the client feels let down or is angry.

- *Look forward.* Once the problem has been aired, facilitate a discussion about the next step(s). Ask the client for suggestions for a resolution, i.e., "What can I do to make the situation better for you?" Try to pin down specific issues or potential solutions. Tell the client exactly what you can do to help, for example, delivering the bad news to the client's board of directors. Ask the client to work with you to determine appropriate moves, allowing him or her to participate in resolving the problem. The result of your discussion should be a determination of how you will proceed.

- *In some cases, you may not be able to fix the problem.* In those cases, thank the client for being open with you and discussing the situation candidly.

- *If the client is terribly distraught, stay until he or she has calmed down.*

- *Follow up.* If appropriate, prepare a memo or letter that summarizes the meeting and outlines the agreed-upon steps. And most importantly, whatever you have agreed to do (e.g., a write-off, a summary report, etc.), do it quickly! Your follow up is the key to client satisfaction and future business. If there was no particular follow-up step required, you may want to think about scheduling a follow-up meeting with the client to talk about the relationship, rebuild confidence in the firm, and demonstrate your interest.

- *Talk to your staff.* Your staff members should be informed and reminded of these techniques so that they will be prepared in the event they pick up client complaint calls in your absence.

V. CLIENTS BEING ACQUIRED

Mergers, acquisitions and consolidations have caused significant shakeouts in legal relationships over the years. In most cases, responsibility for major company legal matters transfers to the parent company's legal staff, although there are exceptions. For example, a financial institution purchased by an out-of-state entity will usually keep its lending work in the local market. Still, the acquiring company may have relationships with lawyers through other channels; in addition, the company's outside counsel may have relationships in your geographic area of which they would like to take advantage.

Before you take any action with the acquiring company, consider the following:

• *Talk openly with your local contacts.* Discuss the situation and get their guidance and approval on any efforts to contact the acquiring company.

• *Be sensitive to the impact that the acquisition is having on your client contacts.* They may have their own anxieties about job security, relocation, etc. and are concerned about their own future, not yours. Consider whether there is anything you can do to help. If, for example, your local contacts are downsized, you might offer to be a reference or to make introductions at other companies.

• *Do your homework on the new company.* Find out as much as you can about the company and, in particular, its in-house legal structure and its relationships with outside counsel. Find out if anyone in your firm has a relationship with the in-house or outside lawyers. If so, you can use those contacts as an entrée to discussing your relationship with the local company.

Once you are ready to contact the acquiring company, here are some activities you might consider:

• *Visit the decision-makers at the acquiring company, such as the general counsel.* Offer to make a trip to visit with the appropriate people at no charge. If you're unable to schedule a face-to-face meeting, offer to send some background information about your firm and its past relationship with the local entity.

• *Make contact with the outside counsel for the acquiring company.* Introduce yourself and explain what your role has been in the past with the local enterprise.

• *Visit any new local people.* If there are new people put in place locally, visit with them immediately to talk about the company, their objectives and what you can do to help.

In each of these instances, your approach should be one of openness and helpfulness. In conjunction with these contacts, you might want to:

• Provide a summary of projects or matters handled in the past as well as those in progress to give the company a snapshot of the relationship

• Ask if there are any short-term projects or other needs for which the company needs assistance during the transition (e.g., overflow work or reviewing contracts)

• Request any guidelines the new company may have for outside counsel, such as billing requirements

• Ask what other needs the new venture might have in the area (e.g., are there other subsidiaries or entities in your area now?)

• Inquire whether the company would like a different type of communication from you, such as a regular status report, either during the transition phase or permanently

• Offer to set up a regular process to evaluate how things are going with the transition and the relationship, at least initially

• Provide information on your firm, the lawyers who work with the local company, and their experience and areas of expertise

> *The bottom line is to see the change as an opportunity, and take the offensive. [D]emonstrate flexibility and don't go in with an entitlement attitude.*

The bottom line is to see the change as an opportunity, and take the offensive. Don't wait for the client to request these steps or impose changes on you. Above all, demonstrate flexibility and don't go in with an entitlement attitude. You need to convey to these new contacts that you are open to exploring new roles for your firm to play, new ways to communicate, new billing methods, or any other issues that they perceive to be important.

Ideas/Notes: Handling Difficult Client Situations

My personal challenge(s) or obstacle(s) in this area:

_____

_____

_____

_____

_____

My goal(s) or objective(s) in this area:

_____

_____

_____

_____

_____

What I need to do to get started:

(1) _____

_____

(2) _____

_____

(3) _____

_____

(4) _____

_____

(5) _____

_____

13

Building Relationships
with Referral Sources

I. INTRODUCTION

For some lawyers, most, if not all, of their business comes through referral sources, as opposed to direct contact with prospective clients. Many times, the quality of the business referred by other professionals or current and former clients can be higher than that generated through firm marketing efforts. For example, personal injury clients referred by orthopedic surgeons often have more meritorious claims than those responding to a television advertisement.

Some lawyers question the effectiveness of targeting lawyers or other professionals in their marketing efforts. It's not unusual to hear a business lawyer state unequivocally that speaking at a CLE program is a "waste of time because you're educating other lawyers." Tax lawyers will say that accountants are competitors more than sources of business. And given the lawyers' practices, these statements might be true.

The value of cultivating relationships with other professionals and the types of professionals to target depend entirely on your practice. An estate planning lawyer can build a substantial book of business through referrals from a few high-performing insurance agents. An appellate lawyer can receive the bulk of his business through referrals from litigators, either within or outside his own firm. Bankruptcy lawyers often find virtually all of their business referred by other members of the bankruptcy bar.

In order to generate business referrals, you will need to identify the kinds of people who come into contact with the kinds of clients you would like to represent, position yourself in front of these potential sources, and then build personal and mutually rewarding relationships with a select number of them. This Chapter discusses the process of developing productive referral relationships.

II. IDENTIFYING YOUR SOURCES OF REFERRALS

In order to identify potential referral sources, you should start by brainstorming about the types of products and services that your clients require. These could range from other professional service providers, like lawyers, bankers, consultants, accountants or venture capitalists, to companies offering other products and services, such as accounting software, financial printing or construction capabili-

> *People with whom your target clientele does business typically will have good information, relationships with many individuals or companies, and potentially opportunities to introduce lawyers.*

ties. People with whom your target clientele does business typically will have good information, relationships with many individuals or companies, and potentially opportunities to introduce lawyers.

For example, an employment lawyer may want to build relationships with employee benefit consultants or human resource training companies. A family lawyer may seek out relationships with family counselors or members of the clergy. A tax litigator will find accountants to be the key to identifying clients with tax-related problems. A patent lawyer might focus on law firms without IP practices but with clients who need those services. And a corporate lawyer serving private businesses might cultivate relationships with business valuation experts.

Are you a generalist? If so, it almost always makes sense to build relationships with other prominent professionals, whether they are bankers, accountants, business people or other lawyers.

There are a number of ways to identify potential sources of business for your practice. For example:

• *Attending conferences.* By going to relevant meetings, you will see and meet the kinds of people or professionals who work in your area. While there, set aside some time to visit exhibit areas. For example, if you attend the bankers' association meeting, a visit to the exhibit area will give you the opportunity to learn more about the vendors that work with financial institutions.

• *Reviewing seminar or conference brochures.* Even if you don't attend the conferences, you should read invitations crossing your desk to see which professionals or organizations are positioning themselves in areas where your clients might have needs or in which you practice.

• *Reading related articles.* Similarly, reviewing articles related to your practice area, industry or clientele will help you determine which people are committed to the area and who are on top of the issues.

• *Reviewing Web sites.* If you are targeting a particular industry, like sports and entertainment law, you can run a search to find out which accounting or other professional firms also have practices in that area.

• *Asking clients.* Find out who your clients use for products and services. Quite often, clients will offer to provide an introduction to their contacts.

When you have an idea of the kind of people with whom you would like to cultivate relationships, you should develop a list. This list might include people you don't know at all (e.g., lawyers in smaller communities for referrals of large, complex litigation matters) and people whose paths you have crossed before, such as clients, professionals involved in past transactions, client deals or litigation, clients' advisors, or people you have met in trade, industry or professional organizations.

Depending on the size of your list, you may need to take different approaches with the potential referral sources. For example, if your list of target referral sources has more people on it than you can realistically contact, you may want to divide them into an "A" list and a "B" list. Those on the "A" list would be people you would target for personal interaction. Logically, they should include those most likely to have the opportunity to refer business to you because of the nature of their contacts, their positions in their organizations, or their existing relationship with you. Relationships with people on the "B" list might be maintained through more of a mass-marketing approach, such as by sending them periodic updates on legal issues related to your practice or inviting them (or their clients) to group events, such as firm seminars.

III. ACTIVITIES TO BUILD RELATIONSHIPS

Once you have identified your potential sources of business, both generally (e.g., accountants) and specifically (i.e., by name), you need to develop a plan of action to generate awareness for you and your practice, and ultimately to build relationships. Some of your activities may be more general, to position yourself before the type of person. Other activities should be very targeted at developing relationships that lead to business. Both of these approaches are discussed below.

A. Getting on the "Radar Screen"

If you have identified types of professionals or contacts that would likely be a good source of business for you, there are many things you can do to position you or your firm in front of them, and to put yourself in a position to begin to establish relationships. For example:

• *Attending professional or industry meetings.* If you are attempting to cultivate referrals from other litigators, for example, you can be an active participant at bar association litigation section or committee meetings. This will give you the chance to become visible to other litigators and meet people with whom you may wish to follow up.

> *Many lawyers find that study groups provide good opportunities to cultivate relationships with potential referral sources.*

• *Forming study groups.* Many lawyers, such as employee benefits or estate planning lawyers, find that study groups provide good opportunities to cultivate relationships with potential referral sources. Study groups typically are comprised of various types of professionals working in an area and meet regularly to present information and discuss changes affecting the practice.

• *Organizing targeted events.* You could plan special seminars, training programs or events for the targeted audience. For example, one law firm that was attempting to cultivate relationships with lawyers in smaller communities for referrals of large personal injury cases sponsored an annual CLE program for the targeted lawyers each year, followed by an invitation to attend a major league baseball game.

• *Speaking.* You can look for opportunities to address the targets through their industry, trade or professional associations. Making presentations on substantive issues of interest to the referral sources is an excellent way to build your visibility and your credibility, and potentially meet new people.

There are other, more passive ways to position yourself or your firm before selected audiences as well. For example:

• *Advertising.* You can place focused advertisements in publications read by the potential referral sources. For example, one IP firm ran an ad in its state bar association publication comparing typical outgoing referrals to a "black hole," and ensuring potential referring lawyers that the firm would not steal their clients.

• *Writing articles for publications read by the targeted audience.* This is an excellent way to build the perception of your expertise.[1]

• *Sending legal or industry updates or newsletters.* By sending written or electronic alerts periodically, you will demonstrate that you are on top of developments in the area.

• *Sending press releases.* You could forward news releases about firm or personal activities related to areas of common interest, such as your appointment to a key committee or a great result obtained for a client.

B. Building Personal Relationships

If you have identified specific individuals to target, there are many approaches you can take to build closer personal relationships with

---

[1] See Chapter 2 *supra* on Writing for Publication.

them. Keep in mind that your efforts should be customized to the person, your relationship, and your respective interests.

Here are some activities you might consider:

• *Collaborate.* There are many potential opportunities to collaborate with good contacts. You can jointly author an article for a related trade, professional or industry publication. You can make a joint presentation at a meeting related to your area of common interest. You can explore having your two organizations offer a joint seminar, and invite your respective clients. You can even set up entertainment opportunities together, e.g., a golf foursome with each of you inviting one client the other should get to know.

• *Entertain.* You can build your relationship through one-on-one social interaction, from breakfast, lunch or dinner meetings to attending sporting or cultural events together. You can also involve spouses, if appropriate.

• *Visit.* Request a tour of the referral source's company, or offer to visit his or her offices before a luncheon meeting.

• *Ask for feedback.* You can use your contacts as a source of information or research. For example, you might ask a few doctors to go to lunch with you, one-on-one, to give you advice on trends or issues that might affect your clients.

> *There are many potential opportunities to collaborate with good contacts. . . . [J]ointly author an article for a related trade, professional or industry publication . . . make a joint presentation at a meeting related to your area of common interest.*

• *Send updates on your practice.* Keep your short list of contacts apprised of things that will add to your credibility. For example, send them copies of articles you've authored, or let them know about your significant speaking engagements or appointments you receive.

• *Invite them to firm seminars or events.* You should be certain selected potential sources of business receive invitations to firm functions, such as open houses or golf outings. In addition, there might be firm seminars or workshops that would be of interest to them or possibly their clients.

C. Obtaining Referrals of Business Generally

Before you start down the path of asking for referrals, you should keep in mind that there must be a benefit to the referral source in having you as a contact. When referring business to a lawyer, the most important criterion for most people is competence; in other words, you will need to convince people that their clients or contacts will be in good hands should they be referred to you. At the same time, there may be other, equally important criteria that need to be addressed before you will receive referrals.

> *[K]eep in mind that there must be a benefit to the referral source in having you as a contact.*

For example, if the referral source is another lawyer, she may be concerned that you will "steal" the client. For some professionals, the opportunity to receive business back from you will be at the top of their list.

For those contacts with whom you believe there is an opportunity to generate business (those on your "A" list), your approach for seeking referrals often can be quite direct. Initially, however, your goal is to learn as much as you can about the potential referral sources and their opportunities to refer business. In order to do so, you might think about the following steps:

(1) *Visiting the referral source's Web site.* Review the description of the practice and look for references to clients or capabilities. This will allow you to ask educated questions when you meet face to face.

(2) *Setting up an initial meeting.* When you call, you should be very clear about the objective of the meeting. Most people respond to an invitation by thinking, "What's in it for me?" As a result, you need to be clear about your agenda for getting together. If you are a health care lawyer targeting a consultant who works in the industry, for example, you could say "I would like to take you to lunch, learn more about the work you and your colleagues do in the health care arena, and explore whether our practices have any synergies." Depending on the target, this meeting could be one on one or involve a group of people from your firm and the organization the referral source represents. For example, if you're an estate planning lawyer, you may have some people

from your firm's trusts and estates department meet with several trust officers from a local bank.[2]

(3) *Conducting an effective meeting.* Your purpose in this initial meeting is to learn as much as you can about the professional or his or her organization, and whether there might be mutually beneficial opportunities. When meeting with potential referral sources, you should explore:

- *Their clients.* What is the make-up of their client base as it relates to your practice? Do their clients fit the profile of your firm's practice? Would their clients be desirable clients for you?

- *Their clients' legal needs and relationships.* Do their clients have a need for your services? If so, how is that legal work currently being handled, and by whom? For example, if you are a patent lawyer, you could say something like, "I saw on your firm Web site that you represent Biotech, Inc. I know you don't have a patent practice, and I was curious who handles patent prosecution for the company now?"

- *Their opportunities to refer business to law firms.* Does your contact's organization make referrals to law firms? If so, are referrals handled by your contact or by someone else in the organization? If your contact does not have the opportunity to make referrals, you may need to ask for an introduction to someone who does. If your contact does make referrals to law firms, you should inquire about his organization's existing relationships with law firms, i.e., where does the organization refer its clients' legal business now and how satisfied is the organization—and its clients—with the way those lawyers are taking care of the clients' needs?

- *Ways you might be of assistance.* Even if you don't have opportunities to do legal work for this referral source, you might be in a position to provide the professional or his or her clients with assistance. For example, you could offer to put on a customized, on-site workshop for the company or its clients.

---

[2] See pp. 213-215 for a discussion of organizing group entertainment.

Once you have learned whether the targeted referral sources actually have opportunities to make referrals, you can determine the best approach for asking for business. For example:

(1) *Ask for an opportunity.* If your contact does have opportunities to refer legal business, you can ask for the opportunity to talk about the work you do for clients and whether you might be able to help your contact's clients. You might conclude with questions like, "What are your reactions to these services? Do they seem to meet your clients' needs?" or "Would you be comfortable recommending me to a client?"

> *If you find your contact's firm has opportunities to refer work but your contact does not control the referrals, you might ask for an introduction to the partners or people that do.*

(2) *Ask for an introduction.* If you find your contact's firm has opportunities to refer work but your contact does not control the referrals, you might ask for an introduction to the partners or people that do.

(3) *Ask for help.* If your contact has relationships with people you would like to meet, you can ask for specific help. For example, if you are an estate planning lawyer and know that a trust officer is working with a particular individual you would like to get to know better, perhaps you can ask whether you can be of assistance with the project or simply ask for an introduction.

In all cases, you need to make certain that you have identified and addressed the key issues for your referral sources. These might include building up your expertise and experience, so they feel comfortable putting a client in your hands, or assuring the referral source, particularly if it's another lawyer, that you will not attempt to develop additional business from the client.

Other tips for meetings with prospective referral sources:

• *Don't be afraid to initiate the contact.* Many other professionals are also seeking win-win relationships. When you call, you simply need to convince them that a discussion might be mutually beneficial.

• *Hold your initial meeting at the contact's office or a convenient restaurant.* If it's a restaurant, make sure it's not too loud or busy; you are conducting business.

• *Be prepared for the meeting.* This takes several forms. First, be prepared with intelligent questions that show you've done your homework on the professional and his or her organization. Second, be prepared to explain the type of work that you do or the kinds of clients with which you come into contact that would be of most interest to the target. Be sure to mention good results you've obtained for other clients. And third, be prepared with targeted materials. These could include a description of the firm's practice or industry experience, lists of representative cases or transactions, lists of representative clients, and a customized résumé.[3]

> *Remember that everyone has existing relationships, and it will take some time and effort to convince anyone to entrust you with his or her clients.*

• *If the contact declines your invitation, don't take it personally.* Remember that everyone has existing relationships, and it will take some time and effort to convince anyone to entrust you with his or her clients.

• *If it becomes clear that the contact has good referral relationships with other lawyers, ask what he or she likes about those relationships.* For example, ask why they are so positive or beneficial. You can express the desire to provide the same type of service or support to your clients and referral sources.

• *Recognize that everyone has self interest.* If there are potential problem areas, address them directly. For example, if you are meeting with an accountant and you practice in an area where lines can be fuzzy between the role of an accountant and the role of a lawyer (e.g., succession planning), put the issue on the table and find out what the CPA thinks are appropriate roles for her and for you.

• *The best relationships involve personal chemistry.* You will not get

---

[3] See Chapter 5, Section IV *supra* for more detail on effective bios and practice descriptions.

along equally well with everyone, so set up enough introductory meetings to increase your odds of finding someone with whom you "click."

Organizing Group Entertainment

Many law firms set up meetings with representatives of organizations with which they would like to build or, in some cases, formalize relationships. For example, a firm's environmental lawyers might get together with representatives of an environmental consulting firm. Litigators might get together with litigation support consultants from an accounting firm. Other lawyers target financial institutions, venture capital companies, insurance companies or brokerage firms.

Group meetings offer an opportunity for the firm's lawyers to present their capabilities, learn about the other organization and start to build personal relationships. Without proper planning, execution and follow up, however, these initiatives rarely result in any tangible returns.

Those organizing the meeting should consider the following activities prior to the get-together:

- *Conduct some research on the visitors.* Visit the company's Web site for information on the firm's capabilities as well as the individuals who will be attending the meeting. Request a copy of the firm's brochure or other related materials. Run an electronic search for recent media coverage about the company or its activities. And make certain all of the lawyers attending the meeting have copies of these materials.

- *Set objectives for the meeting.* In other words, what do you hope to accomplish by the time the visitors leave? Examples might include: to make their principals comfortable with your firm's ability to handle their clients' transactions or to establish personal relationships between your lawyers and their professionals.

- *Make certain that you have the appropriate people attending.* For example, you may want to invite a colleague from outside the

213

host practice group or department who has another connection to the invited firm (e.g., friends with the managing partner, common clients, etc.).

- *Get your lawyers together before the event.* Make certain everyone knows the objective(s) of the meeting. Discuss people's roles. For example, who will make the introductions? Who will make presentations? Who will wrap up the meeting? Everyone attending the meeting should have a role to play. Prepare some questions in advance to "break the ice." And consider making assignments for each lawyer to sit near or act as host to one of the guests.

- *Send information to the visitor.* Send the visiting firm your firm's materials (e.g., a description of the appropriate firm department or practice group, bios of the lawyers who will be in attendance, etc.). If appropriate, include directions, parking information or an agenda.

- *Prepare for the visitors' presentation.* Be certain to inquire about, and make arrangements for, the visitors' presentations (e.g., PowerPoint).

- *Give a proper welcome.* Advise the receptionist when your visitors are expected.

With proper planning, the meeting should take care of itself. However, here are a few additional tips for lawyers to consider during the meeting:

- *Introduce yourself.* As representatives of the host firm, take the initiative to introduce yourself to the visitors and make them feel comfortable.

- *Spend time with each guest.* Try to spend a little time during the social part of the meeting with each person who attends.

- *Be a good listener.* Ask questions that reflect your interest in the visitors' practices, clients or recent projects.

- *Try to identify ways to follow up with them.* Throughout the course of the meeting or presentations, you should be thinking about natural reasons for getting back together or in touch. For example, if someone mentions an industry organization, you might call to suggest attending the next meeting together.

• *Determine a follow-up strategy.* As always, the follow-up activities will determine whether the lawyers develop relationships and ultimately referrals after the meeting. Following the get-together, the lawyers who attended should meet as a group to discuss the meeting and how to follow up, for example:

> • *Individual follow up.* Ideally, each guest will receive a personal contact from a lawyer from the firm.

> • *Internal promotion of the visitors.* There might be opportunities to let the other lawyers in the firm know about the visiting firm or organization, such as circulating information about the group's capabilities in the event others have opportunities to refer business.

> • *Institutional follow up.* You might plan a group event to follow up the meeting, such as getting together to attend a sporting event after six months. At a minimum, you should ensure that individual lawyers follow through with their contacts.

D. Obtaining Referrals from Clients

One of the best sources of business is a happy client. While some clients may take the initiative to refer other people to their lawyer, there are times when you may need to make a more concerted effort to obtain referrals from former and existing clients. In some

> *One of the best sources of business is a happy client.*

cases, you may wish to inform clients of your interest in receiving new business. In others, you may actually want to ask for help.

Here are some things to keep in mind when trying to encourage client referrals:

• *Client satisfaction.* Obviously, you need to make certain clients are satisfied. At the end of each matter, ask your clients to evaluate your services. This is important not just to ensure that those clients will be willing to refer business to you, but to provide yourself with a quality-control process.[4]

- *Exceed client expectations.* Keep in mind that clients who are simply "satisfied" are not likely to refer work. You generally need to exceed clients' expectations before they will start talking to others about you. How do you exceed expectations? It often involves being a great listener, being sensitive to their situation and needs, returning phone calls promptly, communicating regularly and not exceeding your original estimate of fees.[5]

- *Be sure it is an appropriate time to ask for a referral.* For example, you shouldn't expect clients to make referrals until you have completed their project or matter satisfactorily. But, if you haven't had any contact with a client for two years, it may be too late to ask.

- *Don't be afraid to ask.* For example, you might tell clients that you would appreciate a word on your behalf should they have a friend or family member with a need for legal services. Another way to ask is, "If someone you know needs assistance with [a divorce, a litigation matter, an estate plan, etc.], would you feel comfortable recommending me?"

IV. FOLLOWING UP WITH REFERRAL SOURCES

As you've learned by now, follow up is the key to success. You will need to look for ways to stay in touch with your prospective referral sources over time and help them, through referrals or other good deeds.

A. General Follow-Up Activities

In order to generate referrals, you will need to look for ways to stay in touch with your contacts and, hopefully, add value to the relationships. Depending on your relationships and your situation, there are a number of activities you might consider, including:

---

[4] See Chapter 11, Section IV.E *supra* on client interviews.
[5] See Chapter 9, Section II.H *supra* on discussing fees and invoicing.

- Follow-up breakfast, luncheon or dinner meetings
- Social events or entertainment
- Sending information of interest to contacts or their clients (e.g., newspaper or article clippings). For example, one law firm developed an annual cookbook of lawyer and staff favorite recipes to send to former personal injury clients of the firm
- Notes or cards acknowledging personal achievements, such as promotions, or personal events, such as new babies
- Holiday cards

B. Following Up a Referral

After a referral has been made, most referral sources will evaluate the lawyer based on two factors. The first is your performance, i.e., did you take good care of their customer, client or contact? If your referral source is another professional, the second important factor is reciprocity. Most professionals will seek relationships with lawyers from whom they feel they will get something in return. In most cases, this means

> *After a referral has been made, most referral sources will evaluate the lawyer based on two factors. The first is your performance. . . . [T]he second . . . is reciprocity.*

referrals of business; however, there can be other benefits you can provide them if you are unable to send clients or customers their way.

When receiving a referral, think about the following activities:

- *Sending thank-you notes.* At a minimum, you should send a hand-written note of gratitude to the referral source. You might also consider whether some sort of gift would be appropriate. Obviously, the gift cannot be a *quid pro quo*; however, there might be something personal or thoughtful you could send at the end of the year, such as a gift certificate to a favorite restaurant. (Be sure to adhere to the client's policies on gift giving.)
- *Following up on the referred matter.* If it is appropriate, you can keep the referral source informed about the status of your work for his client or contact. You also might think about following up with referral

sources after matters have been resolved, to make certain they feel their clients were satisfied with your services.

• *Reciprocating.* Obviously, the best way to reward a good referral source and to build the relationship is to refer business back.

If you don't have a lot of chances to make referrals to your contacts, you can look for other ways to be of assistance, by positioning them or helping them with their practices or businesses or personally. For example:

• *Get them involved on a panel or as a speaker at a firm seminar or another program with which you're involved.*

• *Get them on an important professional, industry or community board with which you are involved.*

• *Offer to help them place an article in an industry or professional journal where you have some pull.*

• *Make introductions to colleagues.* You might be able to set up a meeting where the referral source can make a presentation to your firm, your practice group or your firm's staff about the company's products and services.

• *Make introductions to contacts.* Similarly, you can set up meetings to introduce the referral source to selected contacts who might be good to know, such as a broker in the industry, a leading industry consultant, a reporter or the executive director of a related association.

• *Make introductions to clients.* Without promising referrals, you may still be able to have your referral source meet clients, such as by extending an invitation to mix with clients in a suite at a sporting event.

• *Nominate them for awards or honors.*

• *Help them solve problems for their own organizations.* For example, if a contact is looking for new office space or a new accounting firm, perhaps you can recommend appropriate advisors.

• *Look for small ways to promote them.* You can ask for pens with the company's name that you can use or give to clients. Or you can use the company's logo coffee mug when in your office.

• *Help them personally.* For example, perhaps you can help a professional get into your country club.

V. OTHER CONSIDERATIONS AND TIPS FOR BUILDING RELATIONSHIPS WITH REFERRAL SOURCES

The following are some additional thoughts about building relationships with people who can refer business to you:

• *Don't take a scattershot approach (e.g., attending meetings periodically, calling people only when you think of it).* Your efforts to cultivate referrals should be organized and systematic.

• *Don't minimize the risk that is involved in making a referral.* Sending a good client or contact to an unknown quantity (you) can be very risky for someone. You need to assure your referral sources that you can help their clients or friends.

> *Sending a good client or contact to an unknown quantity (you) can be very risky for someone.*

• *Develop a few productive relationships.* For example, a close relationship with one successful personal banker is likely to produce much more business than casual relationships of varying levels of success with many bankers.

• *Don't be a pest.* Some people "pop the question" every time they see a contact. That is very annoying.

• *Help referral sources look good to their clients.* For example, if a general practice lawyer has brought you into a client relationship for your expertise, you should show deference to the lawyer in front of the client.

• *Follow up at least twice a year.* One lawyer had twenty contacts on her target list; she had lunch with each one once and then considered herself "done." It would be better for her to have five people on her target list and see them each quarterly.

• *Don't expect exclusivity.* Most professionals have a number of lawyers with whom they interact, so they can match clients to professionals based on personality, needs, etc. You should not expect to receive every piece of business from a contact; similarly you should have a few people in each category with whom you are attempting to build relationships.

- *Be focused.* When you attend seminars, events or conferences, for example, use the time to cultivate relationships with the people on your target list or to meet selected new contacts. Don't attend meetings without a plan.

- *Think about what you bring to the table.* Any relationship needs to work for both parties; one-sided relationships are doomed.

- *Thank everyone who refers business to you.*

- *Be patient.* Building relationships takes time and timing. It takes time to build trust and confidence. A referral source will need to feel very comfortable with you and your skills before making a referral. Timing is also important. You don't know when your contacts will have an opportunity to refer business. Your persistence and your efforts to "add value" to the relationship should ultimately result in referrals.

Ideas/Notes: Building Relationships with Referral Sources

My personal challenge(s) or obstacle(s) in this area:

_____

_____

_____

_____

_____

My goal(s) or objective(s) in this area:

_____

_____

_____

_____

_____

What I need to do to get started:

(1) _____

_____

(2) _____

_____

(3) _____

_____

(4) _____

_____

(5) _____

_____

14

Preparing Effective Proposals and Pitches for Business

I. INTRODUCTION

There was a time when only selected practitioners, such as municipal lawyers or health care lawyers, found themselves competing on the basis of proposals. Today, however, all kinds of clients are employing more formal methods of selecting outside legal counsel.

Larger companies frequently use Requests for Proposals (RFPs) to seek bids for their legal work. Obtaining work from clients of all types often requires some kind of a "pitch" meeting, which can range from formal presentations (frequently referred to as "beauty contests") to informal luncheon meetings.

Unfortunately, many lawyers are not experienced or comfortable with these processes. To improve your odds of success when a proposal or pitch is required, you should consider the guidelines and suggestions discussed below.

II. PROPOSALS AND LETTERS OF QUALIFICATION

Requests for Proposals or Requests for Qualifications (RFQs) may range from fairly informal letters requesting written statements of qualifications to very formal (and lengthy) documents delineating areas to include in the resulting document. One of the first things to remember about these requests is that they are designed to narrow the field. The purpose of the proposal process usually is to help the recipient identify two to four firms to interview before selecting the finalist. A proposal, therefore, should help distinguish you from the other qualified firms that have been invited to respond.

A well-written and well-organized proposal will enhance your changes of making "the cut." The following recommendations should help you when researching, writing and packaging the proposal.

> *One of the first things to remember about [Requests for Proposals] is that they are designed to narrow the field. A proposal, therefore, should help distinguish you from the other qualified firms that have been invited to respond.*

A. Doing Your Research

The first step in preparing an effective response to a request for written information on your firm's capabilities is to conduct due diligence. Your research should involve both the prospective client as well as the opportunity, i.e., the work that will be entailed, the processes that will be required, other activities, etc.

(1) *Researching the opportunity.* Just because you receive an RFP doesn't mean you should take the time and energy to respond to it. You should evaluate honestly whether the type of work or the client itself is of the caliber you are seeking. In addition, and unfortunately, there are many times that organizations send out RFPs with no intention of hiring or changing counsel. The reasons for doing so might include:

- Investigating different options for handling a certain type of work or a particular matter

- Trying to obtain price concessions or other allowances from existing counsel

- Obtaining a number to plug into a projected legal budget

- Meeting the organization's requirements (e.g., a public entity that needs to review its vendor relationships on a regular basis)

Many times, the lawyer isn't aware that the request was not legitimate until after the fact, for example, when the prospect will not return follow-up calls, the project is "put on hold" indefinitely or another firm is hired without an opportunity to discuss the project.

The decision about whether to respond to an inquiry is the firm's, of course, and there may be reasons to submit information even if the request is not a legitimate opportunity. For example, you may want to get on the "radar screen" for the company, to express interest in working with the organization, to show the firm's responsiveness, to do someone a favor, etc. However, it makes sense to try to ascertain the organization's true level of interest and your odds of success before investing a great deal of time and effort in the firm's response.

If the request is less formal (e.g., you receive a telephone call asking for a proposal and projected costs), you should ask some questions immediately. If you receive a formal RFP, you should feel comfortable calling the person who signed the letter or request. If a company is serious about seeking counsel, its representatives usually will take the time to answer your questions.

Asking the following types of questions will enhance your ability to prepare an effective response:

• *What process will be used to make a decision about hiring counsel for this project or area? Who will be involved in the decision?* It is important for you to know who will be making the decision. If the general counsel has final authority, you may speak about your capabilities differently than if it is a board of directors; for example, your approach will be different if the general counsel may be interested in playing a role in handling the matter.

• *What criteria will the company or organization use to make the decision about awarding the work? What is prompting the company to go outside for proposals?* Obviously, you want to know what the key issues are so you can address them head on. Is the prospect most interested in turnaround time or cost? Is the company dissatisfied with a recent result or simply testing the market?

• *Is this project or change something the company has decided it definitely will do? If so, what is the timetable? If not, when can you*

expect a decision to be made? It is good to know the timeline for decision-making, so you can both address the firm's capacity for the work
and plan appropriate follow up. The answer
to these questions also may help you determine whether this is a real opportunity.

> *If you don't know who your competition is, it is very difficult to know how to distinguish yourself and your firm.*

• *Have other law firms been invited to
submit proposals? If so, which ones? Has
the incumbent firm been invited to respond?*
If you don't know who your competition is, it is very difficult to know
how to distinguish yourself and your firm. Are the other firms smaller
or larger than your firm? Are they niche players or general practice
firms? If the existing counsel has a chance of retaining the work, you
may want to think about ways to eliminate the perceived "start-up"
costs involved in changing counsel (e.g., offering to review all files
and integrate the client into the firm's systems at no charge).

• *What are the organization's goals for the project or the relationship? Is there any other information about the organization's needs that
will help you prepare an appropriate response?* Sometimes there is
information that contacts would not be willing to put in a written document (i.e., RFP) that they would be willing to share by telephone,
such as the reason for current dissatisfaction, the real decision-making
process, the politics of the organization or some budgetary constraints.

• *Why has your firm been selected to receive an RFP?* First, it is
good to know what resulted in the company putting you on the list
(e.g., a Martindale-Hubbell search of practice areas, a speech a
member of your firm gave at an industry seminar), so you can track
the source of inquiries. In addition, you may learn about a perception held by the prospect (e.g., "We hear you do a lot of work with
the automotive industry") on which you can build. Conversely, you
may learn that the only reason you received the RFP is because the
organization sent it to the five largest law firms in your city, in which
case you will need to do a good job of educating the recipients
about your strengths.

The answers to these questions will help you craft a more tailored and distinctive response to the request. They may also help you determine if the company is serious about your candidacy for the work.

Is This Business Worth Fighting for?

Before responding to a Request for Proposal or going into a presentation with a prospective client, there are a lot of questions you should try to answer to determine whether the opportunity is a good fit for you and your firm. Here is a checklist of possibilities:

Assess the opportunity:
- What are the client's key objectives for the project?
- Who initiated the project?
- How does this project fit into the client's strategies or business plan?
- Is this project a high priority for the company?
- With whom are we competing?

Assess your interest:
- What is the business worth to the firm?
- What concessions would we need to make in order to get the business?
- How does the company or the work fit with our firm's culture and clientele?
- Do we have the capabilities and capacity to do the work—can we deliver?
- Is there potential for future business?
- Will working with this prospect present conflicts with existing clients or adversely affect existing perceptions of our firm?

Assess your chances:
- Are the prospect representatives amenable to answering our questions?

> • **Do we know who the decision-makers are?**
> • **Do we have established relationships with the decision-makers?**
> • **Have they defined a decision-making process?**
> • **Is there someone in the organization supporting our candidacy?**
> • **What criteria will the prospective client be using to make a decision?**

(2) *Researching the prospect.* Before preparing your response, you should also conduct research on the prospective client and its principal decision-makers. This can be done in many ways:

- Visit the entity's Web site
- Run a Dun & Bradstreet search
- Run a media search
- Check Web sites related to the prospect's industry or type of business
- Obtain annual reports, SEC filings and 10K reports for public companies

The things you should try to uncover include:

- Recent news reports on the organization or individuals
- Insights into business or legal issues
- Information on company principals
- Names of other advisors (e.g., accounting firm)
- Information on the organization's competitors

You also may want to search Martindale-Hubbell, Chambers and Partners, firm Web sites and other resources for information on the competing law firms.

Finally, you should undertake some internal due diligence before preparing your response, for example:

- Run a conflict check to ensure that you can accept the work and to see if others in the firm have relationships with the entity
- Circulate information within your firm about your opportunity to

see if anyone has other relationships or material information that might help with the response

- Solicit input on colleagues' related experience that might be included in the proposal, such as industry expertise or experience with similar matters

B. Writing the Proposal or Letter of Qualification

The days of responding to an RFP by printing boilerplate firm information on letterhead are gone. The more you tailor your proposal to the entity and its needs, the better your chances of success.

(1) *Writing the content.* In most cases, proposals should be written in a conversational style. The writing should be direct and in the active voice. The length of the proposal should be determined by the information sought, and the focus of the proposal should be on the prospective client, not the firm. Remember, the purpose of the proposal is not simply to inform; it is to persuade the reader to select the firm.

In developing a proposal's content, consider the following:

> *The days of responding to an RFP by printing boilerplate firm information on letterhead are gone. The more you tailor your proposal . . . , the better your chances of success.*

- *Focus on the needs of the client.* The client's needs should determine which areas and people to include in your proposal; each proposal should be customized to the prospect.

- *Identify a "selling proposition" or point(s) of differentiation.* These should set you and your firm apart from the competition.

- *Include a lot of detail about your staffing recommendations (i.e., the "team" you are proposing).* Clients generally are very interested in knowing which lawyers and staff will be working with them, and why the individuals were selected (e.g., experience with the type of project, industry background, etc.). At the same time, try to avoid describing the firm's internal organization (e.g., practice groups, departments, etc.); clients are most interested in how you will staff and organize to serve them specifically.

- *Include as much information as possible about your experience with similar clients, similar projects or cases, or similar industries.* Include, for example, a list of recent transactions or cases (if possible), a list of client references (with client permission), or aggregate information on your experience (e.g., number of jury trials, value of deals handled, etc.).

> [T]ry to avoid describing the firm's internal organization (e.g., practice groups, departments, etc.); clients are most interested in how you will staff and organize to serve them specifically.

- *Outline how you plan to help the client.* What solutions do you propose for the problem(s) presented or what strategies do you suggest?

- *Show, don't just tell.* Be specific when discussing your capabilities or services. For example, if you talk about invoice formats, include a sample; if you promise to provide regular status reports, include an example; if you tout your litigation support capabilities, include a redacted report.

- *Highlight other service-related characteristics or proposals to "add value" to the relationship.* This could include things like: developing an extranet; providing free, on-site workshops; working on site (at the client's place of business); or holding annual meetings to discuss how things are going.

- *Address the cost of your services.* In addition to information on how fees are derived or your hourly rates, you should try to give the prospect a "ballpark" fee, if possible, or to budget for phases of the project (e.g., a litigation matter through the discovery phase). In addition, it can be valuable to demonstrate your flexibility and creativity by presenting alternative pricing options or, at a minimum, indicating your willingness to discuss nontraditional options (e.g., flat fees, contingency fees, success fees, discounts for volume, etc.).

- *Express enthusiasm for the engagement in your proposal or letter.* Clients want to work with people who want to work with them.

(2) *Organizing your proposal.* Believe it or not, the form of your response can be every bit as important as the substance, particularly in

cases where the prospect is reviewing a number of lengthy submissions. The proposal should be easy to follow and should clearly present your capabilities and experience. If the proposal is "user friendly," prospects will infer that you are "user friendly" too.

In packaging your proposal, consider the following suggestions:

• If the prospective client has presented a format for you to follow (e.g., I. History of the Firm, II. Personnel, III. Budget), by all means follow it.

• Include a cover letter, thanking the prospect for the opportunity to submit the proposal, outlining the contents of the proposal, and suggesting why your firm is the best candidate for the job. It could invite the prospect to call

> *[T]he form of your response can be every bit as important as the substance. . . . If the proposal is "user friendly," prospects will infer that you are "user friendly" too.*

for additional information, or express your interest in discussing the proposal in person. The cover letter should be concise and convincing.

• Include an Executive Summary. This may be the most important part of your proposal because it will likely be read by the busy executives or in-house counsel who have requested the proposal. The Executive Summary should recap your understanding of the prospect's problem or situation, highlight the benefits of working with the firm, and outline the reasons the firm should be awarded the engagement. It should also touch on strategy, staffing and pricing.

• Package the proposal so it is easy for the reader to review. This means using a table of contents, paginating, including headings and subheadings, employing bullets, having a lot of white space and using tabs to organize information.

• Use exhibits or appendices to provide detailed information such as relevant articles authored by your firm's lawyers, charts or lists, timelines, sample forms, and lawyer and staff bios. This will make the proposal shorter and easier to navigate.

• Organize information into charts or graphs wherever possible. Putting verbiage into a visual form can be very compelling; it also minimizes the length of the proposal and the difficulty in reviewing it. For example, you might use a Gantt chart—a tool used in operations management to define steps and assign timelines—to lay out your expectations for a regulatory matter.

> *[The Executive Summary] may be the most important part of your proposal because it will likely be read by the busy executives or in-house counsel who have requested the proposal.*

• Make the proposal interesting graphically. Incorporate your firm's image and identity program (e.g., logo, colors, etc.) into your materials. Think about taking a picture of the proposed team as a group, instead of including individual bios with photos.

• Be sure to submit the required number of copies when sending your submission.

(3) *Following up.* If you are not selected for the work or for an interview, you should try to learn from your experience. In some cases, it can be very effective to contact the prospective client to learn what influenced the decision. As long as you are not defensive, you might be able to ask, and learn, what you could have done better to improve your document.

III. PRESENTATIONS AND PITCH MEETINGS

The opportunity to make a presentation to a prospective client may come after a proposal has been submitted, or it may be the only step in the prospect's selection process. Most prospective clients will interview three or four law firms, all of which they believe are capable of handling the engagement. The key to a successful interview, therefore, is to form a relationship with the prospect through a meaningful dialogue about the prospect's needs and your services, and to convince the prospect that you are the firm best suited to handle the work.

A. Preparing for the Meeting

If you have not been through the process of submitting a proposal or letter of qualification, you should conduct the same type of due diligence outlined in Section II.A of this Chapter before your meeting or presentation. Once you have done your homework, you should think about the following issues before going to make your pitch:

- *What is the format?* You should feel free to ask the prospective client about the interview plans. How many people will attend? Will it be formal or informal (e.g., what is the dress code at the company)? In most cases, you should wear a suit both to look professional and to demonstrate that you are taking the opportunity seriously. (If the client representatives are very informal, you can remove your jacket.) What type of meeting room will be used? Knowing this will help you determine how you will make your presentation as well as whether the room will accommodate your other needs (e.g., technology demonstration, PowerPoint, etc.).

- *Who should participate?* It is very important to select the appropriate interview team. The factors to consider include area(s) of expertise being sought, industry knowledge and diversity (age, gender or race). You might consider whether it would make sense to involve a nonlawyer staff member (e.g., the HR director for a labor and employment project). Finally, you should think about who the prospect will have at the meeting, so you can factor in relationships and other issues. For example, if the prospect only intends to have three people at the meeting, you do not want to show up with a team of six lawyers; the prospect might infer that you overstaff legal matters.

Like a proposal, the presentation involves both content and delivery. In terms of content, you should be certain to address:

- The prospect's problem or issue, demonstrating an understanding of what is involved and the prospect's concerns

- The services and resources you plan to offer (e.g., including staffing)

- The strategy you propose in terms of service, whether it is for a specific matter or generally (e.g., status reporting, learning the client's business, etc.)

- Your qualifications to handle the project, matter or client (e.g., similar clients, industry expertise, similar matters, etc.)

• *Your "selling proposition."* As with a written proposal, you should try to find ways to differentiate yourself from your competitors for the work. You can assume that the prospect feels all the firms that have been invited to interview are qualified or they wouldn't be there; your job is to help the prospect choose your firm over others.

When considering the actual format of your presentation, you should also think about the following:

• *Who will do what at the meeting.* Each representative of the firm in attendance should play a role in the interview or presentation, whether making introductions, discussing a particular part of the proposal or fielding questions.

• *Whether to use audiovisual techniques.* In some instances, your presentation might be enhanced by using PowerPoint or demonstrating your technology. If you plan to use technology, however, you should determine whether the prospect is expecting a formal presentation and whether the interview room can accommodate the technology.

• *What materials to bring.* Most presentations will benefit from some written materials to augment the discussion. This could take the form of a pitch book, which can be reviewed with the client, or supplemental lists (e.g., representative clients), relevant articles, etc. or charts (e.g., value of cases handled). You might also bring marketing materials to leave with the prospect, such as a description of your practice area and bios of the interview team.

Finally, you should give serious consideration to rehearsing for the presentation, particularly if a number of people are involved or if the presentation is formal.

B. Making the Presentation or Pitch

With the proper research, planning and rehearsal, you should be comfortable with your presentation. At the same time, you should see your face-to-face encounter as an opportunity to build a rapport with the prospective client as well as a chance to pitch your services.

Before your actual presentation begins, start with the following:

• *Shake hands.* Introduce those in attendance from your firm and meet everyone representing the prospective client.

• *Make some small talk.* Try to break the ice with a timely comment or sincere compliment.

• *Explain the agenda.* Tell the client's representatives what you were hoping to cover, and see whether that meets their expectations.

• *Make more formal introductions.* Introduce each member of your firm at the meeting, give a brief statement about his or her experience or qualifications, and explain why each member was selected to attend.

• *Ask a few questions.* Begin by outlining your understanding of the entity's situation or needs. Ask the company's representatives to confirm whether you have summarized the situation correctly and whether there is anything else you should have mentioned. This will give the prospect an opportunity to talk (which is a good thing). For example, "When we spoke by telephone, you mentioned that your primary concerns relate to employee terminations. We have prepared some information about our capabilities in this area but, before we begin, could you give us a few concrete examples of the issues that have been most troubling for you?" By doing this, you will confirm not only for yourself but also for the client that you understand the problems. It will also allow you to make last-minute changes to your presentation if you find the client's needs have changed or your perceptions were wrong.

In making the pitch, you should cover the same type of content that would be covered in a proposal for the business.[1] Generally, this includes:

• The benefits of using the firm

• The proposed relationship with the prospective client (e.g., staffing, pricing, etc.)

• Your strategy for the project or engagement

---

[1] See Section II.B.1 *supra*.

Focus on the most important issues in your presentation. You can always include details or minor points in written materials.

You should engage the prospective client as much as possible in the meeting, asking questions, confirming assumptions or requesting reactions, when appropriate. You should also conclude your meeting with ample time for questions.

Before leaving, there are a few more things to cover:

- *Thanking the prospect.* Be certain to thank the entity's representatives for the opportunity to meet with them and make your presentation.

- *Understanding the decision-making process.* If you are uncertain about next steps, inquire about how or when the entity plans to make its decision.

- *Asking for the business.* Finally, be certain you have expressed your desire to work with the client. You have been invited to bid on the business; don't be afraid to ask for the chance.

C. Following Up

After your interview, send the prospect a thank-you letter for the opportunity to meet. This would be a good time to reiterate your interest in the assignment and why you think you are best suited to handle it. If there were unresolved questions or issues raised during the meeting, follow up with the answers. Also, send anything that might have been promised during the meeting, such as references, an article, etc.

As in the case of a proposal, if you do not get the engagement, you should feel free to contact the prospective client to express your disappointment, but also to try to learn from the experience. You might suggest that if the new law firm ever finds itself in a conflict situation you would be delighted to help out. In addition, you can express your interest in being on the list to receive future requests for pitches or proposals.

> *[E]ngage the prospective client as much as possible in the meeting, asking questions, confirming assumptions or requesting reactions, when appropriate.*

IV. OTHER CONSIDERATIONS AND TIPS FOR PREPARING EFFECTIVE PROPOSALS AND PITCHES FOR BUSINESS

As you try to put your best foot forward in writing or in person, the following tips should help position you for success:

Meet, or better yet beat, the deadline. Prospects will be more likely to carefully peruse the first one or two proposals that arrive. They also will have a perception that you value the work, and that you provide timely responses.

> *Prospects will be more likely to carefully peruse the first one or two proposals that arrive.*

Be on time for interviews and meetings! If you plan to use any technology (e.g., PowerPoint, Internet connections), be certain to get to the meeting room with enough time to test the technology.

- *Check your position.* Like a job interview, it is generally advantageous to be interviewed first or last.

- *If you feel you are losing your audience, change gears.* Ask a question, tell a self-effacing joke or change tactics.

- *Customize your proposal or pitch!* Although prospective clients are interested in your experience, they are most concerned about how you will approach their problem or situation. The more tailored your message is, the more effective it will be.

- *Staffing is important to prospects.* Be sure to introduce the members of the proposed team and adequately explain why they were selected.

- *Clients are buying what you've done for other people.* Wherever possible, provide references, client lists, summaries of transactions or cases, etc. These will also help minimize the perceived risk of hiring you.

- *Be enthusiastic!* Even if you don't get the business, prospective clients will remember your interest in working with them.

- *Build relationships.* Most proposals or requests to interview are received by lawyers who have had previous contact with the entity seeking counsel. As a result, the better you position yourself and the more contacts you make, the greater your chances of receiving requests for proposals and meetings.

Ideas/Notes: Preparing Effective Proposals and Pitches for Business

My personal challenge(s) or obstacle(s) in this area:

_____

_____

_____

_____

_____

My goal(s) or objective(s) in this area:

_____

_____

_____

_____

_____

What I need to do to get started:

(1) _____

_____

(2) _____

_____

(3) _____

_____

(4) _____

_____

(5) _____

_____

15

Following Up with Targets

I. INTRODUCTION

If, through your networking efforts, you meet someone with a specific or immediate legal need, consider yourself lucky. In most cases, your relationships will be with prospects who either don't have a need at the time of your contact or have no compelling reason to change law firms. As a result, the odds of walking away with a new assignment from one particular encounter are slim.

Developing legal work involves both time and timing; it takes time to develop relationships, and it takes timing to be positioned "in the right place" when the prospect is looking for a lawyer. That's why follow up is so important. In fact, there are several theories about the number of contacts needed with prospective clients before you can expect to get business—depending on which one you believe, it can take five, eight or even twelve contacts. For example, the "Rule of Five" in sales asserts that 80% of new business comes after five or more quality contacts with a prospective client.

Success—i.e., new business—will come from consistent and sustained efforts to reinforce the prospect's view of your capabilities and add value to the relationships you have developed. You need to engage in efforts to stay in touch with your contacts over time, ideally through activities that cultivate relationships, educate and provide value.

This Chapter focuses on your opportunities for follow up, the range of follow-up activities you might consider, and ways to make contact with your targets. It also provides some advice for setting up in-person follow-up meetings.

II. FOLLOW-UP OPPORTUNITIES AND METHODS

A. Follow-Up Opportunities

After a certain amount of effort, you probably will have been successful in meeting a number of people and will be turning your attention to cultivating the relationships. There may be some people on your target list who are good enough friends that you can simply call and ask them to lunch, golf or some other occasion. For many of the people you have met, however, you may need a better reason for getting together.

> *One of the secrets to business development success is recognizing opportunities to follow up with people. Most good reasons involve some type of change, for change generates opportunities.*

One of the secrets to business development success is recognizing opportunities to follow up with people. The best reasons to communicate will position you as a valuable advisor and will not feel contrived to you or your contact. Most good reasons involve some type of change, for change generates opportunities.

There are three primary kinds of opportunities that will present themselves to you. Depending on your practice or the nature of your firm, you could discover opportunities to communicate with your contacts almost daily. The kinds include:

(1) *Substantive news or information.* Providing information about legal issues of importance to a prospect is always deemed to be valuable (presuming it's timely and understandable). Your substantive communication opportunities could involve:

- Changes in the law, either pending or final
- New rules or procedures, either proposed or adopted

- Information on client cases or projects (with or without identifying clients) that contain issues of interest to the target

- Materials you write or read, such as articles, seminar materials, PowerPoint slides, etc.

- Announcements or invitations to programs or seminars that might be of interest, either firm-sponsored or organized by other groups

- Results of legal research that might be of interest

- Forms, templates, checklists or other useful tools that targets can use in their businesses or personal lives

- Recommendations for preventive measures to avoid legal problems

(2) *News involving the target.* Whenever there are changes related to your contact or his or her entity, there can be opportunities for you to follow up. These could involve either professional or personal news, for example:

- Your contact receives a promotion

- The entity announces a new venture, such as geographic expansion or a new product line

- The target's competition has interesting news

- New employees join the entity (e.g., a new general counsel)

- Your contact leaves an entity

- Your contact has personal events (e.g., a new baby, a child accepted into a top-notch school)

Of course, you need to use good judgment about using personal issues as a basis for follow up. The more personal the news, the closer the relationship needs to be for you to use it as a communication opportunity.

(3) *News involving the firm.* Finally, frequently there will be opportunities related to your practice or your firm that provide you with chances to contact people. For example:

- Your firm announces new partners or hires some interesting lateral lawyers

- You get inducted into a prestigious association or assume a leadership position in a group

- Your firm ventures into new practice areas or launches industry teams (e.g., oil and gas, pharmaceutical)

- New marketing initiatives are completed (e.g., a redesigned Web site, a new firm brochure)

- The firm hosts an event (e.g., a seminar, an open house)

- New creative initiatives are developed (e.g., a flat-fee pricing structure)

Once you start thinking about it, the opportunities to communicate become more and more apparent. Then the question becomes how to go about it: What will be the best way to contact the prospective client?

B. Methods of Follow Up

Depending on your relationship with the target, your follow-up contact can be casual and easy. For example, you could send a technology buff an e-mail about the firm's redesigned Web site, i.e., "Our firm just launched an upgraded Web site. Here's the link. If you have a minute, check it out and send me your reactions. I'd love to hear what you think." Other contact opportunities might be more formal and time-consuming, however, such as developing a summary of a proposed legislative change and explaining how it might affect the agricultural industry.

(1) *Face to face contacts.* The best way to build personal relationships is through in-person contact. If your target is in your geographic vicinity, there are many ways for you to have face-to-face contact. These include:

- Getting together for breakfast, lunch, dinner or drinks after work

- Playing golf

- Attending sporting or cultural events together

- Making arrangements to attend or sit together at meetings or functions (e.g., a trade association, a bar association section). (Keep in mind that meetings may also present opportunities to see people from other geographic areas.)

- Visiting the contact's entity and taking a tour of the business or plant

- Presenting an on-site seminar or training workshop at the contact's place of business

- Inviting the contact to accompany you to seminars or programs of interest

- Inviting the contact to relevant firm functions, like holiday parties, seminars or open houses

- Inviting the contact to participate in firm activities, such as serving on a panel at a partner retreat, participating in a firm focus group or speaking to your practice group

- Attending events at the contact's place of business or home

- Working collaboratively on a project (e.g., serving on a board together, planning a joint seminar, etc.)

- Hosting a meeting in your offices (e.g., board or committee)

- Organizing a get-together with representatives of the contact's organization and members of your firm

- Arranging opportunities to introduce your contacts to other people with whom they share a mutual interest

- Conducting an "audit" or review of some aspect of the company's operations (e.g., reviewing employment applications or policy manuals, reviewing the standard contract for sales staff). (The scope of the project may allow you to perform this activity without an in-person visit.)

Depending on your relationship with the target and the type of activity you select, your face-to-face contacts might also include your spouses/significant others or families (e.g., dinner at your home, Disney on Ice, etc.).

(2) *Other types of contact.* In addition to face-to-face activities, there are many other beneficial ways to follow up with contacts. These activities might be appropriate if your relationship with the target is not particularly close, the target is located in another geographic area, or you're looking for ways to stay in touch between in-person meetings. The methods below are less intrusive, but also more passive, such as:

• *E-mail or mail.* You can send substantive information of interest to the target electronically or in hard copy (e.g., advisories, alerts, forms or white papers on issues related to the individual or company). Forwarding articles of interest, such as those related to the target's business, occupation, industry or personal interests, is a particularly effective way to follow up.

> *Forwarding articles of interest, such as those related to the target's business, occupation, industry or personal interests, is a particularly effective way to follow up.*

• *Phone calls.* There are many occasions when a phone call can be effective. For example, you could follow up with a contact to see how a particular project or matter turned out. You might call to alert the target to a case, proposed legislation or other legal actions that might affect his or her company. You might even call someone periodically just to check in, say hello and stay top of mind.

• *Finding ways to help.* There are many things you can do behind the scenes to help your targets, either personally or professionally. For example, you could work to get them on an important board or a committee; nominate them for awards or recognition; or offer to make introductions to other people they might like to meet, whether professionally (e.g., a software vendor) or personally (e.g., other fly fishermen).

• *Cards and gifts.* Personal notes and cards or small, meaningful gifts that reflect your knowledge of the contact and his or her interests show your thoughtfulness and are appreciated. These could range from a baby gift to a handwritten card congratulating the target on a promotion. (Keep in mind that some employers have policies that prohibit employees from accepting gifts.)

If your targets include a number of people with similar positions, interests or issues, a well-designed group activity may allow you to target multiple people with one initiative while positioning you as a helpful resource. For example, if you are an employment lawyer, you could organize a small discussion group of HR managers. At each meeting you could present a topic for discussion, allowing the attendees to also network with their peers. If you are an employee benefits lawyer, you could set up a study group or discussion group for benefits managers. If you are an IP lawyer, you could establish a listserver or electronic discussion group for some patent coordinators to communicate with you and each other on issues of common concern.

Focus groups present another good opportunity to gather people together and, at the same time, provide you with insights and information. Let's say you have been representing insurance companies defending their claims but want to shift your practice toward representing self-insured companies in their litigation matters. You could organize a focus group of company decision-makers (e.g., risk managers) to discuss their perceptions of the legal environment—e.g., how they make decisions to hire counsel, their legal needs, your competition, etc. In addition to gaining invaluable information as you reposition your practice, you can build relationships with the individual participants while learning about their individual needs, perceptions and perspectives.

> *Focus groups present [a] good opportunity to gather people together and, at the same time, provide you with insights and information.*

Finally, you could invite a group of targets to participate in some market research and then provide them with access to the resulting information. For example, if you are a commercial real estate lawyer, you could conduct a study to discover the five biggest challenges facing property managers, and then send out the results.

C. Active vs. Passive Activities

When evaluating your options for follow up, keep in mind that the more "active" the effort, the more it will engage the person you are targeting. When given the choice, many lawyers opt for written communication (i.e., letters and e-mail), when telephone or in-person contact is generally more effective. But the effect of written communication can certainly be enhanced if given some thought.

Here are some examples of passive vs. active follow up:

(1) *Opportunity.* Your firm hires a new lateral partner with expertise in an area that might be of interest to a target contact.

Follow Up. The passive (and typical) activity is to send out a written announcement about the lawyer. The active, and more effective, reaction would be to call your contact, talk about your new colleague, and suggest that the three of you get together so you can introduce them.

(2) *Opportunity.* You have an opportunity to speak at an industry association and are given a list of attendees.

Follow Up. The most common, and passive, follow-up activity is to send a letter to attendees thanking them for attending and inviting them to call with questions. The more effective and active follow up would be to identify something of interest to the attendees, such as a paper on the topic you discussed in your presentation or a related case, and send a copy with a personalized letter.

(3) *Opportunity.* You are on the board of directors of a nonprofit organization. You have drafted a document on a *pro bono* basis that the chair, a prominent businessman, needs to sign.

Follow Up. The passive activity is sending the document via mail, e-mail or courier. More effective, and active, would be calling the chair to suggest that you bring the document over for his signature, and see if he has time for lunch or a quick tour while you're there.

Clearly it takes more effort to engage in active follow up and communication, so you generally need to target your efforts. But as you do, your results will grow dramatically. Someone once said that passive activities make you look "interesting;" active, relationship-building activities make you look "interested."

D. Turning a Personal Relationship into a Business Relationship

For many lawyers, targeting friends or personal acquaintances for business can be very awkward. There can be risks to doing this too, of course. For example, you don't want a friend to think your underlying motivation for developing the relationship has been to get his business.

Some people also worry if they are successful in getting business and the legal representation goes badly, they will jeopardize their friendship.

Other lawyers, however, say it only makes sense to work with friends—who better to oversee a legal matter than someone who sincerely cares about you? So it remains up to each individual to determine whether he or she is willing to pursue the notion of doing business with friends.

If you are trying to look at business opportunities involving personal relationships, many of the activities outlined above can be

> *[W]ho better to oversee a legal matter than someone who sincerely cares about you?*

very effective ways to build a relationship and generate business. Let's use the example of a neighbor who is the CFO of a solid and growing technology company. You have gotten together socially on a number of occasions with your spouses and enjoy each other's company. He knows you're a lawyer but you've never talked about doing business together. It would be neither comfortable nor appropriate to approach the subject of doing business together out of the blue. In this kind of situation, it will be necessary to move your interaction from the backyard to the office. For example, you might:

• Call your neighbor at his work number and invite him to go to lunch with you at a place near his office, and suggest that you'd like to stop by first for a quick tour of his company.

• Invite your neighbor to your firm's seminars or workshops on topics that might be of interest to him or his company.

• Do some research about the company and its legal needs or issues so you can reference these activities or ask informed questions when you get together.

• Send information of interest to him periodically, such as relevant articles appearing in trade or business publications.

• Invite him to attend a conference or luncheon program as your guest, such as a meeting sponsored by the Chamber of Commerce or a technology association.

- Invite him to visit your office when he's in the vicinity. This will allow him to see you in your work environment and get a better perspective on the firm as a whole. While he's there, introduce him to lawyers in related areas, like members of your IP group or those who handle financings.

- Invite him to participate in a firm-sponsored entertainment activity, such as a sporting event or a round of golf, then introduce him to other firm clients, good contacts (e.g., venture capitalists) or firm lawyers at the event.

III. SETTING UP FACE-TO-FACE MEETINGS

At some point, your targeting and follow-up efforts will lead to in-person meetings or activities. Many lawyers are uncomfortable setting up these activities, either having difficulty making the call or wondering how to use the time effectively. This Section provides some tips on inviting a prospect to meet, and conducting and following up the meeting.

A. Making the Call

Before you pick up the phone or write an e-mail to invite your target to get together, you need to identify a purpose or objective for your contact. In other words, by the time the lunch, dinner or visit is over, what do you hope to have accomplished? Your personal objective could be:

- To get to know the person better
- To learn more about the entity
- To get to know more about the person's role in the company
- To talk about a recent case in which you or your firm was involved, to demonstrate your firm's expertise in an area
- To educate the contact about an area of concern (e.g., discussing a recent case or ruling that may have implications for the contact)
- To conduct an "informational interview" about the contact's industry, legal needs or other issues
- To uncover areas where you might be able to assist the contact

Having an objective is important. Unless you and the target are personal friends, most people are too busy to get together without a good reason. There should be a purpose for the contact, and, since you're making the call, it's up to you to articulate it. It is very important for you to be up-front about your objectives for getting together. One of the keys to effective relationship building is that there are no pretenses! For example: "As you know, I am spending more and more of my time working in the construction industry. I was hoping to take you to lunch and have you share some of your considerable insights into the local players in the industry and how I might expand the work I do for contractors."

> *Having an objective is important. There should be a purpose for the contact, and, since you're making the call, it's up to you to articulate it.*

There are many reasons that you might reference in extending invitations, for example:

- You've enjoyed working with the contact on a committee or board, and would like to learn more about her business or position

- You're interested in learning more about the contact's company and how it is structured to handle legal matters

- You share an interest in an industry (e.g., health care, oil and gas), and want to get the contact's thoughts on trends in the area and how those trends might affect your practice

- You are interested in expanding your practice in an area, and want to get advice on effective ways to do so

- You (or your firm) recently completed a project, got a good result or learned a lesson that you want to pass along to the organization

- You are interested in getting more active in an organization or association, and would like perspectives on contributions you might make

- You read an article the contact wrote (or an article about him or his firm), or attended a presentation he gave, and you want to discuss the topic in more detail

- The contact knows someone you would like to meet, and you

wonder if he'd be willing to introduce you through a group activity (e.g., a round of golf, a sporting event, etc.)

When making contact, it is important to acknowledge that the person's time is valuable. You can do this by: (1) telling the contact how much you appreciate his willingness to take the time to meet with you; and (2) either asking where the contact would like to have lunch or suggesting a convenient location that will minimize the person's time away from the office.

> *[I]t is important to acknowledge that the person's time is valuable.*

Finally, be prepared to ask informed questions. You should take a moment to learn about the person or organization before your meeting by visiting the company's Web site, reading its materials (e.g., product brochures, annual reports, etc.), conducting a search for recent articles, etc.

B. Conducting the Meeting

When you meet face-to-face, think about the following steps:

• *Thank the contact.* Begin by thanking the contact for her time and promising to keep the meeting to a set or predetermined time limit (e.g., one hour). You should keep your initial meeting short, both to respect the person's time and to show your efficiency.

• *Establish rapport.* Based on your knowledge of the contact or the organization, try to make some conversation before turning to business. This will help you establish a connection. For example, perhaps you went to the same law school as the in-house counsel you are meeting, you have kids the same age or you enjoy the same vacation spots or hobby.

• *Establish the agenda.* Reiterate the purpose of the meeting. Let's say the president of a target company, John, is a personal friend but the decision to hire counsel for the company's labor and employment work, in which you are interested, is controlled by his HR manager. You were able to persuade the HR manager to go to lunch with you, but she has a good relationship with another law firm. You might start by staying, "John tells me your relationship with the Smith & Jones law firm goes back many years and they've done a great job for you. As I told you on the phone, I've been building my own practice in the area, and I appreciate being able to learn from HR professionals like you. I'm most interested in hearing what kinds of issues you have, what's important to you when you work with law firms, and any other insights you have for me."

• *Open the floor.* After stating your proposed agenda, ask the target if there is anything she would like to cover. Occasionally, the prospect may have her own agenda; for example, if she was notified about an urgent matter the same morning and needs some help, you may find yourself in the right place at the right time.

• *Be prepared to ask questions.* You should have a number of areas you would like to explore, depending on your agenda. In this instance, it could range from the types of matters with which her company deals to how she hires legal counsel. The more the prospect talks, the better chance you have of uncovering an opportunity for you or your firm.

> *The more the prospect talks, the better chance you have of uncovering an opportunity for you or your firm.*

• *Summarize.* Repeat the key areas or issues you heard during the meeting. If possible, make a few suggestions or mention a recent client engagement related to a topic raised during the meeting. You should also try to mention something helpful you could do to follow up after the meeting (e.g., sending a copy of an article, sending the name of a good HR trainer, sending a link to a Web site in which she might be interested, etc.).

• *Conclude on time.* Do everything possible to stay on the promised schedule, from having a reservation to being ready to place your meal order to requesting the check promptly when you are finished. Of course, since you extended the invitation, you should pick up the tab.

C. Following Up the Meeting

After the meeting, send a personal thank-you note. In it, thank the contact again for sharing his valuable time with you, and mention the benefit you received (e.g., "Your insights into the construction industry will be very helpful as I continue to expand my practice in that area.").

During the course of the meeting, you should be listening for things that might provide follow-up opportunities. Afterwards, you need to fulfill any follow up promised promptly. If you are lacking a particular opportunity, be on the lookout for possible ways to communicate in the weeks following the meeting, such as sending an article or calling to alert your contact to a new ruling.

IV. OTHER CONSIDERATIONS AND TIPS FOR FOLLOWING UP WITH CONTACTS

The following are some additional thoughts about staying in touch with prospective clients and other target contacts:

• *Keep your antennae up.* You need to be on the lookout for opportunities to communicate so you increase your odds of being "in the right place at the right time." For example, if you read an industry article that you found particularly interesting, you could send it to a few people, write a letter to the editor, send a note to the author or reporter who wrote it, circulate it internally or write a counterpoint article.

• *Understand the target's needs.* For your follow up to be most successful and add the most value to a particular relationship, you need to understand the needs and environment of the target.

• *Show interest in the target's businesses and facilities.* Most people are very proud of their businesses and facilities. If you ask for a tour of a construction site or to visit a plant, your contact will appreciate your interest.

• *Share an activity.* Playing golf, going on a fishing trip or spending a day together at a spa can be very effective ways to follow up; they allow you to spend hours with your target. The caveat is that you need to demonstrate proper etiquette and not let your guard down too much.

• *Give on-site substantive programs or workshops.* Educational programs offer both you and your target benefits. They help position you or your firm as experts on the topic discussion. They provide a free educational program for the prospective client. They allow you to visit a company or organization. And they give you a forum to meet additional employees or executives of the entity.

• *Always bring something of value to a face-to-face meeting.* Try to position yourself so that every contact with a target builds your credibility and the perception that you bring something to the relationship. This might be substantive information (e.g., giving a little free advice), business-oriented advice (e.g., recommending a good consultant in the target's industry) or personal assistance (e.g., recommending a new restaurant).

• *Be a good listener.* One of the mistakes many lawyers make is talking too much. When dealing with prospects, you should aim to listen 80% of the time you are together.

Leveraging a Good Result

One of a lawyer's best follow-up opportunities is obtaining a good result for a client. It is a chance for you to demonstrate your expertise while often enabling you to provide helpful information or preventive advice. Let's say you represented the local affiliate of a television network in a suit filed by a plaintiff claiming damages after a show, and the court dismissed the case, a victory for your client.

The first question you need to consider is how many people (or entities) this decision potentially affects. You can start by developing a list of organizations or people who would benefit from learning about this case, like:

• Other local television stations, and their national network legal departments

• Other types of media, such as newspapers, that might release stories that provoke a similar response

• Lawyers in other cities or states who represent your client's network affiliate or other media (to position yourself for referrals of local work in the future)

• Publications that write about media issues or organizations that follow these issues (e.g., ABA Media Law and Defamation Torts Committee)

The second question to consider is the importance of the result. If it provides people with information—for example, ways to prevent similar lawsuits in the future—it will be worth both your time and the time of those you contact to bring it to their attention.

Finally, you need to determine the most effective ways to distribute the news. To this end:

• Contact your client for permission to cite the case when contacting other entities. The most effective marketing communications tell a story. Keep in mind that without client permission you still may be able to alert people if it is possible to do so without identifying the parties.

• Consider the best way to bring this information to the attention of your targets. In some cases, it may be best to prepare a letter; in others, an electronic, one-page "Alert." Depending on the importance of the matter and your relationships with the targets, you may want to set up meetings to discuss the issues involved.

• Determine whether the issue is of enough interest or importance to warrant undertaking more significant marketing efforts, such as writing an article for a trade magazine or giving a speech to an industry organization.

• Keep an eye out for other articles or cases that involve similar issues, and, if appropriate, send a copy of your case to the parties involved.

Ideas/Notes: Following Up with Targets

My personal challenge(s) or obstacle(s) in this area:

_____

_____

_____

_____

_____

My goal(s) or objective(s) in this area:

_____

_____

_____

_____

_____

What I need to do to get started:

(1) _____

_____

(2) _____

_____

(3) _____

_____

(4) _____

_____

(5) _____

_____

16

"Closing" and Asking
for Business

I. INTRODUCTION

For many lawyers, the result of all their marketing, networking and relationship-building activities is ultimately measured by whether business is developed. While there are many other benefits to the activities discussed in earlier chapters—both for the lawyer and for clients—an effective marketing and business development program should, at some point, result in an increased book of business.

Depending on the nature of your practice, the frequency of changes in your areas, the types of relationships you have developed and a host of other factors, it is quite possible that clients or referral sources will engage you without the need for a more proactive approach. However, for many lawyers, failing to be proactive in seeking work—i.e., never expressing an interest in or asking for business—is the primary reason that they do not get the work.

Asking for business is, without a doubt, one of the most difficult things for many lawyers. This Chapter focuses on how to ask for legal work, or as some people say "close the sale," appropriately and with the requisite propriety.

II. DEVELOPING YOUR BUSINESS DEVELOPMENT STRATEGY

The business development process is similar whether you are seeking to expand a relationship with an existing client into a new substantive or geographic area, or trying to obtain business from a prospective client. At its most basic, obtaining business usually results from the following:

(1) Understanding and identifying the prospect's needs

(2) Understanding the firm's capabilities well enough both to recognize an opportunity to help the prospect and to explain those capabilities

(3) Presenting the information to the prospect and, often, asking for the opportunity to be of assistance

This Section focuses on steps one and two: understanding prospect needs and firm capabilities.

A. Understanding the Client's Needs

Typically if you have gotten to the point where you are ready to ask for business, you will know something about the prospective client. However, you still need to do your homework.[1] You should read company materials, visit Web sites, run searches for media coverage and use your conversations to learn as much as you can about:

- The company—its business, operations, employees, facilities, etc.

- The legal area—legal needs, recent problems, current counsel, etc.

- The decision-makers—in-house counsel, board members, other advisors, etc.

Just as important is to try to use your discussions with the prospect to uncover underlying issues or concerns, which are often less about legal services and more about client services. You should try to understand what prospects value in legal counsel, how they evaluate risk or how they will measure the success of the relationship. For example, what would the prospect like to see improved or changed in its current legal relationship? Perhaps, as a million-dollar client, the contact is upset that the company's "account" keeps getting delegated to younger and younger lawyers.

---

[1] See Chapter 14 II.A *supra* for further discussion on researching a prospective client.

Many lawyers' business development efforts suffer from a "one size fits all" approach to their pitches. You will be much more successful getting business if you can help prospects define and recognize problems and their solutions. In fact, if you are having trouble developing business, it usually has nothing to do with your ability to "close;" it is related to the fact that you haven't identified or met the prospective client's needs.

> *[I]f you are having trouble developing business, it usually has nothing to do with your ability to "close"; it is related to the fact that you haven't identified or met the prospective client's needs.*

But even if you know generally what the problem or issue might involve, you need to drill down even further to understand the decision the client is trying to make, and then tailor your discussion accordingly. In some cases, the client might not even be aware that legal action should be taken; in other cases, a client may have various alternatives and issues to evaluate. Inevitably, clients are most concerned about the very next step facing them, not what might be down the road.

Let's say, for example, that the prospect has received a threatening letter from a supplier. Depending on the company and the individual decision-maker, the decision process could take into account any of the following:

Is it necessary to undertake any action at all? The prospect may be debating whether it even makes sense to take legal action. If that is the case, it does no good to talk about your firm's capabilities; the discussion should be focused on whether it would be prudent for the prospect to pursue the legal issue. You must demonstrate a particular and legitimate benefit to the client of proceeding (e.g., preventing additional lawsuits).

If it is necessary to do something, should we move quickly or should we wait? If the prospect is mulling over the timing of the action, your discussion should focus on the benefits and/or potential ramifications of inaction.

If we do proceed now, can we use our own in-house professionals or staff, or should we go outside the organization? Even if the company proceeds, one of the prospect's options might include having internal staff handle the matter. In this case, your approach should focus on the benefits of having the matter handled by outside counsel, discussing issues like head counts (e.g., not wanting to hire additional staff), capacity, access to the firm's staff or prior work experience, and cost considerations.

If we go outside the organization, which firm should we retain? If the prospect has decided to take legal action and is looking for outside counsel, this is the time to focus on your firm and its track record. Your goal is to differentiate your firm from other law firms potentially under consideration and to establish your credibility and expertise in handling the matter.

By understanding the decision the client is trying to make, you can be much more persuasive in presenting your message. Obviously, if the prospect is mulling over whether taking action on a particular matter is even necessary while you are trying to differentiate yourself from the competition, your efforts will be wasted.

It is also important to understand what is driving a client's decision or needs. Some clients will be most interested in your track record of results; others are more interested in turnaround time or cost. For example, the company may be concerned that if

Some clients will be most interested in your track record of results; others are more interested in turnaround time or cost.

its customer contracts are not drawn up by the end of the quarter, the field staff won't get their commission checks. In this instance, you should be emphasizing capacity and turnaround time.

Usually if you aren't connecting with a prospect, it's because you don't fully understand the prospect's needs. To position yourself for business in the long run, your goal should be to help the prospect make the best possible decision by focusing on the most important factors for whatever step is being considered. Even if you help the client determine that no action is the best action (in which case there is no legal business to be gained), you will have positioned yourself as a helpful resource and built enormous credibility that is sure to pay off in the future.

So how can you understand the needs and issues of the client? One way is to ask probing questions through conversations with the prospective client. Chapter 15 outlined a process for setting up informational meetings with targets to discuss their business, industry or practice, their goals and objectives, and their clients or customers.

Additional activities that will provide a window into the target's world and potential insights into the target's issues include:

- Taking a tour of the target's company or offices

- Tracking matters involving other companies or clients in the same industry or line of business

- Attending open houses, seminars or other functions sponsored by the target's company

- Joining related trade, industry or professional associations and reading related business and industry publications to follow developments

- Talking to other professionals who serve the target or the industry

- Generally having your "antennae" up

B. Knowing the Firm's Capabilities

Once you have identified areas of need for a target, your next step is to determine whether you or your firm can be of assistance. It is astounding how little many lawyers know about their own law firms. The lawyers may have familiarity in a very broad sense about the firm's breadth of expertise or some vague idea about the nature of the firm's

> *It is astounding how little many lawyers know about their own law firms. . . . [F]ew can speak knowledgably about cases handled, matters resolved, industry expertise or other topics that are of most interest to potential clients.*

clientele, but few can speak knowledgably about cases handled, matters resolved, industry expertise or other topics that are of most interest to potential clients.

Part of the problem is that lawyers often look for new business only for themselves. If you don't market the collective capabilities of the firm, you will certainly foreclose opportunities. Even if you don't have great incentives to do so (e.g., the firm's compensation system provides few incentives), developing business for others will help you get better at developing business for yourself. In addition, generating business for others in your firm can result in their willingness to help you in return.

Consider the following example. A client or prospective client asks: "Do you have anyone at your firm who has handled aviation leases?" Many lawyers will respond by saying something to the effect, "I'm sure we do; let me investigate and get back to you," or, worse yet, "I'm not sure but I can find out." This is not a very compelling sales pitch and brings little comfort to your target about your firm's capabilities.

Contrast this approach with the response, "Absolutely. My colleague, Chris Johnson, has handled aviation leases for years. Can we set up a time for you two to talk?" Not only have you expressed confidence in your firm's capabilities, you have seized a business development opportunity.

One key to success in business development is being able to talk to prospects about your firm's track record—names of clients (if possible), representative transactions, successful resolution of litigation, industry developments or other specific examples in the area(s) in which your contacts are interested. Responses like, "We represent 10 of the top 50 largest private companies in town" to a closely held business owner, or "The technology industry represents about 15% of our client base" to an emerging biotech company, will persuade targets that you understand their issues and will be able to handle their legal needs.

Remember, in a law firm your "product" is your people—their expertise and experience. You cannot predict when it will be to your advantage to know that a colleague went to a particular law school or that another heads a bar association section. For example, saying to a client with a tax problem, "My colleague, Jennifer Smith, literally wrote the book on environmental issues for the petroleum industry," not only helps the prospect understand

> *[I]n a law firm your "product" is your people—their expertise and experience.*

Jennifer's expertise, but it shows your pride in and enthusiasm about your colleagues.

The process of educating yourself about your firm's capabilities is continual, and can include activities like:

• Visiting your firm's Web site or intranet on a regular basis to read colleagues' bios and review firm news and other developments

• Reading firm memos, newsletters, seminar invitations or case discussions (from other practice areas) to determine the activities, successes and expertise represented in other areas of the firm

• Reading firm marketing materials, including practice descriptions

• Taking colleagues in other areas to lunch to learn more about their clients and their services

• Attending other practice groups' meetings to listen to their discussions about legal developments or client issues

• Sitting near people other than those you know well when attending firm meetings, retreats or social functions

When you are with colleagues, whether one on one or in a practice group setting, your goal should be to learn the following:

• What is the nature of their clientele? What kinds of companies or entities do they represent? Who buys their services?

• What benefits do they offer clients? What makes them different from their competitors?

• How might you explain their practice to a contact in 100 words or less?

• What recent activities, cases, transactions or events would offer an opportunity to talk about the practice to your contacts?

If you are in a large firm, you may need to focus your internal efforts. If so, it makes sense to look for practices or colleagues that have potential synergy with you. For example, if you are in the construction area, you may want to focus your internal intelligence gathering on the real estate and environmental practice groups.

C. Preparing Your Strategy

After conducting your due diligence on the target and the firm, you are ready to prepare your strategy for obtaining business. You should be in a position to address the following issues or questions when discussing new business with a prospect:

(1) *What is the best opportunity for you to get work or new work?* Many lawyers fail to develop business because they think they need to reel in the whole client; all you need is to obtain one file from a new client or in a new area. Once this happens, you can expand the relationship further. So consider carefully the substantive or geographic area to address based on the risk to the prospect, your contact's area of authority or your firm's expertise.

> *Many lawyers fail to develop business because they think they need to reel in the whole client; all you need is to obtain one file from a new client or in a new area.*

(2) *What objections might you need to address?* Through your conversations, if you sense that there are any obstacles to getting the business (e.g., your age, your firm's size, etc.), you will need to address them before you get the work.

(3) *What are the target's selection criteria?* Again, if you have done a good job of asking questions and probing for needs, you should have determined the most important factors to the prospect, whether it is turn-around time, the cost of legal services or results.

(4) *What are the benefits of using your firm?* You must be prepared to explain why the prospect should use your firm. There are basic benefits upon which you can expound, such as saving time, saving money, getting the prospect out of trouble, keeping him or her out of trouble, etc.

(5) *Which lawyers should be involved?* It is critical to involve the right people, both in the pitch and in the proposed staffing for the new client or new matter.

(6) *What information do you need to provide?* It always helps to have tangible materials that support your approach, whether it is client references, lawyer bios or fee schedules.

III. PRESENTING THE INFORMATION AND ASKING FOR THE BUSINESS

If you have executed these steps well, you inevitably will identify some contacts with needs that you, or someone in your firm, can meet. When that happens, you should be in a position to contact the target to discuss the possibility of doing business together. This Section provides advice on approaching prospective clients.

A. Inviting the Target

Armed with your business development strategy, it shouldn't be difficult to contact the prospective client and propose a meeting. Still, this is one of the biggest obstacles for most lawyers in their quest to develop business. Perhaps it would be of interest to learn how clients react to these types of calls. The following are comments made by law firm clients about direct business development contacts:

- *"If they have done some work for us and call to say, 'Our docket-checker shows you've been sued here but you haven't been served, and we'd like to handle it,' that works."*

- *"People call and want to introduce their partners to me. I'll give them an audience."*

- *"I pay attention to calls if they are very specific and relevant."*

Remember the advice given earlier about articulating your agenda—there should be no pretenses.[2] If you are interested in talking about doing business together, then you need to make that focus apparent to your target when you call, for example:

- *"I've watched your company's growth over the years with great interest since I do a lot of work in the hospitality area. I'd like to talk to you about the services we offer to restaurants."*

---

[2] See Chapter 15, Section III *supra.*

- *"I recently handled some litigation for a company that had not conducted any supervisory training. I'd like to come out and talk to you about how you can avoid this type of employee lawsuit."*

> *The beauty of being forthright about your purpose is that you will get a true reading on the interest level of your target.*

- *"We've appreciated the opportunity to work with you on your estate planning issues and would like to discuss ways we could be of assistance with your business."*

The beauty of being forthright about your purpose is that you will get a true reading on the interest level of your target. If people agree to meet with you, you have been given permission, so to speak, to market to them. If people decline, then you know they are not interested in your services—at least for now.

If your invitation is declined, be sure to handle the rejection graciously. Depending on the prospect's reasons for not meeting, you might respond, for example:

- *"I understand you're very busy. I will look for you at the next board meeting so we can catch up on how things are going."*

- *"I appreciate your relationship with the Smith & Jones law firm. If you ever find yourself in a conflict situation or there is something you think we would be suited to handle, please keep us in mind."*

B. Conducting a Pitch Meeting

There is no right way to organize a pitch meeting. Some people like to discuss business over a meal; others prefer to meet in an office. Volunteering to go to the prospect's office is often the most effective approach. It shows your flexibility in dealing with clients and your interest in their businesses. However, some lawyers prefer to meet at their firm, to "validate" the prospect's perception, showcase other client work or bring other lawyers or staff into the meeting, if appropriate. If you do meet in a public place like a restaurant, make certain it is not too loud or distracting and that tables are not so close together that you will be uncomfortable presenting your ideas.

(1) *Starting the meeting.* In a pitch meeting with a prospective client, or an existing client to discuss additional services, think about the following:

- *Be on time and stay focused.* You might ask the prospect how much time he has allocated for the meeting. Then keep a close eye on your watch.

- *Thank the prospect or client for his or her time.*

- *Introduce the players.* Make certain everyone who is in attendance is introduced and his or her role explained (e.g., "I brought my colleague, Pete, because he is the most knowledgeable person in the firm about trade issues involving China.").

- *State the purpose of the meeting.* For example, "As I mentioned when I called you, we are interested in talking with you about the nature of the preventive work we've been doing for other clients in your industry and how we can be of service to you."

- *Invite the client to comment.* Start your conversation with a brief discussion. This could be an invitation for the client to add to the agenda or perhaps a chance to ask a question about a recent issue of which you are aware (e.g., "How did that termination matter turn out for you?").

- *Get down to business.* While small talk can help build rapport, it can be irritating to a busy prospect pressed for time. Some lawyers use small talk to avoid the business conversation. By setting the agenda, you should be able to get to the discussion quickly and begin the business development process.

(2) *Presenting your capabilities.* When it comes time to present your capabilities, there are two areas of most concern to the majority of prospective clients:

- *Results.* Clients are interested in seeing or hearing what you've done for other people. The most compelling pitches often include things like a list of client references, a list of results, a list of representative matters, etc. These prove a precedent for hiring you; people are motivated to support you when other people they like or admire have already supported you. When a company business owner sees a marquis name on your representative client list, it is a powerful persuader.

- *Staffing/Personnel.* It is extremely important to bring the right people to the meeting and the client engagement. In the legal profession, business development is about selling people, not services. Most people prefer to work with people like themselves. This means you need to relate to them on a personal level, whether this involves expertise, industry knowledge, personality, age, background or ethnicity.

The following client comments support the notion of being prepared to discuss results and staffing/personnel:

- *"To get this business, we would need to know: (1) who has what experience of that type; (2) what the firm specializes in; and (3) the credentials of the lawyers."*

- *"The most important things in the presentation are representative clients and representative cases."*

- *"First, show me who they have done it for before—a case list, a case summary. Second, I'd like to meet the people who will be handling the matter. It's extremely important to me that I'm comfortable with them."*

Remember, when presenting your services, you should limit your discussion to the areas in which the prospect needs help. Some lawyers have a tendency to pitch too many of the firm's capabilities; prospects only want to hear about the experiences that are salient to their current needs.

> *Some lawyers have a tendency to pitch too many of the firm's capabilities; prospects only want to hear about the experiences that are salient to their current needs.*

In addition, you should address any underlying areas of concern that you have uncovered. If, for example, the prospect has raised the issue of the high cost of legal fees, talk about what your firm does to minimize legal expenses. If the prospect has expressed concern about not getting calls returned, you might mention your personal efforts to be accessible.

(3) *Addressing concerns.* In the course of your discussion of services and needs, you may run across the following issues:

• *Fees.* If you haven't talked about money, you probably won't get the work. No client will hire a lawyer with a virtual blank check. So if the question hasn't been raised, you can put it on the table, e.g., "You're probably wondering what it would cost to work with us." Talking about money can be a very good thing; it shows the prospect you can deal with business issues in a businesslike way.

• *Objections.* Objections are things that might stand in the way of your getting business. There are myriad issues that might prevent you from getting

> *Talking about money can be a very good thing; it shows the prospect you can deal with business issues in a businesslike way.*

business—you're a personal friend, the firm seems too small, the firm seems too expensive, the prospect would have to "train" and orient you to handle the business. One of the goals of your due diligence is to identify potential objections; during your meeting, you should be prepared to address and perhaps even raise them. For example, "One question you might have is whether a firm our size has the capability to handle a case of this magnitude. Let me tell you how we have staffed similar matters . . . ." [Objections are discussed in more detail in Section (5) below.]

• *Other Concerns.* It is important not to minimize the client's comments or concerns. If a client says, "Wow, that sounds expensive," you shouldn't be defensive; instead, you might ask how much the client thought he might have to pay or explain the factors on which the estimated fee is based, such as prior transactions.

(4) *Asking for the opportunity.* Finally, after making the case about your capabilities, discussing your approach to the prospect and addressing any concerns, you should be in a position to determine if the prospect will become a client. In some cases, the prospect will take your lead and provide reactions to your pitch. In other cases, you may need to ask the target directly whether he or she is willing to use your services.

Lesson one: Be direct. You may be surprised at the prospect's willingness to give you a chance. Lesson two: Many clients are flattered by the expression of interest.

> **Many clients are flattered by the expression of interest.**

There are many ways to ask for business, and you need to find an approach that fits your personality and style, and addresses the needs you have uncovered. When trying to gauge commitment, the best questions are closed-ended, i.e., requiring a yes or no answer. These will allow you to see where the prospect stands. For example:

- "What are your reactions to these services—do they seem to meet your needs?"
- "Would you like us to work for you?"
- "Do you think this approach might be useful in handling your next product liability issue?"

Sometimes it is best to ask for small commitments that start the process and allow you to see if the prospect is sincerely interested in working with you. For example, you might ask:

- "Should I set up a meeting with your CFO to start the ball rolling?"
- "Would you be interested in having me summarize this approach in a proposal?"
- "Would you like me to review the document and give you some feedback on your options?"
- "Would you like to go over some ideas for how you might address this matter?"

In the latter case, as an example, if the answer is affirmative, you have received a preliminary commitment. After presenting some of your ideas, you might ask:

"Do any of these strategies seem workable to you?"

Again, if the answer is yes, you are closer to obtaining business. A final question might be:

"Would you like me to get started helping you implement this solution?"

(5) *Addressing objections and probing stalls.* After you have "popped the question," you may find yourself with a new client. In other cases, however, you may find yourself facing additional objections or stalls. These need to be handled immediately and deftly to eliminate the client's reluctance in order to gain the business.

The following are some examples of objections and possible appropriate responses:

- "We've been working with James Lopez for 10 years."

By saying this, the prospect could be signaling that he is happy with James, that he is afraid to deliver the bad news to James, or that he is concerned about your "start-up" time. You should ask follow-up questions to determine which of these is correct. If you find, for example, that his concern is having to pay to educate you, your potential response could be: "I understand that he has a lot of information about your company. We would be happy to spend a day on site with you and your managers, at no charge, so we can get up to speed on how you like things handled."

- "We didn't budget for this project and our new fiscal year doesn't start until May 1."

Your potential response could be: "We would be happy to start the project now and bill you in the next fiscal year."

- "Our general counsel needs to approve all hiring decisions."

You might respond: "Would you be willing to introduce me? I'd like the chance to talk about these issues with her."

- "We usually handle those matters in house."

This means that internal staff can handle the work and probably does so less expensively than outside counsel. You could say, "If you find yourself in a situation where your people want or need outside help, we can step in. We understand that overflow work needs to be completed quickly and cost-effectively."

- "I'm concerned because you represent another contractor."

Your response may be to discuss your ethical and business practices (i.e., conflicts and confidentiality) and to highlight the efficiencies to be gained by a lawyer who understands industry issues.

- "I'm not sure whether it makes sense to move the business to your firm."

Your response might be: "It would be really useful if you could give me some idea of how the services we've discussed match up against those of your current law firm."

- "I'm not sure that strategy makes sense for us."

Your potential response: "Would it be helpful for you to talk with some clients of our firm who have benefitted from an approach like the one we discussed?"

Are You Perceived to Be Too Young?

If you are—or look—young, that can present an obstacle to you in your business development efforts. Clients are often reluctant to hire someone they perceive to be "green."

How can you address this if you sense it is an issue? It depends on your personality and your relationship with the prospect, of course, but the most obvious way is to bring it up for the client. You might say, for example: "I'm sure you're wondering whether I've had enough experience to handle this type of matter" or "Don't let my age fool you; I've had considerable experience working with business owners on the precise issue we've been discussing. Let me tell you a little bit about my track record."

By dealing with the obstacle openly, you will demonstrate sensitivity to the client's concern and have the opportunity to address the issue directly. Unfortunately, however, even these actions will not be enough for certain prospective clients; for those, you simply will need to be patient.

Stalling may be a way for the prospect to avoid making a decision. While you may not be willing or able to force a decision, you should make every attempt to understand what is behind the comment. In some cases, prospects are just trying to be nice; they don't want to tell you they aren't interested in your services. In other cases, there may be legitimate issues that need to be addressed. The following are some examples of stalls and how you might respond:

- "I'll think about it."

You might respond: "When do you expect to make a decision?" Then you can follow up after that time.

- "I'm not in a position to make a decision right now."

Your response: "To help me better understand your needs, can you tell me how your company usually goes about making these decisions?"

- "Would you send a written proposal?"

Your response: "I'd be delighted. When can I follow up with you about a decision?"

- "Call me in three or four months."

You might say, "I would be happy to, but only if you think it's worthwhile. Is what we've discussed of interest to you?"

In these instances, the more you can probe into the prospect's response to get to the truth, the better idea you will have about whether the contact represents a real business development opportunity.

(6) *Handling rejection.* When you do work up the nerve to ask for business, the response you get may be "no." For many lawyers, rejection is the hardest part of the marketing and business development process. However, in many cases, a "no" is just no for now, and there may be future opportunities. There are myriad examples of clients who hired a firm some time after an initial approach, and others who make referrals to a law firm even though they don't send their own work there.

[I]n many cases, a "no" is just no for now, and there may be future opportunities.

You need to handle rejection graciously and try to learn from the experience. What might your reaction to "No thanks" be?

- "Thank you anyway for hearing me out. And, your 'no' doesn't diminish my interest in working with you."

- "I appreciate your honesty. I hope all my clients are as loyal as you are."

- "If a project does come up that you believe we're suited for, I'd love the chance to work with you."

You can always position yourself as the backup firm or a conflict alternative. In that way, you can continue to cultivate your relationship and add value while you "wait in the wings."

You can also use rejection as an opportunity to learn from the success of others. Make it clear to the prospect that you are not interested in taking business from someone who is doing a good job, but that you would like to hear why he or she feels the current relationship works so well so you can learn from that.

(7) *Other tips for successful pitch meetings.*

When meeting with a prospective client, you should think about the following additional techniques to improve your success in getting business:

- *Articulate your understanding of the target's need or position.* For example, "It sounds to me like your biggest concern is how quickly we could get this done."

- *Demonstrate flexibility.* For example, "What's most important is that our plans make sense for you and the company."

- *Don't talk too much.* Even in pitch meetings, the most valuable information will come from the prospect, not you. Studies show that the more prospects say, write or demonstrate their views to you, the more deeply they will believe in your ability and the more loyal they will become to you.

- *Demonstrate sincere interest and empathy.* Say, for example, "You must have been very frustrated by that."

• *Make a commitment.* You are asking the prospect for a commitment; is there something you can do to demonstrate your commitment? For example, you might promise not to work for a competitor, or provide your home phone number to show your accessibility.

• *Try not to take rejection personally.* These are business decisions, and often things go on under the radar of which you cannot possibly be aware.

> *Don't be afraid of looking eager for the opportunity.*

• *Be enthusiastic!* Clients want to work with people who want to work with them. Don't be afraid of looking eager for the opportunity.

IV. FOLLOWING UP ON OPPORTUNITIES

The odds that a good prospect will turn into a client the day you meet are not great; however, with proper follow up and relationship development, the odds that a good prospect will turn into a client over time are terrific. In fact, failing to follow up with prospects may signal that you're too busy for more work, that you're not interested in them or that you're not very businesslike in your marketing efforts.

This Section addresses how to follow up calls from interested prospects, and how to follow up after your pitch meetings.

A. Dealing with Cold Calls

There may be times when you receive a call from a prospect requesting a meeting with you. This may be the result of a referral or a Yellow Pages listing. When you receive this kind of inquiry, keep the following in mind:

• *Respond immediately.* If you were not available when the prospect called, you should return

> *Responding promptly to a new business opportunity shows your interest and enthusiasm, and may help you thwart the competition.*

the call as quickly as possible. Responding promptly to a new business opportunity shows your interest and enthusiasm, and may help you thwart the competition.

• *Thank the prospect for calling and ask how she got your name.*

The answer may help you determine if it is a legitimate call. It will also help you learn whether certain marketing efforts are working or identify a referral source who should be thanked. Finally, it might give you some insights into the prospect (e.g., membership in a trade association to which you belong).

• *Check for conflicts.* For example, the caller may be an inventor who currently works for a client employer. (Be certain to review the Rules of Professional Conduct to avoid creating a client relationship on this initial telephone call.)

• *Ask a lot of questions.* Depending on the need, you might inquire about the company's form of corporate entity, ownership, revenues, needs, etc. You can explain that you want to learn as much as possible about the company before the meeting so you can focus your ideas.

• *Learn about the prospect.* Explore the company's Web site and other materials, and investigate the company's industry and competition.

• *Ask why the company is seeking counsel.* The prospect could be inquiring about a new project which he or she believes requires specialized expertise or contacts beyond that of existing counsel, or it could be that the company feels it is outgrowing the existing firm.

> *You will build a lot of credibility by admitting that your firm is not the right fit for certain work.*

• *Be honest about your ability to help.* For example, if the prospect is clearly not suited for your firm, convey this message with empathy and try to assist with another referral. You will build a lot of credibility by admitting that your firm is not the right fit for certain work.

• *If the caller appears to be a good prospect, set up the meeting within three to five business days, if possible.* It is important to seize upon the client's momentum. In addition, you may be in a competitive situation, and you want to appear responsive.

After taking these preliminary steps, you should be ready to set up your meeting.[3]

---

[3] See Section III *supra.*

B. Following Up a Pitch Meeting

After the meeting, you should write a letter immediately, thanking the prospect for the opportunity and reiterating your interest in working with her or the company. If possible, include a reference to something that came up in conversation, such as a pending issue, a question or a common interest. Then, you should consider following up by phone after a few weeks have passed to find out whether the prospect has made a decision about working with you. Again, don't forget to express your interest in working with the company.

Many times, lawyers will have a positive initial experience or meeting with a prospect, but time goes by and no business materializes. It could be that the prospect has filed away the information for the future. It could be that the issue you discussed, which was pressing at the time, has now become less of a priority for the company. Or it could be that the prospect finds it easier to remain with the *status quo*.

Here are some situations you might face, and thoughts about how to respond to them:

(1) *The prospect calls for "free advice" and never hires you.* Giving something of value like free advice can be a great business development technique. At some point, however, you may need to assess whether the prospect is worth the time and effort. Some considerations include:

• *Potentially losing the relationship.* If you cut off your assistance, it may affect your future relationship. Keep in mind that some people may not use your services, but will recommend you to others.

• *Shortchanging clients.* If you are charging clients for the same type of counsel you are giving away free, it is unfair.

• *Confirming advice.* It's quite possible that the prospect is posing the same question to the current counsel and then checking with you. This may suggest a lack of confidence in the current lawyer, which may reflect an opportunity.

• *Ability to make decisions.* It's also possible that the person seeking the advice doesn't actually control the decision about hiring legal counsel. If so, the question for you is whether to continue to invest in the relationship or ask for an introduction to the decision-maker.

After considering these scenarios, if you believe you need to address the situation with the prospect, consider the following approaches the next time you get a request for free advice:

• *Be direct.* Talk to the prospect about the situation, for example: "I'm glad you've felt comfortable calling me for advice. I've been wondering, is there some reason you don't call your company's lawyers about these issues?" What you learn (e.g., the prospect doesn't like the lawyer, isn't comfortable with the lawyer's expertise or likes free advice), may suggest your next course of action.

• *Appeal to fairness.* Explain that, while you've enjoyed building a relationship with the prospect, your existing clients are your top priority, and you don't feel comfortable providing additional services without charging in the same way.

• *Move to a new level.* Finally, suggest that your next response will be billed, e.g., "By the time I research that issue and give you an answer, it will probably result in about $1,000 in fees. Is that acceptable to you?" Who knows? You may end up with a new client.

(2) *The prospect met with you but then never called back.* Let's say you met with a prospective client to discuss a particular need or responded to a request for information by sending a packet of materials. Then nothing happens. What can you do to follow up? Think about the following:

• *Call to ask if your presentation or materials addressed the issues adequately.* You could suggest that many times clients have additional questions after they have a chance to digest the materials, and you would like to know what additional information you might provide.

• *Send some informational materials on the topic you discussed.* For example, if you met with a CFO about financing options, you could send information on filings by competitors or articles on financing options.

• *Call and ask if you can visit the company's offices to learn more about the business.* At that time, you can inquire if there is anything else you can do to help the company's executives. You might be able to offer the name of another professional advisor, for example.

(3) *The prospect asked you to call, and then never returned your call.* It is difficult to know whether the prospect is no longer interested, is too busy to deal with you or is preoccupied with other matters. In any event, keep the following in mind:

• *Don't lose confidence or become angry.* Remember that people are very busy.

• *If the prospect is on the telephone when you call, offer to hold.* This is preferable to leaving a voicemail. Ask for the secretary or assistant, and suggest that you want to avoid starting "telephone tag."

• *Be prepared for voicemail; make sure you have formulated your message ahead of time.* Acknowledge the contact's busy schedule, and suggest a time when you will call back again (don't leave the ball in the prospect's court). Be sure to project confidence and friendliness when calling. If you get the voicemail repeatedly, don't leave repeated messages. It may be best to hang up and try back at another time.

• *Vary the times of your attempts to call.* Maybe the prospect typically has morning meetings.

• *Try to work with the gatekeeper.* Secretaries, assistants and receptionists can often help you in many ways by giving you insights into the contact's schedule or helping you get your call put through.

• *Offer to set up a telephone appointment, so you can pin down the contact.*

• *Vary your approach.* Perhaps you can send an e-mail or a fax in advance of your call. This could serve to remind the contact that your call is in response to his or her request. In addition, some people prefer other methods of communication over the telephone (e.g., e-mails can be responded to at one's leisure). Finally, faxes and e-mails create a sense of urgency.

- *Look for other ways to make contact.* Maybe you can connect with the prospect at a board meeting, trade association luncheon or another social event.

It is important to be patient. When a prospect has had a long-term relationship with another lawyer, inertia is your biggest enemy. Often, it will require an event of some kind to prompt a change, whether this involves a merger or acquisition, changing management within the company or some *faux pas* on the part of existing counsel.

> *When a prospect has had a long-term relationship with another lawyer, inertia is your biggest enemy.*

And when all else fails, move on. Maintain a regular pattern of personal follow up, such as entertainment, mailings or phone calls. Continue to send contacts routine marketing communications, such as firm newsletters or seminar invitations, and hope to generate interest some day. And, if you find out the company has hired someone else or decides to remain with the current counsel, be a gracious loser; wish the prospect well and say you hope to cross paths again.

V. OTHER CONSIDERATIONS AND TIPS FOR "CLOSING" AND ASKING FOR BUSINESS

Except for those rare occasions when a client is actively seeking new counsel, most contacts either have a lawyer or don't have a pressing legal need. So for you to get business from a prospective client, one of the following must occur:

(1) You have related your services to a pressing interest or need of the client.

(2) You have successfully described how you can solve a problem for the client.

(3) You have shown how you can help the client personally.

(4) You have shown how you can help the client save time, money or other resources.

Most people will say that they hate to be sold to, but they love to buy.

And while researching law firms is an intellectual process for a prospect, "buying" legal services is an emotional challenge. Your job is to help the prospect make an informed and safe decision to use your services.

To be successful in generating business, keep the following in mind:

• *Check your applicable Rules of Professional Conduct.* There are rules addressing direct contact with potential clients.

• *Make business development an active, not passive, activity.* Don't assume prospects will read your firm's Web site or take the time to learn about your capabilities. It is your job to let them know how you can help them.

> *The question, "Can you help me?" is very powerful; most satisfied clients will be happy to help you.*

• *Ask clients for help.* Prepare a list of clients who will serve as references when you pitch other business. Ask good clients if they have suggestions for you or are willing to make introductions for you. The question, "Can you help me?" is very powerful; most satisfied clients will be happy to help you.

• *Cultivate many relationships at the prospective client entity.* While you don't want to look like you're going over someone's head, the more people who are your supporters at a company, the better your chance of getting business. This is particularly true if the decision-maker (e.g., general counsel) and "user" of the service (e.g., patent coordinator) are two different people or in two different departments.

• *Don't be greedy.* You only need one file to turn a prospect into a client. So do a good job of analyzing your best opportunity to obtain work. In fact, you might select an area where the company could easily test your services, making the hiring decision low risk for the prospect.

• *Look for opportunities for anyone, not just yourself.* If the need is outside of your expertise or even that of your firm, you still have a valuable asset. There are many professionals who would appreciate the client. You can refer the contact to an appropriate product or service provider, doing both that person and the contact a favor.

• *Focus on the benefits you can offer.* Why should a prospect use you or your firm in lieu of another? If you can't explain the reasons, you shouldn't expect the business.

> *If you can't explain the reasons [a prospect should use you], you shouldn't expect the business.*

• *Always talk positively about your colleagues.* Inadvertent or inappropriate comments can completely derail your efforts to sell or cross sell your firm's capabilities.

• *Project confidence.* If you don't believe you're the best solution to the problem, why should the prospect?

• *Build a relationship.* People prefer to do business with people they like.

Ideas/Notes: "Closing" and Asking for Business

My personal challenge(s) or obstacle(s) in this area:

_____

_____

_____

_____

_____

My goal(s) or objective(s) in this area:

_____

_____

_____

_____

_____

What I need to do to get started:

(1) _____

_____

(2) _____

_____

(3) _____

_____

(4) _____

_____

(5) _____

_____

PART IV:

DEVELOPING A PERSONAL MARKETING PLAN

I. INTRODUCTION

Every lawyer will benefit from a more organized marketing effort, whether he or she is new to business development or has a substantial book of business. Setting out an annual marketing plan for yourself is an excellent idea. It is a fact that things that get written down are more likely to get done.

> *[T]hings that get written down are more likely to get done.*

Many lawyers begin their personal planning process by selecting their marketing activities for the year, such as getting more involved in an organization, participating in a seminar or writing an article for a trade publication. While each of these may be a very good idea, it is important to consider the big picture—the market, the goals and how best to accomplish your objectives.

In fact, a truly effective planning process will include an analysis of the trends, issues and opportunities you face, a statement of your goals and objectives, and then (and only then) selection of the appropriate tools and activities for implementation.

II. PREPARING TO PLAN

Before writing your personal marketing plan, you should spend some time thinking about your situation and your opportunities. This could very well be the hardest part of the task. Consider blocking out a few hours to implement this process—perhaps some time on a Saturday morning.

In preparing to write your personal marketing plan, you should reflect on your interests and commitments, trends and challenges, existing market opportunities, and your various contacts and referral sources.

A. Interests

What are your interests? Think about what kind of practice you want to develop or with what kinds of clients you want to work. For example, you might want to obtain business from larger companies or do more work in a certain substantive area. You should also think about what kinds of activities you enjoy, prefer or can commit to. For example, if you have difficulty planning outings in the evenings because of family obligations, think about breakfast or lunch as better opportunities to see people.

B. Commitments

What are your existing commitments? Take a tally of your current organizational activities, speaking engagements, writing assignments and other commitments, professional and personal. With respect to each commitment, ask yourself whether it is an effective use of your time. You should also consider whether you should be targeting some of these activities more aggressively, to gain a higher profile for yourself or to increase your level of participation.

C. Trends and Challenges

What trends might affect your practice? These could include, for example:

- Changes in client needs or demands (e.g., requesting fixed fee pricing, increased interest in human resources training programs, etc.)

- Trends in client industries or businesses (e.g., market consolidation, expansion of certain product or service lines, etc.)

- Competitive issues (e.g., marketing activities of competing lawyers, your position vis-à-vis other law firms, etc.)

D. Opportunities

What marketing opportunities exist for you? For example, are you working on any cases that will give you chances to write, speak or contact people in the future? Are there pending changes to laws, regulations or rules that will offer you a reason to get in touch with your contacts? Do you have access to research, reports or information that would be valuable for your targets?

E. Contacts

Who do you know? Produce (or create) a list of everyone with whom you should be having some level of communication throughout the year. This list should consist of existing clients and referral sources, prospective clients and referral sources, and other "friends" (e.g., political allies, executive directors of professional associations, selected firm colleagues, etc.). You should consider whether there are people you have met through your outside activities with whom you should be developing closer relationships. While creating such a list may seem like a mundane activity, a good list is crucial to your success.

While creating such a list may seem like a mundane activity, a good list is crucial to your success.

Once you have taken an inventory of your contacts, develop a "short list" of people upon whom you want to focus particular attention in the coming year(s). When you do so, also consider your objectives for contact (i.e., why you are interested in staying in touch) and how (and how often) you will call on them.

Creating such lists helps you to be organized and develop a game plan. It also serves as a reminder to stay in touch—to follow up.

III. WRITING YOUR PERSONAL MARKETING PLAN

After undertaking this assessment, you will be better equipped to write an effective marketing plan. A sample individual marketing action plan is set forth in Table IV on pages 293-295. This Section describes the components of the plan and how to create a good personal marketing plan.

A. Goals

Based on the analysis you conducted in Section II above, you will begin by outlining goals for your practice. Goals involve long-term outcomes (two to three years), and are unlikely to be achieved in a year. For example:

(1) To spend more time working in the area of traditional labor.

(2) To combine my interests in law and agriculture.

(3) To become president of the Young Lawyers' Section of the bar association.

(4) To become recognized as one of the top ERISA lawyers in the state.

(5) To build a niche practice representing nursing home developers.

(6) To become less reliant on CPAs for referrals and generate more business from in-house lawyers.

B. Objectives

Once your long-term goals are set, you should establish some one-year objectives. Generally, objectives are measurable, so you should be able to determine if you accomplished them. Examples include:

> *[O]bjectives are measurable, so you should be able to determine if you accomplished them.*

(1) To bill 50% of my time next year on work in the environmental area.

(2) To achieve total receipts of $750,000.

(3) To have face-to-face contact with everyone on my target "short list" at least once during the year.

(4) To develop referrals from two accountants who have not sent work to me in the past.

(5) To grow my practice 15% next year.

(6) To originate $200,000 in billings.

C. Action Plan

Finally, after setting your goals and objectives, you can identify your plan of action and the steps you should take for the year. The plan of action should be very specific, outlining the activities selected and the persons to be contacted, your deadline, and any necessary follow-up activity.

Remember: different activities produce different results. Some help build relationships; others build credibility; others build skills. The activities you select will depend on your level of seniority, your practice, your location, your time, your skills, your interests, your personality and, of course, your goals and objectives.

The following are examples of relationship-building activities:

- Scheduling working meals with clients
- Entertaining contacts
- Attending industry or organizational meetings to network
- Visiting clients or taking tours of client facilities
- Sending articles of interest to contacts
- Working on collaborative activities with referral sources (e.g., co-authoring an article)

Activities that will enhance your visibility and create a perception of your expertise include:

- Writing and publishing articles
- Speaking at a professional or industry meeting
- Teaching classes
- Sending case alerts or legal communiqués to contacts
- Participating in client seminars
- Presenting internal seminars or circulating internal memoranda on substantive issues
- Sending articles of interest to contacts

Developing your expertise, personal skills or your marketing resources can be a form of marketing (e.g., "product development"). The following are examples of strategies that fall into this category:

- Conducting legal research
- Teaching

- Developing your résumé to be more marketing-oriented
- Preparing substantive materials (e.g., ghostwriting an article)
- Taking courses (continuing legal education classes or business development programs)
- Obtaining certification or an LLM
- Creating a client brochure on a specialty practice area

Finally, examples of organizational and networking activities include:

- Identifying an association or organization to join
- Becoming more active in a group (e.g., running for office, chairing a committee, attending meetings more regularly, etc.)
- Participating in fundraisers or political events
- Organizing a new group or association
- Sponsoring an activity of a group (e.g., hosting a meeting at the firm's offices, sponsoring a cocktail reception for an association, etc.)

> *[A]n effective action plan typically will contain both relationship-building activities as well as other activities, like writing, speaking and organizational activity.*

As you can see from the template that follows in Table IV, an effective action plan typically will contain both relationship-building activities as well as other activities, like writing, speaking and organizational activity. (Usually the more senior a lawyer is, the more contacts he or she will have.)

If you use the following individual marketing action plan template, consider the following tips:

(1) *Contacts.* For the relationship-building portion of your action plan ("Contacts"), indicate the names of your contacts, what you would like to try to accomplish with them or your objective (e.g., introduce them to a firm lawyer in another practice area, learn more about their in-house legal function, build a better relationship, ask for referrals, etc.), the activity you plan (e.g., lunch, attending a football game), and your targeted deadline for the contact.

(2) *Activities.* For the activity portion of your action plan ("Activity"),

indicate the activity to which you are committing (e.g., writing the first firm litigation newsletter, speaking at a trade association meeting, getting on the board of an organization, etc.), the targets for the activity (e.g., an individual, an organization or subscribers to a publication), and your proposed deadline.

(3) *Follow up.* For both sections of the action plan, whenever possible, indicate how you will follow up. For an individual contact, for example, include your proposed follow-up schedule and activity (e.g., schedule a visit after six months, call after three months to ask for feedback on your performance, etc.). For an activity, include your proposed follow-up activity and timetable (e.g., send the published article to selected clients, send another client alert after six months, etc.).

TABLE IV
INDIVIDUAL MARKETING ACTION PLAN

Your Name:_____

(Do not feel constrained by this format or the amount of space given. The goal is to identify a direction for your individual marketing and business development efforts, and some activities to start you down the path.)

I. YOUR GOALS

(1)_____

(2)_____

(3)_____

(4)_____

(5)_____

II. YOUR OBJECTIVES

(1) _____

(2) _____

(3) _____

(4) _____

(5) _____

III. YOUR ACTION PLAN

A. Contacts

Contact	Objective	Activity	Completion Date	Follow-Up Activity

B. Activities

Activity	Target/ Organization/ Publication	Completion Date	Follow-Up Activity

As an example, let's say you practice in the financial services area.

Your goal: Increase your profile in the financial community in order to generate business.

Your objectives:

(1) Meet representatives of three banks with whom you haven't worked before.

(2) Send substantive materials to the local banking community twice a year.

Your action steps:

(1) Become active in the state bankers' association and go to all the meetings.

(2) Set up meetings with the representatives of three banks to discuss their needs and the firm's services.

(3) Develop a database of local bankers and send out three financial services "alerts" this year.

IV. HOLDING YOURSELF ACCOUNTABLE

Done right, a personal marketing plan will make your individual efforts much more effective. However, to ensure that your plan doesn't just sit in a drawer until the following year, you need to develop a system of follow up to hold yourself accountable.

There is no one way or right system for follow up; it depends on your style. For example, you can:

- Use a software package or your Outlook Calendar to docket your activities so they show up on your daily schedule.
- Write your commitments on a day planner or calendar.
- Ask your secretary to keep you on task with monthly reminders.
- Set up a "buddy system" with one or more colleagues in the firm.

• Block out a regular time to make follow-up phone calls or work on your commitments.

It is also helpful to break your commitments into specific, achievable tasks. For example, if your activity involves writing an article, set a deadline for contacting the publication, then for outlining the article and finally for writing.

> *It is . . . helpful to break your commitments into specific, achievable tasks.*

If you have a good secretary or assistant, look for opportunities to involve him or her in your implementation efforts. For example, once they have made initial contacts with people, many lawyers will have their secretaries call contacts to set up follow-up lunches, meetings or social events.

Find the system that works for you.

V. OTHER CONSIDERATIONS AND TIPS FOR DEVELOPING A PERSONAL MARKETING PLAN

The following are some additional thoughts about writing and implementing your personal marketing plan:

• *Play to your strengths.* If you don't enjoy or are not particularly good at writing, perhaps speaking is a better way for you to build your credibility. If you enjoy the theater, consider serving on a theater board as your outside activity.

• *Strengthen your skills in weak areas.* Some activities are important for almost all lawyers, such as being able to make effective presentations or being good at networking and meeting new people. If you are uncomfortable with these activities, think about ways to improve your skills. For example, you can join the Toastmasters to ratchet up your public speaking skills or take a course in networking.

• *Leverage your efforts.* Look for ways to build on your practice or your prior marketing efforts. To leverage a practice, for example, a lawyer who specializes in adoption might get involved in organizations that provide services to children. As an example of leveraging your marketing efforts, after writing an article on a topic, you can send it to a reporter, turn it into a shorter client alert or think about ways to spin it into a speech.

- *Stick with your ideas.* Much marketing and business development success will come from your persistence. As your plan evolves, try to reinforce the activities of prior years. For example, it can take three years or more for you to feel like, and be perceived as, an "insider" in a trade group. Don't fall into the trap of starting and stopping activities before they have a chance to work.

> **Don't fall into the trap of starting and stopping activities before they have a chance to work.**

- *Cut your losses.* At the same time, you need to be honest about your opportunities for a return. If you find yourself entertaining the same person year after year with no measurable benefit, then move on to another target.

- *Be specific.* Instead of vague commitments such as "Socialize with clients," your action steps should include detail like "After concluding the Smith deal, take John Doe of Trust Bank to lunch to discuss our potential representation in the workout area."

- *Be realistic.* You need to be honest with yourself about how much— or what—you can do. If you have done little in the way of entertaining or socializing, for example, set an objective to take someone to lunch once a month.

PART V:
CONCLUDING COMMENTS

In this concluding Section, I have summarized many of the themes that run throughout this book. If you can incorporate these underlying philosophies into your marketing efforts, you should be well on your way to building a book of business.

I. GENERAL ADVICE

- *Use your marketing activities to help people.* The best marketers are those who recognize and fill people's needs, and not just professional or substantive needs. For example, you can help your contacts get interviewed for jobs, get articles published or get on panels. You can introduce them to people you think they should know, sponsor their memberships in country clubs or help them find good professional advisors, like brokers or accountants. You can call the editor of an industry publication to explain an emerging legal issue that might be of interest to readers or send people you know copies of articles you've read that involve salient issues. While it shouldn't be the reason you do it, helping other people will help you in the end.

> *The best marketers are those who recognize and fill people's needs, and not just professional or substantive needs.*

- *Do your homework and prepare.* Before doing anything—speaking, writing, attending a meeting or making a pitch—you need to put yourself in the target's or audience members' shoes. Why should they be interested in talking to, hearing from or reading about you? What do you know about them that will help you make your message more compelling?

• *Ask for what you want.* Maybe it's a position on a desirable board. Maybe it's a chance to get referrals. Maybe it's for a client to introduce you to a prospective client. Many times the best opportunities need to be pursued.

• *Move from passive to active marketing efforts.* As someone once said, passive, positioning activities make you "interesting;" active, relationship activities make you look "interested." The active approach is more time-consuming and therefore needs to be targeted. However, you will be much more likely to see results from your active efforts.

• *Don't forget your internal relationships.* If you are not a solo practitioner, you have built-in referral sources at your firm. Many a good practice was built from a client relationship provided by a firm partner, or an opportunity to work on a novel case or transaction. You can often leverage the opportunities you are given into new opportunities of your own. Ask to make a presentation to another section of the firm, send colleagues copies of your articles, and educate them about things that their clients should know.

> *Many a good practice was built from a client relationship provided by a firm partner, or an opportunity to work on a novel case or transaction.*

• *Avoid pretenses.* Whether you're asking for business, talking about fees or calling someone for lunch, be honest about your intentions. No one likes a "bait and switch."

• *Learn from your efforts and mistakes.* After you make a presentation, try to get feedback from the attendees. Videotape and watch yourself rehearse for a pitch. Ask a client who left the firm what you might do to win back the business.

• *Get out of your office.* To be a good business developer, you need to "see and be seen." That means leaving the firm to go to clients' businesses, meet people for lunch or attend events.

- *Be enthusiastic and positive.* People want to be around people who are genuinely excited about what they do, and clients particularly want a lawyer who is enthusiastic about working with them.

> *To be a good business developer, you need to "see and be seen."*

- *Have an objective for everything you do.* What is the purpose of writing the article? What is the reason for having lunch with an accountant? Articulate what you hope to accomplish so that later you can measure whether the effort was successful.

- *Follow up.* You shouldn't undertake any activity without thinking first about how you will follow it up. For example, how will you follow up with people you meet at a networking event, people who attend a seminar at which you spoke or that advisor you took to lunch?

- *Don't lose hope.* It can take five, eight or twelve or more contacts to turn a prospect into a client. It can take three to five years to build a new practice. It can take years of activity to become a leader in an organization. If you keep your eye on the ball and sustain your activities, however, you will achieve your goals.

- *Just get started.* The more you do, the more you'll be asked to do. Serving effectively on a committee will lead to an invitation to serve on a board. Accepting invitations to parties will lead to invitations to more social events. Writing an interesting article will lead to a speaking opportunity.

II. ADVICE FOR NEW ASSOCIATES

Different firms have different expectations for associates regarding their participation in marketing activities. Some expect associates to get involved from day one; others tell associates not to worry about marketing at all. Regardless of the firm's philosophy, it is often in the associate's best interest to engage in marketing since it will make the associate a better, more client-oriented lawyer.

Few people expect new associates to bring in business, but marketing can still be a little overwhelming. First, it is often difficult to know where to start, and there are so many things that can be done. Second, an associate's time is often not within his or her control. In addition, clients often will perceive associates as being "too green" to give them business.

Associates engaging in marketing activities should keep the following recommendations in mind:

- *Don't lose track of your contacts.* Put your friends, clients, referral sources and others you meet along the way on a list, and review it to determine whether or how you should be contacting someone. For major clients you might have a biweekly breakfast meeting. For law school friends, it might be a quarterly dinner. Put your contacts on the firm's mailing lists, if appropriate, to receive invitations to seminars or copies of firm newsletters. Send holiday cards—personally signed. Establish a schedule to stay in contact.

- *Stay in touch with people.* Throughout your career, most of your contacts will move into new positions or new organizations. Many of the people you know now will become sources of business as their own practices and careers grow, and if you maintain your contact, your odds of being a recipient of business will grow.

> *Many of the people you know now will become sources of business as their own practices and careers grow, and if you maintain your contact, your odds of being a recipient of business will grow.*

- *Express your interests.* Within the firm, let appropriate partners know if you would like more of a particular type of work or to be involved in certain types of activities (e.g., preparing seminar outlines and handouts).

- *Get involved.* If you're not involved in an outside organization, find a place to contribute that is appropriate for your age and interests. Your undergraduate or law school alumni association can be effective, particularly if you are in another community. The Young Lawyers Section of the bar will help you start to network with other lawyers. At this point in your career, you should focus on an area of interest, and learn networking and leadership skills at the same time.

- *Make an impact.* If you are involved in an organization, figure out how you can make a bigger impact. Can you run for office? Lead a committee? Plan the annual meeting program?

• *Learn about your firm.* Your best opportunities as an associate involve other people's capabilities. Do your best to learn about colleagues' practices and clients, so you can talk intelligently about the services of the whole firm, not just what you do.

• *Identify an activity that will help you establish your credibility.* It is important to include things on your résumé that will give clients, referral sources and even colleagues some comfort that you have expertise. Publishing, speaking, teaching and organizational involvements are all avenues to explore.

• *Learn about an industry.* As your practice begins to focus, find out more about the area(s) in which you work. Sign up as a member of client industry or trade groups; subscribe to the relevant magazines or newsletters; and attend conferences and trade shows.

• *Be the best lawyer you can be.* This should still be the primary focus of your efforts as a new associate. But being a good lawyer also means learning how to deal effectively with clients, whether your "client" is a firm partner or an external contact. Learn how to identify needs and expectations, such as the scope of the project or the deadline. Follow up to find out how you did or what you could have done better. Try to take assignments from the same client so that you can build a relationship and gain the client's trust.

> *[B]eing a good lawyer also means learning how to deal effectively with clients, whether your "client" is a firm partner or an external contact.*

III. TIPS FOR LITIGATORS

Some people think that you can't market litigation services. First, you can't predict when litigation will be needed. Second, most clients aren't interested in learning about litigation services. However, while marketing litigation is different than for other practices, it can still be done. Some tips for litigators:

• *Build your reputation as a player in your area.* In addition to coming to the attention of potential decision-makers, you will become better known generally. Most clients will consult with other people in the field (e.g., other in-house lawyers) for a short list of litigators for consideration. By being involved, you will get known and increase the likelihood that you will be on that short list. So, become active in target industries (e.g., the pharmaceutical industry if you're a products liability lawyer). Become visible in

> *Former co-counsel, law school class-mates and alumni of your law firm are all people with whom you should maintain relationships . . . .*

law-related associations (e.g., Defense Research Institute (DRI), the bar association, etc.). Become known as a speaker on targeted CLE programs.

• *Network with judges and other lawyers.* In particular, stay in touch with out-of-state lawyers. Former co-counsel, law school classmates and alumni of your law firm are all people with whom you should maintain relationships so you will be top of mind when they are seeking someone to handle litigation in your area.

• *Focus on niches for marketing purposes.* It is difficult to market "litigation" *per se*; it's a lot easier to market by practice area, e.g., securities litigation, employment litigation or IP litigation.

• *Market your results.* Summarize your experience on your Web site bio by using numbers (e.g., trials, summary judgments, dollars involved, etc.), identifying industries in which you have experience or citing specific cases. In litigation particularly, clients are most interested in what else you have done for similar companies or in similar cases.

• *Obtain some client testimonials.* If you have obtained good results for particular clients, talk to those clients about using them as references or citing the work you have done for them. As one general counsel said, "If the lawyers can attach themselves to visible cases, that makes an immediate impression and overcomes my uncertainty about, 'Did I make the right decision hiring them?'"